EROTIC JUSTICE
LAW AND THE NEW POLITICS OF POSTCOLONIALISM

glasshouse press

London • Sydney • Portland, Oregon

EROTIC JUSTICE
LAW AND THE NEW POLITICS OF
POSTCOLONIALISM

Ratna Kapur

London • Sydney • Portland, Oregon

First published in Great Britain 2005 by
The Glass House Press, The Glass House,
Wharton Street, London WC1X 9PX, United Kingdom
Telephone: + 44 (0)20 7278 8000   Facsimile: + 44 (0)20 7278 8080
Email: info@cavendishpublishing.com
Website: www.cavendishpublishing.com

Published in the United States by Cavendish Publishing
c/o International Specialized Book Services,
5824 NE Hassalo Street, Portland,
Oregon 97213-3644, USA

Published in Australia by Cavendish Publishing (Australia) Pty Ltd
45 Beach Street, Coogee, NSW 2034, Australia
Telephone: + 61 (2)9664 0909   Facsimile: + 61 (2)9664 5420
Email: info@cavendishpublishing.com.au
Website: www.cavendishpublishing.com.au

Kapur, Ratna, 1959–
Erotic justice: law and the new politics of postcolonialism
1 Women – Legal status, laws, etc – India 2 Sex role – India 3 Sex and law – India
4 Feminism – India 5 Postcolonialism – India
I Title
642.5'40878

Library of Congress Cataloguing in Publication Data
Data available

ISBN 1-90438-524-9
ISBN 978-1-904-38524-0

3 5 7 9 10 8 6 4 2

Printed and bound in Great Britain by
Biddles Ltd, Kings Lynn, Norfolk

Acknowledgments

This book owes its creation to the comments and suggestions of innumerable researchers, colleagues, students and friends, who participated in conversations, seminars, workshops and conferences, where I presented different incarnations of the ideas set out in these essays. But the writing, rewriting and reworking of each essay owes a special acknowledgment of its own: Sara Ahmad, Savitri Bisnath, Karen Gabriel, Annalees Golz, Nicola Lacey, Uma Narayan, Jyoti Sanghera and Yasmin Tambiah, who provided careful reading and helped me intellectually to work through one or more chapters; Linda Bosch, Patricia Clough and Kirsten Thomas, who provided me with space at the National Research Council of Women to prepare and present my ideas at several fora and venues; NYU School of Law, Georgetown University Law Centre and Cleveland State University, where participants in my seminars and courses asked hard questions and taught me how to ask better ones; Jayne Huckerby, Angelina Fisher, Connie Chang and Andrea Desouza, for research assistance, helping with editorial changes and proof reading on all the chapters; the Centre for Feminist Legal Research, where Lakshmi Arya, Geetika Bapna and Monica Mody provided comments and research assistance; Sheela Subramaniam and Chunchun Taranibala, who did the indispensable work of assisting with footnoting and citation checking and providing invaluable technical and administrative backup; and Jeet Kumar for staff support and backup. Durbar Mahila Samanwaya Committee and the many conversations I have had with the sex-workers. The Keele Law School, Leeds University and Centre for Feminist Legal Research, Gender, Law and Sexuality Exchange Programme, for providing a forum to present my ideas. I am indebted to those who gave me feedback and comments at the Postcolonialism, Law and Sexuality seminar in July 2003, New Delhi, particularly, Brinda Bose, Mary John and Geeta Patel. Thanks also for the input from friends and colleagues at the International Conference on Cross-Border Movements and Human Rights, January, 2004, New Delhi. My special thanks to my editor, Beverley Brown, whose close readings and insightful comments helped further hone both content and form; Ruth Massey and Sanjeevi Perera, who have guided the manuscript through its various stages. The Rockefeller Foundation, Ford Foundation, Global Alliance Against the Trafficking of Women (Canada), and the Oak Foundation, who provided the material resources and funding at various points in time to make this project possible. The ideas on which these essays are based owe a great deal to the inspiration and guidance I received from Neelan Tiruchelvam, whose cosmopolitanism, intellectual rigour and commitment to a transformative vision have left an indelible impression on my work and life.

For Chapter 3, I am indebted to Kanchana Natrajan for our correspondence on culture, and Marie-Claire Belleau for an important conversation. Thanks to Nathaniel Berman, Brenda Cossman, Dan Danielson, Shohini Ghosh, David Kennedy, Tayyab Mahmud, Martha Minow, Kerry Rittich and Stella Rozanski for their comments, conversations and support on earlier versions of this article. Thanks also to both the Dighton Writers Workshop and the Feminist Studies Group, where I presented earlier versions of this essay. Chapter 4 is a substantially revised version of an article which appeared in (2001) 10 Columbia Journal of Gender and Law 333, 10th Anniversary Volume, and I thank the editors for permission in reproducing parts of the essay for this book.

I am grateful to colleagues who provided feedback on Chapter 4, especially the International Centre for Ethnic Studies, Colombo, Sri Lanka; Cleveland Marshall School of Law, 1999; the International Law Workshop, Columbia Law School, 2001; and the International and Comparative Law Workshop, Cornell Law School, 2001, where I presented different versions of this essay. I am indebted to Karen Knopp, Tayyab Mahmud, Dianne Otto, Tanika Sarkar, Jyotsna Uppal and Leti Volpp for their helpful comments on various drafts of this article. My thanks to Roshni Basu, Deepanjali Kumari, Bridget Kurtt and Aparna Ravi for research assistance. Chapter 4 is a substantially revised version of an article which appeared in (2002) 15 Harvard Human Rights Law Journal 1. I thank the President and Fellows of Harvard College and the *Harvard Human Rights Law Journal* for permission to reproduce parts of the article in this book.

Chapter 5 was written with support from the Rockefeller Foundation Fellowship on Global Human Security. Earlier versions of this article have been presented at the NYU Society of Fellows, December 2003; the UN DAW Expert Consultation on Migration and Mobility and How this Movement Affects Women, Malmo, Sweden, December 2003; Columbia University Human Rights Seminar, December 2003; the New International Law Conference, Birkbeck College, University of London, June 2003; Legalisation of Human Rights Conference, University College, University of London, April 2003; Jawaharlal Nehru University, Women's Studies Centre, New Delhi, February 2003; Queens College, City University New York, November 2002; Vienna Symposium on the International Legal Order, organised by the International Institute for Peace, Vienna, Austria, March 2002; Faculty Seminar, Georgetown University Law Centre, March 2002. My thanks to all those who gave feedback and comments on the essay and presentations. I am particularly grateful for comments provided by Doris Buss, Thuy Do, Susan Marks, Dianne Otto, Lynn Savery and Chantal Thomas. I would like to thank Brigitte Kurt, Aparna Ravi and Connie Chang for their research assistance.

Every book is another journey travelled. I am grateful to Ramma, Kumar and Jyoti who have been constant companions on this journey from the beginning to the end and a source of endless strength and encouragement, especially at moments when the journey seemed never-ending. And finally, my thanks to Palaash for bringing moments of reprieve, lightness of being and frolic during the course of writing this book.

Contents

[P]ostcolonialism is now the main mode in which the West's relation to its 'other' is critically explored, and law has been to the forefront of that very relation.
(Fitzpatrick and Darian-Smith, 1999, p 4)

[I]n creating our own centers and our own locals, we tend to forget that our centers displace others into the peripheries of our making.
(Probyn, 1990, p 176)

'Once upon a time I had everything. There was laughter and happiness in my home. But ever since my father's illness rendered him speechless, life was engulfed in gloom. No one gets into this profession because of choice. Taking advantage of my father's illness, my uncle brought me to the city to get me a job. What job? The bastard forced me into prostitution.' Aman looks distressed upon hearing her story. At which point Chameli breaks into husky laughter and asks him 'So – how did you like it?'. Aman responds, 'Like what?'. 'The story? It was a lie. Tell that story to a customer after three pegs of whiskey, he will pay me 500 rupees as a tip.' Aman is confused and angry – and Chameli breaks into further uncontrollable laughter.

Aman then inquires about her family. 'My mother loved chameli (jasmine) flowers – that's why she named me "Chameli". We had a very big house. We used to dance and play music every night and day … My mother was also in the profession here in Mumbai. She had a huge debt that she needed to repay. One night when I was sleeping with my sister, I was awoken by my mother's screams. Some men were dragging her out of the house. They forced her into a car and drove away. Some folks tell me that they burnt her alive. Her body was found on the seashore. At the tender age of 16, I was initiated into the sex trade to try and pay off my mother's debt. You see this tattoo – (26.6.2000) – it is the day I repaid every penny of my mother's debt. Isn't my story more tragic than a movie?' Aman is once again disturbed. Chameli scrutinises his expression and then bursts into laughter again. 'But this isn't true either. This tale is ruse number two. This story will fetch me 1,000 rupees extra from the client.'

Chameli is a Bollywood film directed by Sudhir Mishra released in 2004 that represents an encounter between Aman Kapur, a well-paid, young investment consultant, and Chameli, a sex-worker, whose life is only revealed through highly orchestrated fictional narratives that may generate income, but never reveal 'her story'. The two meet fortuitously while taking shelter in the underbelly of Mumbai's alleyways, during a dark and stormy night. Chameli is looking for business, and the consultant is looking for a mechanic to repair his car, which has broken down in the storm. But over the course of the night, he finds himself challenged by the character of Chameli, and also exposed to the sordid underworld of Mumbai life, of which he was unaware.

The film operates at two levels. At the level of celluloid entertainment, it solicits its audience by depicting a rather provocative one-night encounter between two strangers who inhabit very different worlds. It also operates at the level of the symbolic, where Aman represents the well-intentioned liberal male, who withdraws from any sexual overtures made by Chameli, but is horrified by her tales of exploitation and abuse. He is pure and untainted, the 'good, respectable man' who is initially disgusted by this 'licentious street woman' and seeks to disengage from her completely. He assumes that she is a tragic victim who has come into the trade on account of unfortunate and violent episodes in her life. He is, however, progressive, morally non-judgmental and seeks, at times, to rescue her from her plight by offering her monetary compensation. Chameli, in contrast, symbolises the very complex, layered sexual subject in a postcolonial setting. With her stories of victimisation and woe, deception and violation of her rights, she plays on the liberal narratives that imagine women in the sex industry specifically, and the third world generally, as invariably in situations of exploitation and abuse. Such narratives simultaneously reinforce conservative sexual morality and the view that women are vulnerable. Their problems can be resolved through legal and moral protection. The difference is that Chameli uses the very device of victim narratives in strategic and normatively challenging ways.

Chameli knows that the client who buys her services believes these narratives, so she sells them for financial gain. She anticipates and fully comprehends the liberal agenda of her middle-class male client, and thus is able to create a product that conforms to this agenda and also brings her benefit. The liberal agenda that seeks this product is shared by the client who pays out of charity, as well as the liberal activist/scholar who will humanise and civilise her through strategies of rescue, rehabilitation and legal reform. While Chameli consciously and carefully represents herself as a conforming object in her narratives, she simultaneously negotiates a deconstructive move. This move involves producing herself as an intricate, multifaceted, thinking subject – one who cannot be comprehended in exclusively liberal terms, humanised and civilised through the conferment of formal legal rights. This manoeuvre is a conscious, manipulative subversion of sex, culture and law, which can only be performed by a subject – not an object, who is merely acted upon. *

Chameli provides me with a trajectory into the contemporary debates on how law has been implicated in the ways in which issues of sexuality, culture and subaltern locations are addressed. Law has been used not only as a site of empowerment, but also as a device for excluding the world's Others, or including them on terms that are quite problematic, both historically as well as in the contemporary context. These inclusions and exclusions have been produced in and through law, either by emphasising the difference of the subaltern subject as incapable of choosing or consenting, and thus incapable of exercising rights, or as backward and uncivilised, to be redeemed and incorporated into the liberal project through the process of assimilation. A third approach is to regard the Other as dangerous and a threat to the security of nation-states, to be either incarcerated or annihilated.

These approaches have served either as a justification for the 'exclusion' and subordination of the Other from the liberal project, or for her inclusion on terms that require that she reinvent herself in ways that are familiar and comprehensible to the liberal project. The colonial subject was denied a host of civil and political rights on the grounds that he or she was backward and uncivilised. Women were denied the right to vote or participate in public life on the grounds that they were biologically inferior, incapable, and infantile. Blacks were regarded as subhuman, as property, incapable of claiming rights and privileges. Apartheid and slavery were both justified and sustained in and through law on the basis of this reasoning. Sexual subalterns have at times been treated as immoral, diseased, or criminal. Sex-workers and homosexuals, for example, have been incarcerated or denied legal rights because of the public nature of their sexuality, as well as the threat they ostensibly pose to cultural and familial norms. In the contemporary moment, a similar logic has been deployed in dealing with new Others, the Muslim as well as the transnational migrant. The Muslim is regarded as fanatical and incapable of being assimilated, and, together with the transnational migrant, cast as a threat to the security of nation-states. These groups have simultaneously been targeted by anti-trafficking and immigration laws, arbitrary detention laws, and racial profiling, through the waging of an elusive and highly dangerous 'War on Terror'.

At the same time, law is a site where these roles and identities have been challenged. I use the term 'subaltern' in relation to law not as a substitute for minorities. The subjects I discuss are minorities in so far as they seek to claim formal equal rights. However, 'the subaltern' is also a device that brings a normative challenge to the assumptions on which law operating from a postcolonial location – with its claims to universality, neutrality, and objectivity – is based. The subaltern is a peripheral subject, and is deployed by postcolonial theory to situate these challenges within a specific historical, cultural and political context, and reveal how critical it is to understand the ways in which colonial discourse informs the postcolonial present. In each chapter I reconceptualise law as a site of discursive struggle, where the role and place of the world's cultural Others who are peripheral subjects – such as transnational migrants, Muslims, homosexuals or sex-workers – have been and continue to be fought out. In each essay, the role of law is exposed as a site of oppression, exclusion and subjugation as well as contradiction and struggle. These chapters demonstrate the theoretical and disruptive possibilities that the subaltern subject brings to law, and to the legal regulation of sexuality and culture. In the process, challenges are offered to the political and theoretical constructions of the nation, cultural authenticity, and women's subjectivity.

The theoretical framework

Postcolonial feminist legal theory provides the overarching theoretical framework for these essays. Postcolonial feminism is an emerging area of scholarship that seeks to account for women's conditions of subordination within the conditions of postcolonialism. It cannot be articulated as a new, monolithic theory, given the problem of yoking together the theories of women in countries as diverse as India, Kenya and Jamaica, with those of the first world postcolonial nations such as Canada, Australia and New Zealand. One major distinction, of course, lies in the fact that Canada, Australia and New Zealand are white-settler colonies. The heterogeneity of postcolonial feminist theories and practices precludes the formulation of a grand theory. It is a scholarship articulated within the politics of positionality – that is, within the location of both the theorist and the audience – and not merely articulated by third world scholars located in Western academia (Dirlik, 1994; Sunder Rajan, 1997). An awareness of who speaks for whom, how and where, as well as of who is listening and to what end, informs the politics of postcolonial feminism (Mani, 1998; Sunder Rajan, 1997). The postcolonial feminist position in this collection is articulated from the location of the Indian subcontinent, yet it speaks to broader global politics and relations of domination that inform those politics.

Postcolonial feminism provides a critical and necessary challenge to explanations of women's subordination that have been furnished from liberal and Western feminist positions, especially those that have come to occupy the international human rights arena in their understanding and articulation of concerns of third world women. For example, in this book I examine how engagements with trafficking, violence against women and sexuality in the context of human rights, have served to reinforce the first world/third world divide between women. Postcolonial feminism exposes the imperial and essentialist assumptions about third world women and culture that have come to characterise the debates on women's rights, and which rely on a centre-periphery model of world culture. It not only challenges the 'us and them', 'here and there' divides along which liberalism and 'global feminism' have operated. It also challenges attempts to universalise women's experiences primarily along the lines of gender, which perpetuate the exclusions that have been the hallmark of 'universalising strategies' since the colonial encounter. Strategies that celebrate some notion of 'global sisterhood', or argue that all women are similarly oppressed, obscure the universalising and hegemonic moves on which such claims are historically based, at times perpetuating the exclusion of the very constituency they claim to represent, through cultural, religious or sexual 'Othering'. The search for universal solutions to women's concerns continues to ignore both the significance of the colonial encounter for the situation and understanding of women in the postcolonial world, and also how their struggles for rights are tethered to the legacy of this encounter in the contemporary moment.

Postcolonial feminism is not merely a counter to 'Western feminism' (Bulbeck, 1997, pp 97–128). Such a position would only add to the entourage of binaries – us and them, first world/third world, here and there – that already characterise a large amount of the scholarship that attempts the 'global move'. Postcolonial feminism is in part a challenge to the systems of knowledge that continue to inform feminist understandings of women and the subaltern subject in the postcolonial world, and seeks to create a project of inquiry and interrogation that will better inform feminist projects that speak to and for these subjects (Spivak, 1990, pp 62–63). The scholarship thus engages with feminist projects, especially liberalism, that fetishise the third world woman, treating her as an object of study or a subject to be rescued and rehabilitated by the feminist mission.

The scholarship also challenges feminists in the postcolonial world who continue to reinforce the divides between 'us' and 'them' by constantly scrambling to secure an 'authentic' primordial identity to distinguish their positions from Western feminism. For example, arguments that seek to speak from an 'authentic' Indian feminist position, or a 'culturally distinctive' position, can land themselves in a number of traps, including cultural essentialism, homogenising the location and politics of Western feminism, reinforcing right-wing agendas and women's victim positions in the postcolonial world. Efforts to naturalise boundaries and distinctions produce mythical differences that have informed the political and legal strategies of feminists and others in the postcolonial context. Boundaries must be engaged as sites of historicised struggle, where differences are deconstructed and knowledge is produced about shifting identities and multiple subjectivities that are neither essentialised nor universalised (Gandhi, 1998; Loomba, 1998). There is a need to avoid slipping into a 'native' or 'authentic' feminist position of culturally relativist knowledge production, which serves only to erase or marginalise the heterogeneity of the Others.

There is a striking feature of postcolonial feminism that is rarely present or evident in its Western counterparts. Education, celluloid and the ease of travel force the acquisition of knowledge about the West at the same time as postcolonials are beginning to know their own contexts. It is a sense of inquiry and curiosity that I have not seen present in Western scholarship, which either continues to operate in terms of the binary oppositions, assumptions and stereotypes that this book sets out to challenge, or merely assumes that the metaphysical and ontological pursuits are identical – that the starting point of knowledge is the same. As Gayatri Spivak states, there is a distinction between the superficial desire to 'learn about' the Other and the desire to 'know' the non-West through conscious and assiduous study and participation (Spivak, 1991, p 228). The location of the postcolonial feminist produces a double consciousness that is a central feature of the postcolonial imagination and of postcolonial scholarship. The desire to know the West does not stem exclusively from a desire to be like the West. In fact, it is this desire that provides a location from which to develop a critique of the partiality of the universal truth claims and cultural assumptions of those who speak for the 'global', and to expose any dominant hierarchy or hegemonic use of the word 'gender'.

Feminist positions, including postmodern feminism, do not adequately interrogate the colonial trappings and hegemonic first world formations on which law is based, which continue to exploit women and the subaltern subject and exclude or ignore the non-West from their discussions (Grewal and Caplan, 1994, p 2). They do not adequately address how the colonial past continues to inform the postcolonial present, contemporary relationships of domination and subordination, and understandings of difference. The non-West is included in this literature either as a traumatised subject who is maimed, brutalised or discriminated against by her cultural context, or as a 'global sister' celebrating the cause of the 'universal' feminist agenda, fighting for an emancipatory goal that is defined purely in terms of a liberal framework. Feminist scholars and activists always operate from within a cultural space. Postcolonial scholarship has revealed that culture is not merely a negative or deplorable attribute of the Other, but is an attribute of the West as much as the rest. For example, the responses of liberal feminists to alterity or the third world woman have to be understood as emanating from a culture where the treatment of difference is deeply connected to the history of British and European colonial expansion in the 19th-century. This expansionist project saw the subjugation of two-thirds of the world under white rule, justified partly on the grounds that the native non-white subject was regarded as culturally backward, inferior and civilisationally immature (Young, 1990, pp 1–20). And the very notion of a 'global sisterhood' needs to be problematised, as it simply assumes that we are all headed towards a progressive end, expressed in terms of human rights and democracy, and that women's needs and desires are both uniform and universal. It is a concept that is limited, as it does not rigorously engage with the complexities of the contemporary political, economic and cultural formations that structure the global arena and operate along a first world/third world divide.

Postcolonial feminist legal theory offers another cosmology within which to understand the world's 'Others', and diverse locations from which they can speak. Although there are several echoes of postcolonial theory and subaltern studies scholarship in other schools of thought, postcolonial feminist scholarship brings a new and unique perspective to a book on sexuality, culture and law. It illustrates how a locational analysis and an understanding of historical processes bring a critical challenge to the assumptions about the Other that have informed scholarship and legal initiatives in the area of sexuality, at the domestic, regional and international levels. It also provides the insight that certain assumptions of liberalism and modernity – a progressive narrative of history, a fixed and stable sovereign state and sovereign subject – are not received as uninterrogated universal truth claims. The view of the world based on a unitary, reasoning subject, and on a set of dichotomies of the world, is exposed in liberalism's encounters with the world's constitutive Others, which have disrupted any claims made in favour of a narrative progress of human history. The idea that liberal values have liberated the world from its primitive past and forged ahead towards a more emancipated and equal world order further crumbles when confronted with these challenges.

This book is not focused on developing legal strategies for liberating the Other. Instead, my endeavour is to force an interrogation of, and a sense of accountability within, the scholarship produced by and on behalf of women and subaltern subjects who inhabit the postcolonial world, and to evaluate the justice-seeking projects formulated by and on behalf of these groups in the legal arena. Each chapter examines the strengths and limitations, the perils and paradoxes, of legal engagements by subaltern subjects from a postcolonial feminist perspective. I question the divides, myths and truth claims – remnants of colonial discourse – that have frequently been reinforced through legal scholarship and legal interventions. The chapters are specifically directed towards de-linking feminist scholarship and legal strategies and proposals from some of their homogenising claims, while at the same time engaging with alterity without falling into a relativist position (Grewal and Kaplan, 1994).

Erotic justice

This book is concerned with interpreting postcolonialism broadly, in order to reconceptualise the processes of Western modernity as they relate to the formation of the West through the world's Others. I focus mostly on how these concerns play out in the context of women, though I also address other subjects, such as homosexuals, migrants, and Muslims. Each chapter challenges the dominant narratives of modernity that do not pay attention to the uneven development and variously disadvantaged histories of nations, races, communities and peoples. It is a challenge that does not consider imperialism as a thing of the past, but observes that colonialism's methods of domination are reproduced in different ways in the present, in and through the techniques of liberalism and through the discourse of rights. Erotic justice therefore requires a revisiting of historical claims and dominant narratives. The chapters are linked by a postcolonial feminist legal analysis, though they were written at separate moments and not with the intention that they read as a tidy narrative about the condition and legal situation of the subaltern – especially the sexual subaltern – in the modern era.

In Chapter 2, 'New Cosmologies: Mapping the Postcolonial Feminist Legal Project', I set out some of the claims made by liberalism, looking specifically at the notion of liberal internationalism, developed especially by Martha Nussbaum, as providing a universal remedy for the injustices experienced by women around the world. I discuss how some of the assumptions on which liberal internationalism are based have been challenged by postcolonial theory and subaltern studies scholarship, and how it cannot necessarily account for the complex relationship between law, culture and sexuality in a postcolonial context. I set out the main features which have come to be associated with postcolonial theory, including its challenge to progressive narratives of history, the relationship between power and colonial knowledge production, and the foregrounding of the complex and layered subject produced in and through the colonial encounter.

In the second part of the chapter I discuss some issues relating to the subject of law and sexuality that are familiar to feminist legal theorists and other critical scholars, and address these from a postcolonial feminist legal perspective. Specifically, I examine the construction of the public/private distinction, and evaluate feminist engagements with law and sexuality, and the contemporary challenges posed by the rise of the religious right in India. Each of these themes emerges at various points throughout this book. The legal regulation of sexuality in postcolonial India has operated along a public/private divide that was partly constituted by colonial legal regimes. This divide has been central to the ways in which issues of sexuality are implicated in understandings of culture and the very identity of the nation-state. Feminist engagements with law and sexuality have produced mixed results for women and sexual subalterns, partly because of the integral relationship between culture and sexuality, and assumptions about law that do not account for the way in which colonial legal histories continue discursively to infuse the present. I examine the contradictory impact of such engagements by looking specifically at the issue of sexual harassment. And finally, I discuss how the Hindu Right has pursued issues of sexuality in and through a liberal rights discourse. The Hindu Right is a contemporary right-wing religious and nationalist movement that is dedicated to the establishment of a Hindu state. Through its political wing, the Bharatiya Janata Party (Indian People's Party), which led a national coalition government between 1999 and 2004, the ideology of the Hindu Right exercised considerable influence on policy and the formulation of laws (Ahmad, 2000; Hansen, 1999; Jaffrelot, 1998; Kapur and Cossman, 2001). The legal strategies of the Hindu Right have built on the integral relationship between sexuality and culture, and they have been remarkably successful in advancing their agenda. The discussion demonstrates how a postcolonial analysis throws up challenges and obstacles that remain unaddressed by claims to universality, and by an uninterrogated liberal project. The analysis builds on existing critiques of the law's lack of emancipatory and transformative potential, as well as its discursive function, and exposes how these elements play out in a postcolonial context.

In Chapter 3, 'Erotic Disruptions: Legal Narratives of Culture, Sex and Nation in India', I explore the different understandings of culture that characterise the current debates on law, culture and sexuality. I expose how cultural essentialism is deployed to reaffirm dominant sexual ideology by those in positions of power, and how such an approach views culture as static and immutable. I also examine the ways in which cultural arguments are being made by those attempting to challenge this dominant narrative of culture, sex and nation. I argue that although the arguments may, at first glance, appear to deploy the same cultural essentialism used by those in positions of power, these arguments can be seen to be based, at a deeper level, on cultural hybridity. I attempt to reveal the ways in which this cultural hybridity is deployed, though in subtle ways, to counter the stagnant, fixed and immutable approach to culture that characterises the essentialist approach. I examine the possibilities of cultural hybridity in accommodating, or creating greater space for, the sexual subaltern and sexual speech.

My discussion looks at the ways in which these contemporary tensions are being played out in the legal domain, and how law is implicated in the formulation and reformulation of culture and sexuality. The results of the discursive struggles in this arena have been inconsistent, and the alliances they have thrown together depend upon the issues involved, often producing contradictory results for women and sexual subalterns. The idea of culture as hybrid is an important tool of the postcolonial intellectual project. It is a tool that exposes the essentialism inherent in imperial discourse, which produced an orient or a cultural Other or a native subject, as inferior reflections of the West. It also continues to inform our assumptions about Others in the contemporary moment.

In Chapter 4, 'The Tragedy of Victimisation Rhetoric: Resurrecting the "Native" Subject in International/Postcolonial Feminist Legal Politics', I turn to the international arena and how it is reinforcing assumptions about gender, culture and sexuality – especially of the third world female subject. I discuss how the international women's rights movement has reinforced the image of the woman as a victim subject, primarily through its focus on violence against women (VAW). I use the example of India to illustrate how this subject has been replicated in the postcolonial context, and the more general implications this kind of move has on women's rights. My main argument is that the focus on the victim subject in the VAW campaigns reinforces gender and cultural essentialism in the international women's human rights arena. It also buttresses the claims of some feminist positions in India that do not produce an emancipatory politics for women, and that thus fail to take advantage of the liberating potential of important feminist insights. These insights have challenged both the public/private distinction, according to which human rights theory has operated, and traditional understandings of power as emanating exclusively from a sovereign state.

In this chapter, I challenge the idea of the disempowered, tragic subject that has come to dominate the imaginations and responses of legal scholarship and legal interventions, especially when that subject is located in the third world. I want to think about ways in which we can create a space especially for the erotic subject, who exists in many contexts though she expresses herself in culturally specific ways. This subject can shatter any claim to a universal sexual or cultural truth, as sexual subalterns are diverse and pluralistic. I bring into the foreground the desire of this subject not as a way to deny that violence and exploitation that surrounds her life, but as a heuristic device to challenge the representation of her exclusively as a victim. Making the erotic subject visible not only challenges the dominant story about sex in the domestic context as something that is negative and culturally alien; it also challenges the stereotyped representations of the third world subject in the first world as an abject subject.

In the final chapter, 'The Other Side of Universality: Cross-Border Movements and the Transnational Migrant Subject', I examine the legal regulation of the border-crossings of transnational migrant subjects. I examine how the liberal subject and the nation-state are challenged through the contemporary phenomena of migration and border-crossings. I explore how the legitimacy of the transnational migrant subject, who is a subaltern, is reshaped and reconfigured in the process of crossing borders: rendered vulnerable, stigmatised, and even outlawed, in an effort to stop him or her from crossing borders through the operation of the anti-trafficking, anti-migration and anti-terror initiatives.

I examine three types of initiatives that states are adopting in the regulation of cross-border movements. First, I evaluate the international legal regulation of trafficking, as well as the impact of the US Anti-Trafficking Act 2000, on women's rights and their cross-border movements. These initiatives encourage protectionist responses from states, which restrict women's movement. They also reinforce assumptions that women's movement is coerced and primarily for the purposes of sexual exploitation, and that women themselves are helpless victims, incapable of choosing to move. Secondly, I address recent policy and legal initiatives by the UK government to encourage the assimilation of the transnational subject through new emotional, cultural and citizenship criteria. These measures target distinct cultural practices, such as arranged marriages, and require people who want to become UK citizens to take a compulsory English language test and an exam on British society, institutions and ways of life. These initiatives fortify a sense of British identity and penalise those who refuse to conform to dominant cultural, national and familial norms. Finally, using the example of Australia's recent treatment of refugees and asylum-seekers, I analyse how the status of the transnational migrant subject has been further corroded and delegitimised by their being cast as the Other in the emerging discourse of the conservative or religious right, as well as in and through the pursuit of the recent War on Terror. The overarching concern with security has afforded some states an opportunity to demonise the Other, who is projected as dangerous and a threat to the security of the nation. The redrawing of these boundaries at the rhetorical and political level has prompted legal proposals that perpetuate the fear of the Other, justifying his or her disenfranchisement, incarceration, and at times expulsion. It has also conflated issues of trafficking, migration and terrorism.

A recognition of the multi-dimensional aspects of subaltern lives in the postcolonial world creates the possibility of a dialogue between our worlds, though this dialogue will continue to be riven with conflict and contestation. A well-rounded, universal strategy is not a possibility, as such a project can only be sustained through erasures and marginalising conversations. An engagement with the postcolonial world on issues of law, culture, and sexuality cannot be viewed primarily through a lens that constructs the Other exclusively in terms of his or her disadvantage. Reiterating the location of Chameli and her strategic and normative challenges, these essays turn the gaze of universality back onto legal scholarship and legal interventions. At times, these betray a lack of respect for women and other subaltern subjects by assuming that they are defined only in terms of their disadvantage, that they do not have the capacity to choose, and that their liberation lies in the form of rescue and rehabilitation, law reform, or even military campaigns.

The critique offered in this book of the liberal and utopian project is not intended to result in despair, pessimism or a sense of hopelessness. It is intended to be productive, and to articulate a different cosmology within which to understand the relationship between postcolonial subjects, law, culture and sexuality, that does not reproduce universalising agendas or fall into a cultural relativist trap. This book also moves beyond the issue-based activism and identity politics that have come to replace transformative political movements. Earlier cosmologies, such as the socialist left, have withered or been reborn as 'New Labour', 'New Democrats' or 'New Socialism'. Long-awaited class antagonisms have failed to emerge in a world order where capital has become ubiquitous and new non-state actors have emerged, which are disparate and scattered (Brown, 2001, p 9). These developments have further exposed the internal contradictions and partiality of liberalism's claims to progress and universality. Despite this knowledge, there is a continuing appeal to rights discourse and a commitment to the idea of progress, as so much political hope has been invested in this narrative. It is an approach that Wendy Brown characterises as a 'Yes I know. But...' politics. The critique is suspended, out of concern that it will create anxiety, fear and even nihilism. Yet this is where I support Brown's contention that a position that equates critique with pessimism, and progress with optimism, is quite mistaken (Brown, 2001, p 15). This claim is exposed when we recognise that the idea of working towards a good society, a good family, a good woman, and a good man, are amongst the most dangerous, normatively speaking.

Erotic Justice engages with the question: what is the theoretical basis of our politics – especially in terms of our engagements with law – once the faith in liberalism and modernity have been eroded? Does it lie in a return to the past, a search for some 'golden era'? The 'golden era' position is being successfully lobbied for by various right-wing groups across the globe, stretching from the neoconservatives in the United States to the Hindu Right in India. Yet what vision do those who oppose the right have to offer as an alternative? The current political space, as evidenced in some of the chapters in this book, seems to be occupied by an activism that has not been thought through, which is producing reforms and proposals in the legal area that are proving increasingly problematic for those whom these movements seek to empower. There is an absence of deeper thinking in the area of law, thinking that looks into the genealogy of the truth claims on which law is based, and engages with the legal arena as a site of discursive struggle and normative challenges, rather than remaining committed to the idea that more rights lead to more freedom and greater equality, and that the meanings of such terms are uncontested. Although feminist legal theory more generally has provided a significant challenge to some of the claims about gender and sexuality on which law is based, it is not evident that its radical analysis has translated into anything other than the reinforcement of a liberal agenda. This book contributes to a critique that emerges from a postcolonial perspective, and is advocated as productive, as opening up the space for new political possibilities and imaginations. I argue that our postcolonial present needs to be understood by revisiting the colonial past and its encounters with the native subject. The colonial encounter issues into the present, fracturing political thinking that revolves around totality and completeness. It is not a project which claims to be universally applicable or relevant. However, it does provide openings and possibilities in the present that cannot be explained in terms of a continued embracing and acceptance of the terms of liberalism, progressive history, and the autonomous sovereign subject.

My hope is that this book will contribute to the development of a theory of erotic justice that would bring erotically stigmatised communities from our respective worlds into an inclusive conversation. I express a caution against strategies that advocate the superiority of assimilation over non-assimilative politics, or of uniformity over diversity, because as the following chapters demonstrate, such positions only lead to an exclusionary politics. A transformative politics can only emerge if we are willing to think from different locations and more creatively. The strategies we formulate and the assumptions we challenge today are critical, not so much for the present, but for the fact that there will always be another Other who will come along.

Chapter 2
New Cosmologies: Mapping the
Postcolonial Feminist Legal Project

In this chapter I elaborate on the postcolonial feminist legal project and how it provides an analytical lens through which to view issues of sexuality and law, and a locational framework that decentres the 'West' and the liberal venture in their role as providing the primary grid of analysis. The first section briefly discusses the arguments presented in favour of 'liberal internationalism' as a device for addressing violence and discrimination against women. I specifically examine the arguments presented by Martha Nussbaum in *Sex and Social Justice*. This text is of interest partly because it addresses the themes of sexuality and law that are relevant to this book, and also because it provides a strong endorsement of the liberal project as an international project with a universal recipe for 'women [in the third world] fighting against hunger and illiteracy and inherently unequal legal systems' (Nussbaum, 1999, p 6). I then examine the features of postcolonial theory and subaltern studies that expose some of the assumptions on which liberal claims are based, especially its claim to provide a universal remedy for the injustices experienced by women, particularly in the global South. More importantly, the discussion provides an analytical framework that is better equipped to address the rights and claims of women and other subaltern subjects in the postcolonial world and elsewhere.

In the second section of this chapter, I bring a postcolonial feminist legal analysis to bear on three issues that are quite familiar to feminist legal theorists and other critical scholars, but that play out quite differently in postcolonial India. I analyse the role of the public/private distinction, how it has been produced partly in and through the colonial encounter, and its implications on the relationship between law, sexuality and culture in the postcolonial present; I evaluate feminist engagements with law and sexuality, focusing by way of example on sexual harassment, and on how these engagements have produced contradictory results for women and sexual subalterns; and finally, I discuss the role of the religious right in advancing its agenda on sexuality in and through rights discourse, exposing how sexuality continues to be an important site of struggle over claims to cultural authenticity, the definition of Indian national identity, and the role of women within that state and culture. Although some of the issues and debates may look quite similar to those in North America and Britain, they play out very differently in a postcolonial context. As discussed in this chapter and elsewhere in this book, encounters with law are shaped in part by the relationship between culture and sexuality produced during the colonial encounter, which continues to impact on the way in which sexuality is taken up and developed in the legal arena.

Liberal internationalism and the capabilities approach

[T]he widows who gathered in Bangalore were learning to think of themselves not as *discarded adjuncts* of a family unit, *half dead things*, but as centers of thought and choice and action, citizens who could make claims against the state for respect and resources. All this is liberal individualism, and liberal individualism, consistently followed through, entails a radical feminist program. (Nussbaum, 1999, p 67; emphasis added)

In *Sex and Social Justice*, Martha Nussbaum develops an argument in favour of a capabilities approach to human development. Nussbaum's theory of justice and human rights is developed from her reading of Amartya Sen's concept of substantial freedoms or *capabilities*, which he developed to address questions of justice and human development (Sen, 1999). The capabilities approach identifies 'a kind of basic human flourishing' based on a list of central capabilities drawn up by Nussbaum, from which she generates some specific political principles. The list includes the following 10 central human functions: to live for a normal human life span; to have good reproductive health, nourishment, and adequate shelter; to have bodily integrity, which is the ability to move freely from place to place and be free from sexual violence; to have integrity of the senses, imagination, and thought, that enable one to think and reason in a 'truly human way'; to have the ability to express emotions, which includes the ability to love, grieve, experience longing, gratitude and justified anger; to have practical reason, which is the ability to form a conception of the good and reflect critically on how to plan one's life; to live for and in relation to others and have a social basis of self-respect and non-humiliation; to live with a concern for and in relation to animals, plants and nature; to play, which includes laughing and enjoying recreational activities; and finally, to have control over one's political and material environment (Nussbaum, 1999, pp 40–41; Nussbaum, 2000). The capabilities approach emphasises that the central goal of public policy must be to promote the capabilities of each citizen to perform these important human functions. Each capability must be equally promoted by society in order to ensure an individual's claim to a good life in which 'the dignity of the human being is not violated by hunger or fear or the absence of opportunity' (Nussbaum, 1999, p 40). The capabilities approach considers people one by one, and does not lump them together in families or communities. It can lead to the emergence of new communities which are embedded in the local context, and are not submerged in the aims and wants of the husband and family. Nor is it an approach concerned with the distribution of resources, because resources, as Nussbaum argues, do not have value in themselves when they are disconnected from their promotion of *human functioning* – that is, what humans actually do and are. The capabilities approach is also based on choice, where the government does not direct the citizen into acting in a specific way, but simply makes sure that the citizen has all the resources and conditions that are required for acting in those ways. Thus, the central feature of the capabilities approach is that it shifts governmental action from what individuals should think or do, which can be oppressive and tyrannical, to a focus on how to assist individuals to think and do what they want. Society is obliged to provide individuals with the basic infrastructure in order to enable them to make choices. 'Once the stage is fully set,' Nussbaum states, 'the choice is up to them' (Nussbaum, 1999, p 45). Nussbaum advocates this capabilities approach for all members of humanity – a liberal internationalism, that is not just confined to one's own context. As she writes, 'I believe that individuals have moral obligations to promote justice for people outside their national boundaries and that their governments do also' (Nussbaum, 1999, p 6).

Nussbaum's analysis draws quite specifically on the work of Kant as represented today in the political thought of John Rawls, and also the work of John Stuart Mill, thinkers who she says best exemplify liberal tradition and doctrine. There are two primary assumptions about humans at the heart of the liberal tradition as articulated by these scholars: that all individuals have worth because of their power of moral choice; and that society and politics must respect and promote this choice and the equal worth of the choosers (Nussbaum, 1999, p 57).

Nussbaum acknowledges that there are some important critiques of liberalism put forward by feminists that must be confronted for her argument to be persuasive. The first is the idea that liberalism is based on individualism, and treats the subject as existing prior to social relations, outside of any social ties (Nussbaum, 1999, p 59). Nussbaum's response to this critique is that feminists should be concerned about the fact that liberalism has not been nearly individualist enough when it comes to women and family. Liberalism has tended to focus on the autonomy of males and the development of the public and private spheres. It has not taken the tenets of individual autonomy to their 'socially radical conclusion' (Nussbaum, 1999, p 65). Nussbaum relies on JS Mill's argument in *The Subjection of Women* to illustrate how this liberal thinker was in fact concerned with the well-being of the individual in the family and argued that law should be used to advance the fair treatment of every individual in the family, including women (Mill, 1997). She acknowledges that some liberal thinkers have been reluctant to intervene in the family, or to follow Mill's lead. Yet she states that this reluctance lies not in liberalism *per se*, but in fact reflects an abuse of the liberal tradition and runs against its true tenets (Nussbaum, 1999, p 65).

The second critique put forward by feminists is that the liberal vision is abstract and formalistic, and does not take account of important differences such as class, caste, religion, gender and race. It relies on a formal model of equality that ignores these important social differences. Nussbaum acknowledges that the liberal principle of formal equal treatment, 'if it is applied in an excessively abstract or remote manner', fails to demonstrate equal respect for all persons (Nussbaum, 1999, p 68). Such an approach could, for example, justify segregation. But Nussbaum argues that it is a mistake to think that liberalism has been committed to ahistorical abstraction, even though some liberal thinkers have been guilty of such an error. Liberal philosophers, she argues, have rejected such notions of pure formal equality, while liberalism affords individuals the right to demand equality from their government in ways that take into consideration material prerequisites, so that it aims at 'equality of capabilities'. A true liberal position on equality promotes equal worth, which requires that society work towards promoting the capacities of people to choose a life that accords with their own thinking.

Nussbaum also poses the question of whether focusing on the idea of women as members of different groups – families, religious traditions, ethnic groups – is better for women than 'abstract individualism'? She argues that feminists who focus on the differences between race and class should heed the liberal tradition's emphasis on looking at human dignity in a 'fully general way' – that is, to adopt a holistic approach consistent with a feminism that does not put the interests of women above all other marginalised groups, but rather fights hierarchy across the board (Nussbaum, 1999, p 71).

A third feminist critique is that of liberalism's emphasis on human beings as reasoning subjects. Although reasoning – specifically practical reasoning – has helped women to secure their equality, it does tend to place much emphasis on something that is considered a male trait, and denigrates traits such as emotion and imagination that are traditionally associated with females (Nussbaum, 1999, p 72). Nussbaum once again argues that this is a misrepresentation of the liberal argument, at least as presented by JS Mill, who combined love and emotions with rationality: 'Let her love others and give herself away – provided she does so freely and judiciously, with the proper critical scrutiny of social norms' (Nussbaum, 1999, quoting Mill, p 77). Nussbaum argues that this proposal does not kill love through male rationality, but 'indicates the conditions under which love is a healthy part of a flourishing life' (Nussbaum, 1999, p 77). Nussbaum does not reject the liberal emphasis on reason, though she does reject excessive male rationalisation. She seeks to create a liberal construction of emotions which represents a balance between reason and feelings – as opposed to emotions, which are imposed on women through tradition, convention, and patriarchal social conditioning. This wonderfully balanced liberal subject is not visualised as a man, but as a female who is able to centre her life on the experiences of love and other emotions which are consciously given through the employment of reason.

Nussbaum argues that the thing women must most mistrust is habit, disguised in the form of tradition, as it has invariably been used to their disadvantage. Women need to recognise that tradition has often been articulated by men and used to subordinate women to do men's bidding (Nussbaum, 1999, p 79). And the most regressive traditions are located in the third world. She proclaims that 'We [American women] would never tolerate a claim that women in our own society must embrace traditions that arose thousands of years ago – indeed, we are proud that we have no such traditions. Isn't it condescending, then, to treat Indian and Chinese women as bound by the past in ways that we are not?' (Nussbaum, 1999, p 37). Nussbaum is willing to suffer the label of Western imperialist, rather than to 'stand around in the vestibule waiting for a time when everyone will like what we are going to say' (Nussbaum, 1999, p 30). She states quite categorically that any tradition that objects to the universal obligation to protect human functioning and its dignity, and the dignity of women as being equal to that of men, is unjust (Nussbaum, 1999, p 31). Liberalism must be used to challenge tradition and the social formation of sexual desire, to ensure that women think first before they give themselves away to another. Their desire for pleasure must be acted upon with conscious reflection and out of an exercise of choice, and not habit or tradition. It is in the context of habit and tradition that women have the most need for reason.

A recurring refrain in *Sex and Social Justice* is that the liberal position as such is not flawed, but that there has been a profound inconsistency in what liberalism stands for and how it has operated in relation to women. Nussbaum says that what we see here 'is not a failure intrinsic to liberalism itself. It is, in fact, a failure of liberal thinkers to follow their own thought through to its socially radical conclusion' (Nussbaum, 1999, p 65). For example, subordination by sex has been deemed to be natural, and the subject of sex ignored by political philosophers and theories of justice. It is only feminism and the unmasking of inequalities in familial arrangements that are bringing about the implicit promise in liberalism (Nussbaum, 1999, p 10).

Nussbaum provides an important defence of liberalism, and a response to the feminist critiques of liberalism. However, her responses still fail to engage with the critiques of postcolonial feminists, postcolonial theory and subaltern scholarship, which have exposed the limitations of liberalism – in particular its inability to transcend assumptions about the Other on which legal reasoning and the liberal project are based. Liberalism has been able to operate partly because it has been able to justify the denial of rights and withholding of benefits from a vast subsection of people. And the idea that progress is being made, that more and more people are included within the discourse of rights and that the ideals of liberalism are being realised, is not borne out in practice. There remains a deep ambivalence in the liberal project, which seeks to include the 'wretched of the earth' and all those left behind in the inexorable march of progress. Yet the project is unable to transcend the need for an Other, and continues to deny rights and benefits to a host of subjects, who are excluded either because they exist in opposition to and threaten the liberal project (such as those accused of being 'Islamic terrorists') or because they are incapable of being redeemed, unable to comply with the cultural, familial, religious or sexual norms that inform justice-seeking projects, such as sex-workers, migrants and homosexuals. The problem is not that liberalism fails to live up to its own practice, but rather that failure is constitutive of the tradition.

The aim of restoring liberalism to its pristine, original elegance is an elusive one, for its history belies the possibility of any such origins. Liberals must be willing to embrace the history of liberalism, not excavate some supposedly pure form of it. Resorting to some 'authentic' version of liberalism simply denies the reality of those whom it claims to represent, disclaiming their histories and imposing another's through a hegemonising move. Returning for a moment to the work of JS Mill, Nussbaum refers to his text *The Subjection of Women*, which is undoubtedly a very progressive document for its time, but Mill's work also exhibits a propensity towards approval of Empire. For example, in *On Liberty*, which is hailed and cited as a crucial text in the liberal tradition, and has informed the more absolutist stands on the right to free speech, especially in the United States, Mill justified the exclusion of the 'native' or 'colonial' subject from the enjoyment of this right, based partly on the argument that this subject lacked the capacity to reason, and had not fully reached the stage of civilisational maturity (Collini, 1989, pp 13–14). Mill supports the market place of competing ideas, in which reasoning subjects are able to differentiate between good and bad ideas. However, as Paul Passavant has argued, quite specific moral geographies constituted an integral part of Mill's arguments on speech and liberty (Passavant, 1999, pp 61–85). Passavant traces the genealogy of the right to free speech, arguing that Mill's use of this concept was constituted in a Eurocentric context, and based on internal and external borders. The external border was inscribed upon a map of the 'moral geography' of the civilised and the barbaric. A line was drawn between those who deserved liberty and free speech and those who did not. Mill's argument was based on the assumption that the right to free speech could only be exercised by the thinking and reasoning, autonomous liberal subject. It was a right available to the civilised West. The very conditions of discussion and debate required a civilisationally mature society and persons who had the ability to consent:

> For the same reason, we may leave out of consideration those backward states of society in which the race itself may be considered as in its nonage ... Despotism is a legitimate mode of government in dealing with barbarians provided the end be their improvement ... Liberty, as a principle, has no application to any state of things anterior to the time when mankind has become capable of being improved by free and equal discussion ... (Mill, quoted in Collini, 1989, p 13)

Thus the right to free speech is marked as a distinguishing feature of the civilised West, in contrast to the disentitled, external, distant, and chaotic non-West.

Mill's views were no doubt heavily influenced by his father's major work on the *History of British India*, a 19th-century account of Indian manners and morals. In this account, James Mill sought to demonstrate why India was ineligible to be numbered among the civilised nations. He discussed the past deficiencies that made India backward and incapable of being reformed except through foreign rule and despotism. The argument served to relegate the subcontinent to the primitive end of the civilisational spectrum. Thus, the specific liberal tradition referred to by Nussbaum not only incorporates arguments about freedom and equal worth, it also incorporates arguments about civilisation, cultural backwardness and racial superiority.

It seems important for liberal feminists, wherever they are located, not merely to assume that the starting point of the analysis is always the same. There is a critical need to reposition our thinking when engaging with the postcolonial world, and to understand the double-consciousness that informs the perspectives of postcolonial feminism. It is a position that emerges from historical processes, processes that have been contested, complex and contingent. Many feminists, women, and sexually and socially marginalised or stigmatised communities in the postcolonial world (and elsewhere) have simply not imbibed the liberal response in its 'pure form', for its legacy has not been a liberating one. It is of course possible to work with poor, widowed or illiterate women in the postcolonial context and expose them to the possibilities of liberal individualism that the 'widows in Bangalore' were exposed to, and to transform them from 'dead things' into citizens imbued with agency and choice. But it is also possible to sit with these same women and other disadvantaged groups to talk about the strengths and limitations of liberal rights claims and choices, and how the project of universality and 'liberal internationalism' is a deeply problematic and, at times, exclusive one. Women who have been excluded from the universal project of liberalism are also the first to understand and be critical of claims of universality and for reform. This form of critical knowledge is extremely empowering, and provides a tool with which to challenge the assumption that the starting point of knowledge is always and already the same.

Given the extent to which exclusion has been justified in the name of liberalism, arguments that remain confined to pointing out its faulty application, or the abuse of the tradition by some liberal thinkers, begin to ring hollow and force a deeper interrogation of a position based on liberal internationalism, as well as a greater willingness to work with whatever such critiques produce. In my view, this process of interrogation is essential if we are to move towards a political project that deals with the messiness of the world, and the inequalities that surround us. This process also forces the ball back into the court of liberalism, which must take responsibility for the way in which it has operated in different parts of the world, and must acknowledge its untidy and exploitative history, rather than deny it. The story of liberalism's lofty goals and values can only be told by those who have benefited from its application – those who historically held two-thirds of the world in subjugation, or enslaved people on the grounds of colour, or denied them rights on the grounds of their inferior sex, or who today use pre-emptive strikes against countries deemed 'uncivilised' and 'hostile to freedom', in the name of freedom, justice and democracy. In the contemporary moment, while some liberal philosophers continue to polish and shine the liberal stone, others continue to exploit the 'dark side' of liberalism, pursuing their narrow, myopic, self-perpetuating agendas, under the guise of equality, freedom, justice, and the idea of immutable human values.

Contemporary liberal thinkers might seek to learn from the double-consciousness that is produced when these arguments are raised in a postcolonial context. Law and the liberal project on which it is based have had a troubled reception from their very introduction into the postcolonial world. The project served to subordinate the native, deny him or her rights to sovereignty and at times to any recognition of humanity (Anghie, 1990). These ideas were received into the colonial context as culturally specific to the colonial power, and as exclusive. They cannot be explained away by a position that the liberals just got it wrong or failed to fulfil their promise of equal respect and equal worth. I argue in several chapters in this book how these values are and remain highly contested and their meaning contingent on prevailing, dominant ideologies. For example just as the imperial project was able to shape liberal values in ways that enabled colonial expansion, similarly the religious right in the contemporary moment has been able to advance its rather conservative agenda in and through liberal rights discourse not in opposition to it. The terms of liberalism do not simply exist in some social and cultural void, but are shaped and determined by the context in which they are located. In India, the Hindu Right, a religious right-wing nationalist movement that until recently led a coalition government, supports the right to make choices, build new communities, right wrongs, develop an active citizenship, improve the state, and recognise common needs/problems/capacities.[1] It shares all the principles and ideals articulated by Nussbaum. The Hindu Right has also used these principles to advance its agenda effectively through liberal rights discourse – to assimilate Muslims, build a monolithic nationalistic, Hindu state, and to recognise women's

---

1 The Hindu Right refers to the main organisations and political parties in the current phase of Hindu communalism in India – namely, the Bharatiya Janata Party (BJP – Indian People's Party), the political wing of the Hindu Right; the Rashtriya Swayamsevak Sangh (RSS – Association of National Volunteers), which is the main ideological component of the movement; and the Vishwa Hindu Parishad (VHP – World Hindu Council), which promotes the religious ideology of the party (Chandra, 1984; Pandey, 1990; Prakash, 1995). Other smaller bodies include the militant and virulently anti-Muslim Shiv Sena ('foot soldiers of Lord Shiva') and the Bajarang Dal (Hanuman Squad).

rights, but within the terms of dominant sexual, cultural, and familial norms. Those who espouse a liberal project to advance women's rights and the rights of other minorities have failed to address how equality, freedom of (and from) religion and speech – which are all important rights that 'real' liberals would endorse – have been susceptible to ideologies and visions that are indeed quite distinct from feminism (Buss, 1998; Kapur and Cossman, 2001, pp 232–83).

Rather than producing more universals that attempt to 'fix' the derailed liberal tradition, legal analysis and strategies need to address law as a site of discursive engagement, and not merely as capable of promoting universal norms and values in which everyone will ultimately be included. Rather than turning to a follow-through project of more individualism (Nussbaum, 1999, pp 60–67; Okin, 1989), the starting point of an empowering politics should commence from a critical position. As I stated in the introduction to this book, such a possibility is provided for by postcolonial feminism, which is not co-dependent on Western feminism, or for that matter on a tightly bound notion of liberalism. It emerges from an appreciation of the meanings of history for the current political, cultural and legal present. It understands that historical wrongs and traumas are not resolved, healed or brought to closure simply through reformist projects, apologies or reparations. What is important to interrogate and understand is how colonial histories discursively suffuse the postcolonial present so overtly (Brown, 2001, p 141). By engaging with this tension, postcolonial scholarship exposes how scholars from the metropolis, including liberal feminists, either adhere to a hegemonic historical narrative and the idea that objectivity can serve as a form of historical and political repair, or engage in a theoretical critique of the hegemonic project only up to the point where it encounters the world's Others – that is, to the point where it simply includes more Others (Bhabha, 1991).

In the following section, I focus by way of example on how liberalism has operated in postcolonial India, by proceeding to unpack three core attributes of liberalism and exposing how this history reveals the contingent foundations of the liberal project. The analysis exposes how the liberal project lacks an emancipatory potential, and forces us to revisit feminist legal histories and the politics of meaning from a postcolonial perspective. At the same time the postcolonial project must not be regarded as merely a response or reaction to liberalism, but rather as produced in and through the colonial encounter. The relationships of domination and subordination continue discursively to infuse the present, albeit in different ways, and to provide an analysis and critique that can account for the complex relationships between law, sexuality and culture that are not explained through older, tattered frameworks.

Postcolonial theory and subaltern studies

Postcolonial feminism, which forms the theoretical framework that informs several chapters in this book, has derived several of its features from postcolonial theory and subaltern studies. Postcolonial theory has emerged through a complex interdisciplinary dialogue in the humanities, and through the incorporation of theories as antagonistic as Marxism and poststructuralism (Gandhi, 1998). As a result, much like postcolonial feminism, postcolonial theory has not emerged through a consensual dialogue, nor is it a cohesive project. Thus it is more appropriate to use the term to denote multiplicity and heterogeneity (Appiah, 1992, pp 221–54). Yet there are some features that have come to be associated with postcolonial theory which underscore the analysis in these chapters. The first is the critique of the linear, progressive narrative of history that occupies the citadel of liberal doctrine. The second is the relationship between power and colonial knowledge production, and how assumptions about the Other have come to be produced. The third feature is the question of agency and the resistive subject, produced in response to the pressures of the colonial encounter. This feature is influenced by the subaltern studies project, which exposes the complex and contradictory location of the subject in a postcolonial context.

Questioning narratives of progress

Postcolonial theory identifies the ways in which the devices and processes of Empire continue to inform our present, and it also identifies the ways in which these processes have been and continue to be challenged and altered. Postcolonial theory thus sets itself up against the idea of linear time and modernity's assumptions about the integral relationship between history and human progress. It challenges the modernist narrative of human progress based on the idea that the world has emerged from a darker, more uncivilised era. Such accounts use the Enlightenment as a starting point, and argue that law, the emergence of the nation-state, and individual sovereignty reflect the gradual transition of civilisation from the primitive into a modern and evolved form (Brown, 2001, p 6). This view regards history as a grand, progressive narrative through which Eurocentric narratives are totalised as the accurate account of all humanity. It is a position that views human history as moving forward, towards a single and common goal, frequently defined in terms of liberal democracy, good governance and the rule of law. The market is also included in this model, as it maximises choice and is the ultimate expression of freedom. Law is situated in this vision as an objective, external, neutral truth that propels us into the future, providing stability to the societies in which it operates and steering us carefully along the path of maturity, development and civilisation. The role of law in excluding or subjugating Others such as the colonial subject, women and blacks is not regarded as intrinsic, but rather as a result of manipulation that can be corrected through the gradual process of inclusion of these previously excluded groups. This perspective does not engage with the terms on which inclusion is determined, nor with the complex political problem of the relation between the past and the present, and of both with the future, which is the core tension that resides in law and its impact on the world's constitutive Others.

As Dipesh Chakrabarty has argued, Western historical study has posited a singular future for the masses of the world, in which justice and modernity are equated with being European (Chakrabarty, 2000, p 33). Cultures are marked as being in the process of transition, sitting in the 'imaginary waiting room of history' before they can claim the right to be modern (Appiah, 1992; Chakrabarty, 2000, p 8). Postcolonial theory provides the space for unmasking this view of history as emanating from the heart of Europe. It is a view that ultimately served the colonial enterprise, justifying intervention in societies deemed primitive and backward.

Postcolonial scholarship, together with other forms of critical scholarship and new international legal scholarship, challenges this position and the idea that human progress, and the emergence of the rule of law as a signifier of such progress, is such a neat and tidy project (Anghie, 1996; Berman, 1999; Jameson, 1991; Kennedy, 2000; Scott, 1999). Rather, it is a system that, based on a Eurocentric vision of the world and on Enlightenment ideals that have come under serious challenge by the world's Others, has not been inclusive. From this point of view, modernity's thesis of 'history as progress' is a fiction – and an exclusive one. Law, meanwhile, is understood as the mechanism for sustaining unequal structures of power – such as in the form of slavery or Empire – and as a subordinating or 'civilising' tool of the superior power.

The questioning of the historical narrative emerges partly from the debate about the very meaning of the term 'postcolonialism'. Postcolonialism is more than a temporal marker, as some scholars argue, that describes the moment of separation between colonialism and its aftermath (McClintock, 1995; Parry, 1997). Such a chronological approach does not address the ways in which colonialism continues to reverberate in the postcolonial moment, long after the Empire has been dismantled. As Albert Memmi has stated, 'the day oppression ceases, the new man [sic] is supposed] to emerge before our eyes immediately … this is not the way it happens. The colonized lives for a long time before we see that really new man' (Memmi, 1968, p 88). Despite the yearning at the point of independence to forget the past and look to the future, the break with Empire does not dispel the cultural, economic, political and legal implications it has had for the postcolonial world. The past remains present, albeit in a different form, and the historical relationship with Empire continues to inform the way in which relationships of dominance and subordination, inclusion and exclusion, are played out in the contemporary period.

By disrupting the dominant narratives of modernity, the postcolonial project denaturalises the relationships of dominance and subordination that underlie them. It exposes how master-narratives have failed to pay attention to the uneven and layered histories of the world, and how history has been produced through moments of rupture, crisis and disruption. Postcolonial theory captures these complex relationships of domination and subordination that mark the features of Empire, and reveals how its devices and processes continue to inform our present. These processes are not confined to the political, but also include the legal, cultural and economic. Thus some states might have transformed their former political relations with the West by winning independence, while their material subordination has continued. Powerful countries, which were also postimperial states, or never had colonies, continue to exercise some forms of control over weaker states through legal, economic and cultural processes (Marks, 2003, p 451; Said, 1993; Said, 1995). Hardt and Negri argue that today the processes of imperialism stand in contrast to the imperialism of the 19th-century. The previous form of imperialism was state-focused, whereas in the current moment the processes of imperialism are flexible and decentred, operating through the new sites of information technology and the new processes of capital. According to these authors, the nation has now been superseded by these new processes (Hardt and Negri, 2000, pp 187–90) – but their argument does not seem to take account of the

fact that earlier processes of Empire were also disparate, and incl
forms of local and indirect power-sharing (Fitzpatrick, 2004, p 42). The
imperialism in the contemporary moment is acknowledged and impli
relations of power between state and non-state entities, at both globai
levels. The 'post' in postcolonial does not merely mark an end to the .ionial
moment. It provides the opportunity to interrogate and elaborate on how the past
continues to inform the present.

The Other

The second, related strand of postcolonial theory examines the relationship between
power and knowledge-production, and how the Other came into being. In
epistemological terms, this involves the ways in which non-European objects of
knowledge were reconstituted in the colonial encounter through a range of
disciplines, including law, to make them comprehensible to the West. In other
words, this feature tells us how the Other came to be produced, constructed, and
made intelligible to the West. 'Orientalism' was a central discursive and institutional
mechanism that endowed colonised people with identities (Foucault, 1972;
Foucault, 1980; Foucault, 1984a; Said, 1995). These identities were not imposed
merely through the use of armies, but through textual knowledge and education,
historical writing, anthropological accounts, and law (Cohn, 1996; Mahmud and
Kapur, 2000, p 6; Viswanathan, 1989). This knowledge was constructed against
definitions and assumptions about colonial masculinity, culture and historical
difference (Sinha, 1995; Vijayan, 2002). The colonial power was able to give material
effect to the imperial enterprise by structuring the ways in which knowledge was
developed, received and understood. This process of the production of knowledge
was a site of tension and contest, and is critical to understanding how assumptions
about culture, difference and the Other came to be produced and continue to
operate in the present.

Postcolonial theory exposes how certain subjects have been excluded from the
terms of liberalism that justified the subjugation of Others. Indeed, when Europe
was in the midst of a struggle for liberty, equality and freedom, and there was an
assumption that these ideas were universal, these values seemed to stumble and
falter at the moment of their encounter with the unfamiliar. These unfamiliar
subjects came to be constituted as Others by being brought into systems of
knowledge and representation that justified difference in treatment. For example,
tradition and antiquity served at times for making moral judgments about the
native subject, and as one justification for establishing colonial rule in India.
Difference in treatment was justified by the placing of the society at the primitive
end of the civilisation scale, in need of being civilised at times through strict
discipline and punishment. In the present day these values meet with some of the
same difficulties in their encounters with difference – certainly in the case of sexual
and religious subalterns, and of transnational migrants. The postcolonial critique of
liberalism and the liberal subject has brought into question the ontological and
epistemological foundations of liberalism on which the rule of law is based.

Uday Singh Mehta has unpacked the ways in which liberalism was based on
promises of universality, while justifying exclusions in practice (Mehta, 1999). He

sets out how liberalism has enabled the production of Others. It makes specific assumptions about human nature: that all people are born equal, free and rational; that the subject is atomised and exists prior to history and social context. These assumptions link the capacity to reason with adherence to some notion of a universal natural law applicable to all. The claims of liberalism are transhistorical, transcultural and transracial. There is an assumption, for instance, that everyone is free, equal and rational – a view articulated by Locke in the 17th-century. This is the common basis for liberalism, from which its normative claims arise.

Mehta relates how 17th-century thinkers such as John Locke set out the justification for excluding certain individuals from the universal ideal. Locke used the example of children. If consent was fundamental to the legitimacy of political authority, and consent entailed the capacity to reason, then a subject who lacked the capacity to reason also lacked the capacity for consent. Such a rationale could be used to justify exclusion from the political constituency. Inclusion and exclusion in the liberal project were thus contingent on the ability to reason. Mehta then examines how Locke's thesis came to influence certain assumptions about the colonies in the 19th-century – in particular India – and how colonialism could quite comfortably justify the exclusion of a whole population from participating in the political sphere within the framework and logic of liberalism.

India inspired the theoretical imagination of a range of British political thinkers. In the 19th-century, writers focused on how India was different. Mehta draws specific attention to the work of James Mill, whose publication on the history of India in 1817 focused on difference, in contrast to Locke who focused on commonality. Mill depicted India as chaotic, unfathomable and inscrutable, which made the Indian different. India was distant and removed in civilisational terms, India was infantile and backward and Mill argued that a society so different from the ruling power should not be entitled to liberty. It was a society that could not become internally democratic, and the only choice available to it was despotism, as Indians were incapable of benefiting from free and equal discussion.

James Mill's logic is sometimes regarded as an argument for the permanent subjugation of India and of the native. In light of India's extreme difference, it is relegated to the primitive end of the civilisation spectrum, regarded as incapable of being entitled to self-government. Indians are infantile and childlike, so, in Lockean terms, incapable of reason and thus incapable of consent – the core requirement for a liberal subject, for liberal democracy, and for representative government. Imperialism was justified on the grounds that certain individuals and groups could not be included in the universal ideal, on the grounds that they were by nature incapable of consenting, or lacked reason, or were uncivilised. Mill's work contributed to the conclusion that the native subject was not entitled to liberty, primarily because he was so different from the ruling power, and incapable of becoming part of a democratic society.

Mehta thus illustrates how the universalist claims of liberalism discussed by Locke play out in practice a century and a half later to justify political exclusion in practice. In the 19th-century James Mill and other British liberal thinkers made clear that political institutions such as representative democracy were dependent on a

society having a certain state of development or maturation, and on a subj̲
capable of exercising reason. Empire was one way in which to rectify the
deficiencies of the past – what has frequently been described as the 'civilising
mission of Empire', in societies that have been stunted by history. 'The Empire ... is
an engine that tows societies stalled in their past into contemporary time and
history' (Mehta, 1999, p 82). Civilisational achievement became a necessary
prerequisite to progress and entitlement to the benefits of the universal project.
Mill's *History of British India* thus provided part of the theoretical basis for the liberal
endeavour to liberate India from its own culture (Majeed, 2001).

The much more sophisticated and younger JS Mill subsequently argued that
progress with respect to the individual refers to a life in which the 'higher quality
faculties' are expressed, and in which such expression is possible through a
commitment to representative democracy and other egalitarian institutions (Collini,
Geuss and Skinner, 1989, pp 14–15). Despite the more capacious form of liberalism
articulated by JS Mill, there are nevertheless aspects of his work that are consistent
with the imperial project (Bhabha, 1994, pp 93–101). Mill himself worked with the
East India Company for over 35 years, drafting policy documents that, once they
had been approved by the directors of the Company and the Board of Control, were
forwarded to the Governor-General of India (Zastoupil, 1994). These dispatches
became important in the formulation of colonial discourse, and also reflect how JS
Mill, amongst others, attempted to reconcile a universalist approach to liberty with
the subjugation of the Asian subcontinent (Lal, 1998; Parekh, 1994, pp 11–13; Parekh,
1995).

As Mehta argues, the principle of liberty was limited in its application by a
primitive evaluative scale of civilisational achievement. The clearest statement of
this position comes from Mill's essay 'Civilisation', in which he draws a distinction
between backward and civilised societies, arguing that all features of civilisation
reside in 'modern Europe, and especially Great Britain, in a more eminent degree ...
than at any other place or time' (Mill, 2002, p 132). This classification determines
whether savages can be members of democracies and share in the principles of
liberty that Mill argues need to structure societies. It is this civilisational argument
that constitutes part of Mill's defence of the British Empire and the imperial project.
It is, as Mehta argues, 'a principle of liberty whose applicability is limited to those
adults who are members of advanced civilisations' (Mehta, 1999, p 102). The logic
does not contradict Mill's liberal doctrine. In setting out his principle of liberty, his
purpose is to specify the necessary conditions under which that principle would
enable the maximisation of utility. In a society that is backward the principle would
not lead to the maximisation of utility, and this analysis is quite consistent with
Mill's position (Mehta, 1999, p 103). In other words, he sets out the terms on which
inclusion is to be determined, and justifies the resort to mechanisms that exclude the
Others until they have been trained into civilisation.

The significance of Mehta's analysis lies in its demonstration of how the
universalist claims of liberalism and the rational subject justified political exclusions
in practice, and also set out the terms for political inclusion. The subject of colonial
rule was regarded as different, infantile, primitive, an Other, and hence denied the
benefits of liberalism until he or she was trained into civilisation. This analysis was

with the terms of liberalism, and creates a logic that continues to
sent, justifying a host of exclusions, whether these are blacks,
and religious subgroups. Exclusion is thus inherent to liberalism,
f inclusion demand the erasure of difference. Both are based on
d on racial, cultural, and civilisational criteria.

Agency and the resistive subject

The third important feature of postcolonial theory is its challenge to the unitary
liberal subject. The liberal project has been successfully built on the idea that the
subject is atomised, decontextualised, ahistorical, and reasoning. 'He' is also a
universally valid subject.

The postcolonial project affords the possibility of conceptualising the subject in
ways that directly challenge the autonomous, reasoning subject of liberal rights
discourse (Nessiah, 2003). It focuses on the resistive subject – that is, one who
produces resistance in coercive circumstances, a deeply layered and multifaceted
subject. It is at this juncture that postcolonial theory joins with subaltern studies
(Said, 1988, pp v–x). The subaltern studies project further complicates our
understanding of the subject who is excluded by the liberal project and the imperial
narratives of history. The subaltern project exposes how certain voices have been
excluded from the dominant narratives of history. The project regards hegemonic
history as part of modernity's power/knowledge complex, which in the context of
colonialism has been deeply implicated in imperialism's violent encounters with
other regimes of power (McClintock, 1995, p 6). In the context of law, the subaltern
project also brings a normative challenge to the assumptions about universality,
neutrality and objectivity on which legal concepts are based, exposing such
concepts to be products of the ruptures produced in and through the colonial
encounter.

The subaltern studies project was initially launched in Britain in the 1960s, when
Gramsci's writing exercised a significant influence on the shape of English
Marxism. It triggered an analysis of peasant societies based on the position and
location of the subaltern subject. This project of writing history from below was
subsequently taken up within postcolonial contexts, including in India (Guha, 1982,
pp vii–viii; Sarkar, 1985). The early focus of the subaltern studies project argued in
favour of a theoretical framework capable of capturing the nuances of the agency of
the colonised by foregrounding the spaces of resistance in the discourses around
colonialism and nationalism. The project was initially grounded in historical
materialism and the search for an essential peasant consciousness, but this focus
seemed, for some, too limited and restrictive. During the 1980s other writers,
increasingly influenced by poststructuralism, challenged the search for an essential
peasant consciousness. The project could not simply be reduced to an account of
those who were left out of the telling of history.

The influence of Michel Foucault came to affect the subaltern project, producing
subaltern critiques that challenged all those who continued to adhere to the
'Enlightenment ideals'. The project splintered, coming to be divided between those

who continued to write histories 'from below' and those who adopted a more Foucauldian analysis, focused on contesting Eurocentric, metropolitan and bureaucratic systems of knowledge (Chakrabarty, 1995). The new tradition was concerned with challenging all traditions and disciplines that were defined within the logic and rationale of the Enlightenment project. One aspect of this new tradition was the effort to unmask the universal subject of liberal rights discourse. Such critique destabilised the humanist subject and brought into critical consideration a host of other categories, including gender, class, ethnicity and race. Subaltern studies no longer remains preoccupied with the idea of a peasant rebel as an autonomous political subject who writes her own history. It has shifted away from economic analysis as the primary zone of power, and begun to unpack the multiple locations of power through a discursive and textual analysis. The scholarship has expanded and begun to address and challenge the neo-imperialism of the late 20th-century and problems of agency, subject-position, and hegemony in the era of globalisation (Beverley, 1999; Bhabha, 1994; Chakrabarty and Bhabha, 2002; Lal, 2002; Ludden, 2002; Mignolo, 2000, pp 171–97).[2]

The subaltern subject provides a normative challenge to the subject of liberal rights discourse. It is a subject who occupies an ambivalent position, whose resistance or presence can be read in different ways. The subaltern project analyses the terms in which the formerly colonised subject comes to engage with her past, as well as how she challenges the simple dichotomies of 'us and them', of the invader and the native. A complex relationship is established, partly shaped and troubled by the desire on the part of the colonised to return a voyeuristic gaze upon Europe, as well as by the desire on the part of the colonial power to civilise and normalise the native subject. The colonial subject pursues the West, desires to mimic or even own it at the cost of disowning her own subjectivity. Yet this desire to mimic produces what Homi Bhabha describes as an ambivalence. The 'mimic men' are 'almost the same but not white' (Bhabha, 1994, p 89). By returning the gaze, the 'mimic men' expose both the fissures and cracks in the liberal subject, and its culturally specific location. At a minimum, we are left with a subject who aspires to mimic an identity that she cannot fully assume, who cannot be normalised and assimilated into a universalising (European) standard. The mimicry also exposes how the liberal subject is culturally specific, and cannot be fully replicated in a non-European context, but is altered and rendered ambivalent in a colonial context. An example of this are the efforts of Christian missionaries to teach Indian Hindus to take Christian communion: the vegetarian Hindu is horrified by the idea of eating Christ's body and drinking his blood, and thus renders the missionary as a cannibalistic vampire (Bhabha, 1994, pp 145–46). She thus denaturalises the liberal subject, revealing its instability and culturally specific location. At a more radical level, this subject brings about a conscious normative challenge, intent on resisting the assimilative gestures of the imperial and liberal project, and producing a subject that is quite distinct and unlike the sovereign, autonomous subject of liberal rights discourse. Law has served as an important site of the constitution of this subject, and exposed liberalism's

---

2   See works in *Subaltern Studies*, Volumes I–XI, published by OUP: Chatterjee and Jeganathan, 2000, Volume XI; Bhadra, Prakash and Tharu, 1999, Volume X; Amin and Chakrabarty, 1996, Volume IX; Arnold and Hardiman, 1994, Volume VIII; Chatterjee and Pandey, 1992, Volume VII; Guha, 1989, Volume VI; Guha, 1987, Volume V; Guha, 1985, Volume IV; Guha, 1984, Volume III; Guha, 1983, Volume II; Guha, 1982, Volume I.

assumptions about the sovereign, atomised subject as distinctly European and constituted partly in and through its encounters with difference. Indeed, it is this ambivalence which provides a central lens through which the constitution of the postcolonial subject through the process of law can be understood.

The legal regulation of sexuality in India: a postcolonial feminist reading

Postcolonial feminism draws on postcolonial theory and the subaltern studies project, which foregrounds a host of subjects who have been excluded by normative discourses. However, neither postcolonial theory nor subaltern scholarship has brought an adequate account of gender or sexuality to its position, nor do they address feminist participation in these discourses. They have consistently failed to engage the sexual subaltern subject.[3] Sexuality remains extraneous to this theoretical project except when it is taken up within the context of law and violence. The challenges that sex and the sexual subaltern subject bring to normative understandings of culture and sexuality, which in turn underlie the legal regulation of sexuality, have simply not been addressed. Yet the insights of both postcolonial and subaltern studies scholarship assist in providing a more complex articulation of the subject-position of the sexual subaltern, of the relationship between sexuality and culture, and analytical tools for understanding the assumptions and paradoxes produced by legal engagements over sexuality.

In examining the legal regulation of sexuality in the context of India, the debates and issues at times appear to be very similar to those in North America or Britain. This similarity results partly from the emphasis on sexual violence, and from the way in which sexual violence has become a centrepiece of the global women's human rights movement. Also, there is considerable funding available from domestic and international sources to support these causes, partly because states are willing to address issues of sexual wrongdoing without necessarily supporting a rights agenda, or displacing dominant assumptions about sexuality and sexual subjects. This support has produced a considerable amount of law in the area of sexual violence, and has at times marginalised efforts in other areas. However, despite the similarities and the pressures of discursive homogenisation, the postcolonial framing of these issues produces a different analysis and outcome. For example, a close reading of the legal responses to the issue of sexual harassment in India belies assumptions that they have had a liberating or transformative impact. The explanation does not lie in the fact that the reforms have been inadequate, or in the fact of under-enforcement. The outcomes can only be understood against the history of colonial legal encounters with sexuality, which have produced complex and ambivalent results for women and sexual subalterns.

Contemporary legal engagements with sexuality highlight how the legacy of the colonial encounter continues to influence the way in which this issue is addressed in

---

3 Some recent work has been published on the issue of queer identity and postcolonialism. See for example Hawley, 2001 – a collection of essays which focuses on the implications of globalisation on gay and lesbian identities from a postcolonial and queer perspective.

postcolonial India. I discuss below three aspects of this engagement. The first is how the legal regulation of sexuality in postcolonial India has operated along a public/private divide that has been constituted partly by colonial legal regimes. This divide has been central to the ways in which issues of sexuality are implicated in understandings of culture and the very identity of the nation-state. Secondly, I look at how contemporary feminist engagements with law and sexuality have produced mixed results for women, partly because of the integral relationship between culture and sexuality and assumptions about law that do not account for the ways in which colonial legal histories continue discursively to infuse the present. I examine the contradictory impact of such engagements by looking specifically at the issue of sexual harassment. And finally, I contrast feminist strategies with those of the Hindu Right, which has had a profound impact on the way in which issues of sexuality are addressed in law. Their legal strategies build on the integral relationship between sexuality and culture, and they have been remarkably successful in advancing their agenda in and through the discourse of liberal rights.

The public/private divide

Since the 19th-century, social reformers and women's rights activists have sought to extend legal intervention, particularly of the criminal law, to areas dealing with women's sexuality – in particular, sexual violence (Kapur and Cossman, 1996, pp 118–33). These engagements have sought a renegotiation of the public and private spheres, through the incremental encroachment of the public – the state-sanctioned criminal law – into the 'private' sphere of the family (Nair, 1996a). The public/private divide represents the 'ideological marker that shifts in relation to the role of the state in different historical moments, in particular contexts, and in relation to particular issues' (Boyd, 1997, p 4; Boyd, 1999). The efforts of social reformers in the 19th-century to prohibit violent and oppressive cultural acts, such as early child marriage, and support the rights of widows to remarry, were constantly resisted by political nationalists or cultural revivalists as undue intervention in the 'private' sphere of the family, which constituted the space of Indian cultural values, a space that needed to be secured from colonial intervention. Indeed, the conjugal space became a central site of nationalist struggle in the late 19th-century (Sarkar, 2001, p 191). The realm of legitimate sexuality was to be determined by the colonial subject and not the colonial power, and the resistance to law reform served as a symbol of Indian resistance to colonial rule and a challenge to subjugation. The native woman became the symbol of the incipient Indian nation (Ray, 2000).

At the same time, the nationalist resistance to reform and the selection of the home and women's sexuality as the spaces of Indian cultural autonomy from the Raj needs to be understood against the backdrop of the colonial canvas, and assumptions that Indian women were victims of a backward culture and in need of rescue and rehabilitation (Burton, 1994; Liddle and Rai, 1998). In *Mother India*, Katherine Mayo's invective against the unhappy condition of the Indian woman provided a justification of the imperial presence in the subcontinent (Sinha, 2000). She lists the brutal nature of Indian men, the horrors of child marriage, widow subjugation, and the illiteracy and slavish habits of Indian housewives. Mayo's book made the argument for the continuation of the Empire in order to rescue atavistic, abject women from the brutality of the Indian male. Such arguments, with their focus on the injured subjectivity of the Other, continue to find expression in contemporary feminist discourse (Bumiller, 1990; Daly, 1978, pp 113–33; Dworkin, 1991).

These competing views found expression around the issue of rape, which was a site of intense contest in the 19th-century debates, quite specifically in the context of child marriage. I do not provide a comprehensive discussion of this campaign, but attempt here simply to highlight the role of law and the contradictions produced by engaging in law reform on issues of sexuality through the colonial regime, and its implications for the public/private divide. The issue of child marriage was taken up in the later part of the 19th-century by some leading Indian reformers, such as Behram Malabari and Ranade. The practice of child marriage came to be regarded by reformers as a social evil that needed to be eliminated. Hindu marriage had traditionally involved two components: (a) a wedding ceremony that took place anytime during a girl's childhood; and (b) the consummation ceremony (*garbhadaan*), which took place within 16 days of the girl's first menstruation. In 1860, the age of consent to marry had been raised to 10 years, with little or no controversy. However, the issue was raised again in the 1880s, when the spirited social reformer and journalist, Malabari, led another campaign to increase the age of consent to 12 years. An intense struggle emerged between the social reformers and the political nationalists. Social reformers sought legal changes from the colonial administration to improve the status of Indian women. The women's question was raised as part of a broader agenda of social and political reform, in which social reformers sought to eliminate a host of practices, from *sati* to the prohibition of widow remarriage, to child marriage. The position of women within the Hindu tradition was simultaneously exploited by the British to continue their rule. Attention was directed at the most extreme cultural practices as evidence of the 'barbarity' of Indian society, and of its resulting need for foreign rule. The political nationalists who opposed reform on the age of consent argued that law was an ineffective means of changing practices within the family, and that education was the primary tool for bringing about such change. More significantly, they also fiercely opposed the law reform, as it was viewed within the colonial context as an instrument by which the British intended to legitimise their rule. Women were strikingly absent from this debate. At no point, however, were the legal measures sought based in any sense on the argument for equal rights for women. They were purely protectionist, and articulated against a broader contest over the definition of the nation-state.

Two high-profile legal cases had a significant impact on the outcome of the age of consent controversies. The first was the 1886 case of Rukmabhai, who was married at a very young age and refused to live with her husband, on the basis of social, economic and personal incompatibility. Her husband brought a petition for restitution of conjugal rights. The court ordered Rukmabhai to return to her husband, and when she refused the court threatened her with imprisonment. The threat was only removed after a vocal campaign by the social reformers, and the personal intervention of Queen Victoria (Sarkar, 1993). But it was the horrifying and tragic case of Phulmonee that galvanised public support for the Age of Consent Bill that was passed in 1891, and which in many ways silenced the opposition, at least temporarily. Phulmonee was a girl of about 10 or 11 years who was raped by her 35-year-old husband, Hari Maiti, and died as a result of the injuries she sustained. Since the girl was over the age of consent – that is, 10 years – the husband could not be found guilty of rape. He was charged with her murder but subsequently exonerated by the court. The outcome in the judicial forum gave an impetus to the law reform campaign and the subsequent change in the age of consent. The British finally enacted the legislation in 1891, partly as a result of these two cases.

The effect of the child marriage campaign was contradictory where the legitimacy of law itself was at issue. Although the age of consent was ultimately raised by legislation, the political nationalists were enormously successful in their efforts to rearticulate the domestic sphere as beyond the reach of colonial intervention. The controversy succeeded in mobilising a resistant discourse that insisted on non-intervention in the private realm, which was to be cordoned off as a site of production of Indian cultural values. The legislation of 1891 condemned the practice of child marriage by raising the age of consent, but the outcome of the discursive struggle was to mobilise very effectively the political nationalists, and to undermine the legitimacy of the efforts of the social reform movement in seeking legislative change from the colonial state. Further, as Tanika Sarkar has argued, what was at stake in the age of consent controversy was no less than the definition of conjugality, which was in her view 'at the very heart of the formative movement for militant nationalism in Bengal'. In other words, political nationalists sought to redefine Hindu conjugality and renegotiate the public/private divide, placing the domestic realm of the family and the home beyond the reach of colonial intervention. The family was reconstituted as a 'pure space' of Hindu culture and tradition, uncontaminated by colonial intervention. Women who occupied this place, in turn, came to represent all that was pure and untouched by colonialism. Indian womanhood became the embodiment of nationalism, as the nation came to be constructed as a divine mother, and women in general became the mothers of the nation. The glorification of women's roles as wives and mothers, as chaste and sexually pure, came to infuse the very discourse of nationalism (Chaudhuri, 1993, p 78). Social reformers, who were attempting to redefine Hindu tradition to exclude child marriage, were thereby trying to introduce change into the very sphere that in the eyes of the political nationalists was most representative of Hindu culture and tradition. The contest between the social reformers and the political nationalists was not simply over the legitimacy of engaging with the colonial state, but was also a contest over the power and authority to define Hindu culture and traditions, and over the line between the public and private spheres.

The relationship between issues of sexuality, culture and the public/private divide continued to remain integral in subsequent controversies, including the efforts to reform the laws that applied to the familiar and personal affairs of Hindus in the independence movement, and subsequently to reform other personal laws in the 1980s. All of these interventions involved change in the domestic realm and women's roles within it, which generated a great deal of resistance. The efforts of social reformers historically, or feminists in the contemporary period, to prohibit violence and oppressive practices within the family have time and again been resisted as an undue intervention into the private sphere of the family, and have frequently met with cries of 'religion in danger', or charges of anti-nationalism and foreign intervention. The relationship between culture and the public/private divide continue to inform a number of the contemporary debates on issues of sexuality, and the way in which these issues are addressed in both the legislative and judicial arenas.

The relationship between sexuality and culture remains as germane in the postcolonial present as it was in the 19th-century, and continues to inform the legal regulation of sexuality and the public/private divide. However, the issues are somewhat different today, with the increasing visibility of sexuality in the public domain through satellite broadcasting, the assertion of rights claims by sexual subaltern groups, the Aids pandemic, and the high-voltage song-and-dance sequences in Indian commercial cinema. Sexuality is somewhat more difficult to contain in the contemporary moment. Yet sexuality continues to be the subject of extensive legal regulation in the name of 'Indian cultural values', despite the proliferation of sex talk, sexual imagery and sexual expression in the public arena. Few aspects of sexuality are exempt from some form of regulation, whether it is laws governing sexual speech, determining who is the subject of legitimate sexual relations, which sexual acts constitute assault or violence, and what constitutes public sex, and is hence subject to criminal or other legal sanctions.

The cultural arguments are partly informed by the public/private distinction, which continues to shape the way in which the law intervenes in familial and sexual relationships. The criminalisation of some activities – such as rape, adultery, and sodomy – and the non-criminalisation of other activities – such as the rape of a woman by her husband – are marked by the idea that there are certain forms of sexuality that are private, culturally accepted, and exercised legitimately within the family. The family and the marital relationship are legitimate areas for containing women's sexuality in the name of protecting it, and thereby defending Indian cultural values. Despite the intense feminist lobbying to reform laws relating to sexual violence, these laws continue to sustain the public/private distinction, and the dominant sexual ideology and cultural assumptions on which they are based. The result is that the sex laws work at times in highly contradictory ways for women and other sexual subgroups. Sometimes, the refusal to intervene is based on the construction of some sex as private, as part of a cultural and sacred space, and beyond legitimate intervention; and at other times legal intervention is justified if the sex is public, and transgresses cultural and sexual norms. The law is not used to protect public sex, and may even penalise it. There are also times when even private sexuality, such as homosexuality, is constructed as public and therefore subject to legitimate intervention by the law. Running through the shifting use of the public/private distinction lie assumptions about the private as a space for the articulation and preservation of Indian cultural values, and women as the central repositories for these values.[4] The distinction is simultaneously informed by

---

4　For example, in the context of rape, the extent to which the rape laws continue to reflect traditional assumptions about women's sexuality, chastity, virginity and honour has been well documented (Agnes, 2002; Kannabiran and Kannabiran, 2002; Menon, 2000).

dominant sexual ideology, which is pure, chaste, reproductive, non-commercial, heterosexual (in fact, marital), and held sacred.

The private space is thus both a space of cultural production and a re-inscription of sexual norms that are consistent with women's sexual purity and honour. For example, the contemporary legal regulation of rape is concerned only with sex within the public realm – that is, with rape that occurs outside the realm of the family, quite specifically the marital relationship. And even when the rape has occurred in the public sphere, the legal regulation can be seen to be further shaped by whether women's sexuality is of a public or private nature. Where a woman's sexuality is considered private, guarded within the confines of the family, where she is a Hindu, a virgin daughter or a loyal wife, the criminal law may protect her. So long as she adheres to dominant norms, she receives protection. But when she deviates from these sexual norms and cultural values by having consensual sex outside of marriage, same-sex relations or commercial sex, the law considers her sexuality to have become public, to have transgressed cultural norms, and thus not to be within the purview of the protection of the criminal law. Public sexuality is conflated with being Western, contaminating, and corrupting – forces from which the Indian nation, cultural ethos and traditions need to be protected.

Another example is the legal provision that, until recently, permitted the defence to introduce evidence in a rape trial to demonstrate that the victim was of 'a generally immoral character'.[5] The purpose of this section was to provide the defence with the means to discredit the testimony of the witness. It was based on the assumption that an 'unchaste' woman could not be believed, at least not when it came to matters of sex. As soon as it was demonstrated by the defence that the woman was sexually promiscuous, that she has transgressed dominant cultural norms, her sexuality belonged to the public sphere and was no longer entitled to the protection of the criminal law. Instead it was penalised. The case law is filled with similar examples of this distinction between women's private and public sexuality, and how it continues to operate along cultural assumptions. The outcome of the Mathura rape case, in which the Indian Supreme Court overturned the conviction of two police officers on the basis that the young woman had not demonstrated utmost resistance and thus must have consented, can also be seen in light of the fact that Mathura had run off with her lover and had thus transgressed cultural norms.[6] She was no longer a good woman within the private confines of the family. In 1989, 10 years later, in the equally controversial Suman Rani rape case, the Supreme Court reduced the mandatory minimum sentence of two police officers, partially on the basis that Suman Rani was 'a woman of questionable character and easy virtue with

---

5   Indian Evidence Act 1872, s 155(4), which was repealed with effect from 12 December 2002.
6   *Tukram v State of Maharashtra* [1979] All India Reports 185 (SC).

lewd and lascivious behaviour.'[7] Again, in this case Suman Rani had eloped with her lover; as a woman who was 'used to having frequent sexual intercourse' she placed herself beyond the protection of the law. By way of contrast are those cases where women were considered to conform to prevailing norms. The Supreme Court has held that an 'Indian woman attaches maximum importance to her chastity' and is therefore unlikely to lie about a rape.[8] In other words, corroboration of her testimony is not essential in a society where sexual permissiveness is not the norm, unlike in the 'West'.[9] In fact a girl or woman from a tradition-bound non-permissive society such as India may be reluctant to bring a complaint of rape, as it could reflect on her chastity.[10] The same assumptions operate, but with different results. In the courts' view, the dishonour and shame inflicted by rape upon the innocence of virgin daughters and the loyalty of chaste wives is such that these Indian women would be unlikely to make false allegations, would be predisposed to delaying a report of rape, and/or unlikely to be able to resist rape. In each of these cases, the cultural arguments underscore the decisions and inform the construction of Indian women's sexuality – as chaste, pure, monogamous, honourable and confined to the private/domestic sphere.

At the same time, regardless of how much a woman conforms to dominant norms, she is still not protected within the family if she is raped. Marital rape is not recognised under current legal definitions of rape. Section 375 of the Indian Penal Code 1860 (IPC) provides that 'Sexual intercourse by a man with his own wife, the wife not being under 15 years of age, is not rape'. The origin of the exclusion of marital rape from the purview of the criminal law is based on a compilation of law prepared by Sir Matthew Hale CJ, in 1736, entitled *History of the Pleas of the Crown*:

> The husband cannot be guilty of a rape committed by himself upon his lawful wife, for by their mutual matrimonial consent and contract the wife hath given up herself this kind unto her husband which she cannot retract.[11]

In other words, a woman surrenders her right to consent to sexual relations at the time of entering into a marriage, and the husband is given an unconditional, unqualified right of sexual access to her. Every act of sexual intercourse is deemed to be consensual. The continuing exemption of marital rape from the purview of the

---

7 *Premchand v State of Haryana* [1989] All India Reports 937 (SC). In a subsequent review petition, the court held that, in referring to the 'conduct' of Suman Rani, it was neither characterising her as 'a woman of questionable character and easy virtue nor [making] any reference to her character or reputation'. Rather, the court tried to argue that in fact it had been referring to her conduct 'in not telling anyone for about five days about the sexual assault perpetrated on her' (p 938). The court's effort to backtrack in the wake of considerable public controversy was difficult to sustain, in the face of the explicit reasoning of the initial decision. Moreover, the Supreme Court has since held that any delay in reporting a rape should not count against a rape victim, since there are many reasons why women, particularly rural women, may be unable to report the rape right away. It is difficult to understand the Suman Rani case outside the traditional assumptions about women's sexuality, cultural norms, and the distinctions between illegitimate (public) and legitimate (private) sexuality.

8 *State of Maharashtra v Chandraprakash Kewalchand Jain* [1990] All India Reports 658 (SC), para 17.

9 *Bharwada Bhognibhari Hirjibhai v State of Gujurat* [1983] All India Reports 753 (SC), para 9.

10 *Ibid*, para 10.

11 Volume 1, p 621.

criminal law sustains the definition of the wife as exclusive property of the husband. The marital exemption has since been narrowed by the introduction of s 376(a) of the IPC, which states that the rape of a woman by a husband from whom she is judicially separated constitutes rape, and is punishable by up to two years' imprisonment. The mandatory minimum sentence in non-custodial rape cases is seven years, and 10 in the case of custodial rape. The relatively low sentence in the case of judicially separated men convicted of raping their wives creates a hierarchy of the crime. It is thus only when there is a judicially recognised rupture in the marital relationship that a wife is assumed to have revoked her consent to sexual intercourse with her husband. There is thus no challenge to the assumption that the act of marriage gives rise to unqualified and unconditional consent on the part of the wife to sexual intercourse with her husband. And the exemption is once again cast in terms that are regarded as invoking contemporary Indian cultural values, though its origins, paradoxically, are entirely Hanoverian.

Not all sexuality located within the private sphere is considered by the criminal law to be private, especially if it seems to contravene Indian cultural values or definitions of tradition, purity and authenticity. Sodomy and homosexual sexual activity have long been penalised under the provisions of the IPC. Section 377 provides that:

> Whoever voluntarily has carnal intercourse against the order of nature with any man, woman, or animal, shall be punished with imprisonment for life, or with imprisonment of either description for a term which may extend to ten years, and shall also be liable to fine.

> Explanation – Penetration is sufficient to constitute the carnal intercourse necessary in this section …

When it comes to particular kinds of sexuality that, in the law's view, are 'against the order of nature' and against Indian cultural values, the location of that sexuality is irrelevant. Rather, the so-called 'perverse' nature of this sex is such that it becomes public, and thus the legitimate subject for state intervention. Unlike marital rape, where the private nature of the sex and cultural assumptions about the marital bond immunises it from any criminal intervention, in the case of homosexuality the fact that it may be conducted in private is irrelevant, since it cannot, by definition, be conducted with the right kind of privacy – that is, within the heterosexual, marital family, between a husband and wife, and within the boundaries of Indian (with the contemporary meaning of 'Hindu') culture. Private sex is thus only immunised if it is legitimate private sex – that is, sex within marriage, familiar and culturally grounded.

In summary the public/private distinction is a shifting, and at times contradictory, one. Sometimes the criminal law constructs the family and the marital space as public and in need of protection; for example, it criminalises adultery. At other times the family is private and beyond the reach of the criminal law, as in the case of marital rape. Yet running through the legal regulation of sexuality is the understanding that the marital relationship is the exclusive site of legitimate sexuality, and a cornerstone of Indian cultural values. Indeed, the latest report of the Law Commission rejected any proposal to repeal the marital rape exception, on the grounds that it would amount to 'excessive interference with the marital relationship'.[12] In contrast, the legal regulation of homosexuality is unconcerned with the location of the sexuality in question, since the nature of the sexuality renders it public. And the legal regulation of non-marital rape can be seen to vacillate between the public realm of illegitimate sex and the private realm of legally sanctioned sex. The legal regulation of rape remains concerned with the location of a woman's sexuality. If her sexuality has been contained within the confines of the family, it is private and protected. If not, it is public and subject to considerably less protection. Despite the shifting nature of the public/private distinction, running throughout the various areas of criminal intervention is a dominant sexual ideology, which draws a line between good sex and bad sex, and dominant cultural assumptions about sexuality, which construct women as chaste, loyal wives who maintain the integrity of the Indian family, culture and nation. They are good women. Bad women transgress these dominant norms, and they are either unable to secure the protection of the law or their sexuality is regarded as public, and hence illegitimate, and is criminalised and punished.

In many cases, the idea of sexuality operating according to a culturally determined distinction between public and private spheres undermines the effectiveness of some legal provisions. And even when the courts do convict an accused under one of these criminal provisions, the grounds on which they do so are often shaped by, and in turn sustain, the dominant norms that construct women's sexuality. The intervention of the criminal law into the private sphere can thus be seen to be informed by, and to reinforce, the moral regulation of women and sexuality in and through dominant sexual ideology and conservative cultural norms.

Feminist engagements with 'sexual wrongs' and legal rights

Feminist engagements with law and sexuality illustrate the specific challenges presented in this area in a postcolonial context. Reflecting on these legal engagements exposes how such initiatives have neither been altogether transformative nor necessarily even empowering. In India, the law reform campaigns of the contemporary women's movement have focused in part on sexual wrongs, including rape, domestic violence and dowry murders, sexual harassment, obscenity, and trafficking. Lobbying and campaigning on these issues has created a considerable amount of public awareness about issues of violence against women, and has resulted in the emergence of non-governmental organisations and other services to assist women who are victims of violence. This focus on sexual violence and victimisation has been critical, producing debates and scholarship, and mobilising the international community on these issues. The campaigns on violence against women, with their focus on law reform, have had some extremely important and beneficial consequences for women. This movement has drawn attention to the lack of domestic governmental responses to women's demands for more effective laws against rape, child sexual abuse, and domestic violence. The campaigns have been overwhelmingly successful in translating very specific violations experienced by individual women into a more general rights discourse.

---

12 Law Commission of India, *Review of Rape Laws*, 172nd Report, 2000, Chapter 3, p 14.

Yet 30 years later, despite all of these engagements and successful law reform campaigns, violence against women continues to occur on a staggering scale. The rape, domestic violence and harassment statistics have only increased.[13]

This situation forces an interrogation of the relationship between feminist goals and rights discourse in the area of sexuality. Are rights something 'we cannot not want'? (Spivak, 1993, pp 45–46). Postcolonial feminism, together with other critical traditions, has critiqued the liberal project, by exposing its lack of emancipatory potential, as being incapable of delivering on its promise of justice. More rights do not necessarily equate with more empowerment. Legal campaigns and initiatives on violence against women have done little to displace the dominant sexual norms which inform the law. In fact, I suggest that these initiatives have reinforced negativity about sex and sexuality and moralism around sex, and have failed to dislodge the conservative cultural moorings that anchor issues of sexuality in law. Thus, initiatives that, at one level, are being pursued in order to advance rights to sexual or bodily integrity have not necessarily proved to be progressive, and have had paradoxical implications.

A recent example of this paradoxical effect of the legal initiatives pursued by feminists concerns the issue of sexual harassment. The emergence of sexual harassment as a wrong and a form of discrimination against women has been articulated exclusively by the Indian courts, and has not been enacted into any statute. The issue of sexual harassment entered into the public arena when a complaint was filed by a senior member of the Indian Administrative Service, Rupan Deol Bajaj, against KPS Gill, the Director General of Police in the northern state of Punjab. The complaint was filed under s 354 of the IPC, which criminalises any act that outrages the modesty of a woman, as well as under s 509, which penalises the use of force or intimidation, and the making of sexual gestures to insult a woman. Gill was charged with slapping the complainant on her posterior and sexually intimidating her at a dinner party. Although the High Court quashed the complaint, it was reinstated by the Supreme Court and ultimately Gill was fined a large sum of money, to be paid to Bajaj as compensation in lieu of spending three months in harsh imprisonment. However, the framing of a harassment case within the discourse of modesty failed to address the wrong as a form of discrimination and violation of women's rights to equality. 'Outraging' a woman's 'modesty' is not defined in the IPC. It was interpreted by the court in the Bajaj case as referring to 'womanly propriety of behaviour; scrupulous chastity of thought, speech and conduct'. It has also been defined as including any 'act done to or in the presence of a woman' which 'is clearly suggestive of sex according to the common notions of mankind', 'common notions of mankind' being gauged by contemporary societal standards.[14]

---

13 For example, there has been a 54.4% rise in the number of rapes in India between 1991 and 2001: Raghavan, 2003, p 129. See also the Table of Incidence of Cognisable Crimes (IPC) under different Crime Heads, between 1999 and 2001 NCRB website at http://ncrb.nic.in/Crimecomp.htm, which indicates an increase in the number of rapes from 15,468 in 1999 to 16,075 in 2001.

14 *State of Punjab v Major Singh* [1967] All India Reports 63 (SC).

The inability of the 'modesty' provision to address adequately claims of sexual harassment ultimately led to the filing of a class action petition in 1997 in the Supreme Court of India. The petition was brought by a number of social action groups and non-governmental organisations seeking legal redress for women whose work had been obstructed or inhibited because of sexual harassment in the workplace.[15] The Supreme Court decision accepted that sexual harassment in the workplace violated women's equality rights, and that employers were obliged to provide mechanisms for both the prevention and for the resolution, settlement or prosecution of sexual harassment. The court set out guidelines on sexual harassment in the workplace, and declared these as constituting the law of the land until further action was taken by the legislature. The guidelines defined sexual harassment as including: unwelcome physical contact and advances; a demand or request for sexual favours; sexually coloured remarks; the display of pornography; and any other physical, verbal or non-verbal conduct of a sexual nature.

The *Vishaka* judgment is significant at a symbolic level for its validation of the problem of sexual harassment, and its recognition of the fact that it is an experience many women are almost routinely subjected to in the workplace. A primary ingredient of sexual harassment as defined by the Supreme Court guidelines is that the sexual conduct must be unwelcome. A second requirement appears to be that the conduct must disadvantage a woman, such as by affecting her recruitment or promotion, or creating a hostile work environment. Under this definition, there are certain clear cases of sexual conduct that constitute sexual harassment – for instance, what has been called *quid pro quo* sexual harassment, in which a threat is made or a benefit offered in order to obtain sex. Unfortunately, the second leg of the definition seems to have been dispensed with in a subsequent Supreme Court decision, leaving open the possibility that any kind of sexual remark can be impugned under the guidelines.

The early signs in India indicate that sexual harassment law will produce some of the same problems that have occurred elsewhere. A tendency to focus on sexual conduct, suppressing sexuality in the workplace and deflecting attention from the more common non-sexual forms of discrimination and abuse in the workplace are already becoming apparent (Schultz, 1998). But there are also some concerns emerging around the issue of sexual harassment that are specific to its postcolonial context. In the first major decision after the *Vishaka* judgment, the Supreme Court not only broadened the scope of the sexual harassment test, it also delivered a decision that seems to reinforce the policing of women's sexual conduct within the boundaries of traditional, culturally determined sexual behaviour, without necessarily remedying women's claims of sexual harassment. In the *AEPC (Apparel Export Promotion Council)* decision, the complainant was a private secretary to the chairman of the company.[16] The chairman tried to molest the complainant on several occasions during the course of her work, including trying to sit beside her when she did not desire it and attempting to molest her in a hotel elevator. The chairman was dismissed after a departmental inquiry. He challenged the order through the courts, arguing that he had never actually touched the complainant.

---

15 *Vishaka v State of Rajasthan* [1997] All India Reports 3011 (SC).
16 *Apparel Export Promotion Council v AK Chopra* [1999] All India Reports 625 (SC).

The High Court held that 'trying' to molest a female employee was not the same as actually molesting her, and that the chairman's conduct could not therefore be impugned. The company appealed to the Supreme Court.

The court accepted the definition of sexual harassment as laid out in *Vishaka*. However, it went on to determine the content of the sexual harassment, holding that 'any action or gesture which, whether directly or by implication, aims at or has the tendency to outrage the modesty of a female employee, must fall under the general concept of the definition of sexual harassment'.[17] The court accepted that sexual harassment violated a number of international conventions, including the Convention on the Elimination of All Forms of Discrimination Against Women. The court further held that the conduct of the chairman in trying to sit next to the complainant and touch her, despite her protests, constituted 'unwelcome sexually determined behaviour' on his part, and was an attempt to 'outrage her modesty'. His behaviour was against 'moral sanctions' and did not withstand the test of 'decency and modesty', and therefore amounted to unwelcome sexual advances. Together, his actions constituted sexual harassment.

In the *AEPC* decision, the complainant's pristine conduct, including her lack of knowledge about sex (as she was not married) were factors that redeemed her credibility. Had she been knowledgeable, and described in minute detail what happened to her (it is not in the least bit clear from the reading of the decision what happened to her), then presumably her sexual knowledge would have damaged her credibility. Had she used abusive language or sexual language in her interactions, it could have undermined her claim that the conduct was unwelcome. Had she spoken in language replete with sexual innuendos, presumably that would also have diminished her claim that the conduct was unwelcome.

The core ingredient of the definition is that the sexual conduct must be 'unwelcome', which remains for the complainant to prove. However, this burden is conditioned by dominant norms and the complainant's conduct. More specifically, it means that the complainant's sexual past, mode of dress and conduct, and conformity to cultural prescriptions may be introduced as relevant evidence in determining whether the conduct was 'unwelcome'. Dress, behaviour, cultural conformity, and even profession may thus be used to demonstrate that the accused was incited to the conduct, and may be sufficient evidence to disqualify a claim of sexual harassment. Waitresses, bar-room dancers, and other performers are all vulnerable to such claims. Indeed, the definition seems to provide scope for reproducing and reinforcing dominant assumptions about sex, women's sexuality and sexual practices, as well as reinforcing the sexual segregation of jobs, as has been pointed out by feminist legal scholars in Western contexts (Halley, 2002, pp 80–104; Schultz, 1998). However, in the postcolonial context it simultaneously reproduces assumptions about women's sexual conduct that are based on cultural idealisations of women – as in this instance – as guardians of Indian cultural values, and hence entitled to legal protection. Chastity and its implicit cultural connotations were critical in determining the outcome of the case.

---

17 *Ibid*, p 675.

The particular definition of sexual harassment does not displace dominant assumptions about sex and sexuality. The requirement that the behaviour be 'unwelcome' is informed by stereotypes about women's behaviour and sexual conduct. If the complainant's speech or dress is found to be sexually provocative, it can be relevant in determining whether she found particular sexual advances unwelcome. The defence could well argue that her dress and manner invited sexual attention. There are also aspects of this decision which can only be explained by the postcolonial context of the claim. For example, despite the fact that the new guidelines were intended to de-link sexual harassment from Victorian assumptions of modesty, the *AEPC* decision reintroduces the notion of modesty and the idealisation of the Indian woman as chaste. The court read the notion of 'outraging the modesty of a woman' into the definition of sexual harassment, and interpreted this to mean any action that could be perceived as one which is 'capable of shocking the sense of decency of a woman'. Given that the origin of the standard of 'outraging the modesty of a woman' is both Victorian and colonial, it represents an understanding about women's sexuality as chaste, pure, asexual and uninterested in pleasure. The conflation of Indian women's sexuality with colonial or Victorian norms, with modesty being cast as a core 'Indian value', limits the potential of the sexual harassment law as a liberating or sexually transformative device.

This decision is indicative of the way in which sexual harassment law may operate when formulated exclusively within a liberal framework, without sufficient attention to the Indian context and the way in which colonial legal histories discursively infuse the postcolonial present. The arguments presented in the *AEPC* case were framed within the discourse of conservative sexual morality and dominant cultural assumptions about appropriate sexual and conduct. This suggests that sexual harassment law is not necessarily a positive force for change for women. The *AEPC* decision highlights how the definition of sexual harassment is contingent on a woman's sexual status and knowledge, as well as her conformity to cultural prescriptions. A victim's narrative of the encounter is substantially qualified by the framework of dominant sexual and cultural norms. If she transgressed any of these norms, then her story of sexual vicitmisation could be converted into a narrative of agency, invitation, provocation, cultural transgression, and 'welcoming'.

A second implication of the definition is that it is over-inclusive, to the extent that all sexual speech and expression could be implicated as sexual harassment. Unfortunately, this line was further extended by the Supreme Court in the *AEPC* decision, in which it greatly weakened the second leg of the definition of sexual harassment – the requirement that the conduct result in an abusive and hostile working environment. By including the outraging of the modesty of a woman in the sexual harassment standard, the court did not build on the idea that sexual harassment was a violation of women's rights to equality, life and liberty. Rather, it assumed that evidence of an offence against a woman's modesty – a creation of the 19th-century Victorian and colonial mentality – was sufficient to succeed in a claim of sexual harassment.

The legal responses inspired by feminists and articulated by the Supreme Court do not address the problem of sexual harassment. Rather, these responses are emerging as tools for repressing sexual speech and expression. The law appeals to employers to enforce the sexual harassment codes, a move that can lead to the sexual sanitisation of workplaces and university campuses, and also strengthen the efforts of the right wing to continue to link sexuality to prevailing sexual norms and clearly defined cultural boundaries. The definition covers, for example, sexually coloured remarks. At what point does a remark become sexual? In which language? And when is it unwelcome? In conversation? Or when it is overheard by the complainant? Given the pressure on employers and the desire to avoid being subjected to litigation, employer-drafted codes can often decree that the workplace be completely sexually sterile, and employers can announce a 'zero-tolerance' policy on sexual humour. What space is left for sexual rights and sexual expression once we consider that sex *per se* must only be framed within the language of protectionism, cultural conservatism, modesty or violence? Who determines whether an action has crossed the boundary of cultural modesty or is unwelcome? Sexual harassment law within the context of an increasingly censorious climate, sexual puritanism, and cultural conservatism can operate to deter sexual expression – a form of communication that can be valuable, educative and affirming.

At one level, the language and debates in the area of sexual harassment are similar to those current in the West. The problematic application of the sexual harassment law could be ascribed to the fact that India is in need of reform in its cultural practices, and of liberation from a sexually conservative past. Yet, at another level, to give the cases such a 'straight' reading is to disregard the way in which the relationship between sexuality and culture has been a site of contestation since the late 19th-century, as well as having been integral to assertions of nationalism and resistance to colonial rule. The cases reveal how colonial legal histories and the integral relationship between culture and sexuality inform current debates on law and sexuality. Constructions of sexuality are deeply implicated in the boundaries that are drawn between legitimate and illegitimate sexuality, which are further displaced onto expressions of national identity.

Despite 'victories' in the *Vishaka* and *AEPC* cases and others like them, there was no challenge to dominant cultural norms nor displacement of dominant sexual ideology. What exactly is dominant sexual ideology as constructed in the law? It is based on the assumption that sex is something from which good and decent people ought to be protected. Sex and sexuality have long been constructed as a bad, dirty and corrupting force that needs to be constrained, lest it otherwise undermine the social fabric. There is absolutely no affirmative articulation of sexuality in the case law – it remains undefined and ambiguous, and is what remains after 'bad sex' has been eliminated or suppressed (Lacey, 1998, pp 98–124). And 'bad sex' is determined by an appeal to an underlying conservative sexual and cultural morality, which divides sex into good and bad, and establishes a hierarchy of sexual practices. This reinforces the negativity in which sex is framed, and includes nearly every activity in the spectrum from brutal gang rape to sexually explicit images, or even sexually coloured remarks. Sex is something to be feared, which is corrupting and contaminating (Rubin, 1989, p 283). Sex, when it is not monogamous, heterosexual, non-commercial, marital, chaste, pure and confined to vaginal intercourse, can legitimately be understood only within this negative framework. Similarly, there is no challenge to the cultural norms according to which sexuality has been constructed. The cultural concerns which informed the *AEPC* decision reframed the issue of sexual harassment in terms of modesty and the cultural construction of women's sexual behaviour as chaste, passive, pure and virginal.

What are the consequences of the failure to make challenges to the normative in our engagements with law? The failure makes it possible, despite feminist efforts and engagements with law, to re-inscribe sexuality within dominant norms. Indeed, this is precisely what has occurred under the Hindu nationalists who until recently, led the coalition government at the centre. The government set up the Mailmath Criminal Law Amendments Committee, which in March 2003 recommended that the adultery provisions be made applicable to women, along with men, in the interests of equality (rather than of course abolishing the crime of adultery altogether); and that the provisions dealing with cruelty by the husband against his wife be made compoundable and bailable, in the interests of reconciliation, to preserve the sanctity of marriage and ensure that the wife is not left economically destitute.[18] The recommendation is also intended to protect the husband from adverse consequences if the wife should file a trivial claim against him. The committee understands that a wife should be supported in the marriage – but to remain in the marriage, not to exit from it. 'True to the Indian tradition the woman quietly suffers without complaining many inconveniences, hardships and even insults with the sole object of making the marriage a success. She even tolerates a husband with bad habits. However, when her suffering crosses the limits of tolerance she may even commit suicide. For the Indian woman marriage is a sacred bond and she tries her best not to break it.'[19]

Apart from creating the possibility of reinforcing dominant norms, a related concern is that the excess – that which does not constitute dominant sexuality and is regarded as culturally transgressive – is subject in law to restraint, persecution, censorship, social stigma, incarceration and even annihilation. Thus notions of chastity have been used to deny women maintenance under the Hindu Adoption and Maintenance Act 1956, which does not entitle a Hindu wife to receive maintenance from her former husband if she is unchaste (s 18(3)). A sex-worker is treated either as a victim in need of rescue and moral rehabilitation, or a moral contaminant to be punished and incarcerated, specifically because of the sexual nature of the work in which she engages; the gay man is targeted primarily as an active sexual subject who is disruptive of prevailing sexual norms. Public sex is penalised or/and criminalised through the sodomy laws, vagrancy laws, narcotics provisions, and some provisions of the state Acts dealing with railways. And of course sexual images are constant targets of censors and the moral brigade, panicked over the impact of such images on Hindu culture, families and our sexually sanitised universe. Sexually explicit images are invariably described as 'vulgar', 'obscene' and 'lascivious', reinforcing the sexualisation of women's bodies and the idea that sex is dirty. This view in turn encourages the idea that women's bodies are somehow dirty. Negativity about sex and sexuality inadvertently

---

18 Government of India, 2003
19 *Ibid*, pp 190–91.

reinforces the perception of sex as something about bad women, as whores, and that of good women as sexually pure and chaste, as wives and mothers. These views further strengthen the inference that in order to protect women from harm we need to protect them from sex, and that in order to protect Indian culture from erosion we need to protect it from sex.

The legal reforms proposed and enacted have come down heavily against victimisers through the use of the criminal law, or by focusing on strategies that are not necessarily liberating, such as instituting sex codes on university campuses that are based on punishing sexual wrongs without simultaneously articulating sexual rights for women. Protectionist responses continue to treat women as weak and vulnerable, incapable of taking decisions – in fact, inferior – while the state, in its *parens patriae* capacity (or even non-governmental actors) take actions on behalf of women. And these responses are invariably packaged in a cultural box that seeks to restrict affirmative expressions of sexuality and sexual speech, lest these destroy the fabric of Indian cultural integrity, once again colonised by the 'contaminating West'.

Cultural nationalists and sexual shakedowns

The Hindu Right has been able to advance its agenda effectively on issues of sexuality and women's rights, in and through the discourse of liberal rights. Some of the justifications used by feminists addressing issues of sexual violence are the very same arguments deployed by these considerably less progressive groups to support the increased censorship of sexually explicit representations and the scrutiny of public sexuality, including heterosexual intimacy, and to target and harass sexual subalterns – namely, sex-workers, gays, lesbians, and other Others.

It is important to stress that the Hindu Right is not a monolithic and homogeneous entity, and that different components, though they are all communal, advocate more extreme or moderate positions depending on both the issue and their own roles within the movement.[20] Thus, the BJP, which depends on electoral politics for its existence, advocates a more moderate stance in relation to the Muslims or on the construction of a temple for the Hindus at Ayodhya, a town in the northern state of Uttar Pradesh on the site where the Babri Masjid, a 16th-century mosque, was destroyed by the mobs of the Hindu Right in 1992. The VHP, a vast grassroots organisation that has been extremely effective at mobilising Hindus both in India and from the diaspora, is more militant in its appeals to religion and its invective against Muslims. It is the most vociferous and continuous advocate of the construction of a temple, and it is strident in its anti-Muslim rhetoric. In the national elections held in May 2004, the BJP-led coalition was defeated at the centre,

---

20 See note 1 above. Communalism has been defined as a discourse based on the 'belief that because a group of people follow a particular religion, they have as a result, common social, political and economic interests' (Chandra, 1984, p 1). It is a discourse that attempts to constitute subjects through communal attachment – particularly through religious community. The construction of communal identities – most notably, Hindu and Muslim - has been a central characteristic of the modern Indian polity, and continues to be an important source of political fragmentation. Through communal discourse, subjects come to understand the world around them as one based on the conflict between religious groups, and Indian society is understood as fractured by the conflict between these groups. Although India is characterised by many other equally compelling sources of division – class, caste, language, region – communalism has been, and remains, amongst the most politically divisive and explosive of discourses.

though the party continues to hold power in a number of states in India. The defeat of the BJP in the national elections does not constitute a defeat of the Hindu Right, whose existence does not depend exclusively on electoral outcomes. The VHP and RSS continue to operate in the public arena mobilising communities through grassroots participatory processes in support of their movement and their central ideology of Hindutva. Hindutva, which binds together the various components of the Hindu Right, seeks to establish the political, cultural and religious supremacy of Hinduism and India as a Hindu nation. Thus, I use the term Hindu Right in this essay not to obscure the important differences between the groups within this movement, but rather to capture their underlying shared vision.

A central but paradoxical strategy of the Hindu Right is to install religion and culture as primary attributes of nationalism and national identity, while at the same time deploying the discourse of secularism, free speech and equality to pursue what is in fact an anti-secular agenda – that is, the establishment of a Hindu state. The Hindu Right works in and through the discourse of rights, including secularism, equality and free speech, to pursue its religious and cultural vision, a vision that corresponds to the Hindutva agenda of casting the Muslim Other as intolerant, and suspect in terms of his loyalty to the nation and the threat he poses to the security of the Hindu majority and the Indian nation. This strategy reflects how the Hindu Right is engaged in a discursive struggle in which it is attempting to establish its vision of Hindutva as ideologically dominant. Through its collective efforts, it is seeking to naturalise the ideas of Hindutva, by making these ideas a part of the common sense of an increasingly large segment of Hindu society. The Hindu Right's struggle for ideological dominance stretches across a broad range of fields, from history to politics, religion to economics. My focus is on the struggle for meaning within the field of law, and on the ways in which the Hindu Right has sought to deploy a host of legal concepts and constitutional principles in order to advance its political agenda. In particular, there has been a highly significant development in how the Hindu Right has infused the constitutional principles of secularism, equality and free speech with new meaning, consistent with its vision of Hindutva.[21]

The Hindu Right has its basis in revivalist and nationalist movements of the 19th-century, which sought to revitalise Hindu culture as a strategy for resisting colonialism. As it developed through the 20th-century, it began to take on its distinctively right-wing, anti-minority stance – particularly in the 1920s, with the publication of VD Sarvarkar's *Hindutva: Who is Hindu?*, and the founding of the RSS (Sarvarkar, 1949; and see Pandey, 1990). Sarvarkar developed the idea of Hindutva, a communal discourse which seeks to construct the political category of Hindu in opposition to non-Hindus, particularly to Muslims and Christians. As Basu, with others, has stated:

---

21 See for example *Prabhoo v Prabhakar Kasinath Kunte and Others* [1996] All India Reports 1113 (SC), where the court conflated the term 'Hindutva' with Hinduism, holding that Hindutva reflected the way of life of the people in the subcontinent (p 1,130). For a discussion on the implications of this decision on the meaning of equality, see Kapur and Cossman, 2001. For a discussion on the discursive shifts brought about by the Hindu Right in the meaning of the constitutional right to equality, see Kapur and Cossman, 1996, pp 236–46.

[a]t the heart of Hindutva lies the myth of a continuous thousand year old struggle of Hindus against Muslims as the structuring principle of Hindu society. Both communities are assumed to have been homogeneous blocks – of Hindu patriots, heroically resisting invariably tyrannical, 'foreign' Muslim rulers. (Basu, Datta, Sarkar, Sarkar and Sen, 1993, p 2)

Muslims and Christians are to be considered suspect because, unlike Hindus, their holy lands lie outside India. Even though they share the same 'Fatherland' – that is, India – their allegiances are often questioned on the grounds that they have religious fealties to foreign lands. Thus, the Hindu Right and the political philosophy of Hindutva is antagonistic to difference. For example, MS Gowalkar, who led the RSS from 1940–73, stated:

All those … can have no place in the national life, unless they abandon their differences, adopt the religion, culture and language of the Nation and completely merge themselves in the National Race. So long, however, as they maintain their racial, religious and cultural differences, they cannot but be only foreigners … the strangers have to acknowledge the National religion as the State religion and in every other respect inseparably merge in the National community. (Gowalkar, 1939, pp 45–46)

The nationalism of the Hindu Right and its vision of the nation are narrowly religious. The political category of Hindu has been constituted in opposition to religious minorities, and premised on the very elimination of these minorities, through assimilation or considerably more violent means. Religious minorities are constituted in this discourse as presenting a threat to the integrity of the Nation and cannot be recognised or accommodated as a legitimate part of the Hindu Nation. Gowalkar was very clear that there was no place for religious minorities who failed to assimilate: they must 'lose their separate existence to merge in the Hindu race, or may stay in the country, wholly subordinated to the Hindu Nation, claiming nothing, deserving no privileges, far less any preferential treatment – not even citizen's rights' (Gowalkar, 1939, pp 47–48). The Hindu nation was thus constituted in the writings of Gowalkar through an attack on the very legitimacy of religious minorities, and on a denial of any protection of minority rights within it.

This thinking has translated itself in the contemporary period into the Hindu Right's position on religious difference, in which the special constitutional measures for the benefit of Muslims are deemed to be a violation of the Indian version of secularism based on the equal treatment of all religions, and its formal approach to the right to equality. The Hindu Right complains that the policy of appeasing minorities has perpetuated the oppression of Hindus. The contemporary social, economic and political malaise that is allegedly gripping Hindu society is seen as the result of this policy of appeasement, and the solution to this crisis is the establishment of a Hindu state. The Hindu Right's position on secularism and equality is driven by its political agenda of Hindutva – of establishing a Hindu nation based on a Hindu way of life. Right-wing Hindu religious orthodoxy is not being pursued in opposition to the constitutional principles of secularism and equality, but rather in and through them.

Hindutva continues today to be a political category that at its core is an attack on the legitimacy of minority rights in India. At the same time, the Hindu Right has exposed itself as very much a product of the conditions of postcoloniality. Today it also derives a considerable amount of economic support and fealty from the diaspora. For example, in the United States, the VHP or World Hindu Council of America receives funding in the form of considerable charitable contributions from non-resident Indians in the United States, who are keen to retain some notion of 'roots' in their 'motherland'. These funds are remitted back to India in the form of financial support for the RSS and the BJP, and their ideology of Hindutva.

The postcolonial period has also witnessed dramatic shifts in the economy since 1991, when the period of economic liberalisation was ushered in and added a new dimension to the consolidation of Hindutva political ideology. The Hindu Right has begun to place an emphasis on Indian society being 'modern but not Western', responding to the material and historical shifts of the late 20th and early 21st centuries in India. Hindutva is today being redefined to address the fundamental transformations in the social, economic and political landscape by reinforcing the boundaries of control over the nation, which also entails reinforcing boundaries of control over women. Hindutva is providing an important new legitimating ideology, designed to protect the (Hindu) cultural integrity of the nation at a time of economic restructuring and the opening up of the market.

The Hindu Right has sought to promote the spread of its communalised discourse to an increasingly large segment of Hindu society, particularly with the creation of the VHP in 1964. Founded at the behest of the RSS, the VHP was intended to infuse the politics of Hindutva with a specifically religious vision. Unlike the RSS, which functioned as an elite organisation, the VHP was intended to popularise the Hindutva ideology among the masses. And this phase of populism has been characterised by an increasingly extreme and violent anti-Muslim rhetoric. Although the rhetoric of the earlier leaders of the Hindu Right, such as Gowalkar and Savarkar, was certainly characterised by a strong anti-Muslim stance, the rhetoric of leaders such as Bal Thackeray (who leads the Shiv Sena) seems to have reached new heights. For example, in an exchange that took place shortly after the Bombay (Mumbai) riots of January 1993, following the destruction of the Babri Masjid, he responded to a charge that 'Indian Muslims are beginning to feel like Jews in Nazi Germany' by saying: 'Have they behaved like the Jews in Nazi Germany? If so, there is nothing wrong if they are treated as Jews were in Germany.'[22] His comments reflect the long-standing admiration of the Hindu Right for the Third Reich. More recently, he called on the government to form Hindu suicide squads to fight terrorism, suggesting that there were Muslims present in India bent on the destruction of the nation.[23]

Central to the Hindu Right's nationalist vision is the position of women. Although the Hindu Right does not speak with a single and homogeneous voice on women, there is a moderate position promoting women's equality within its discourse and pursuant to its nationalist agenda. It promotes a vision for women that is deeply imbued with dominant sexual ideology, such that the Hindu Right is able to advocate seemingly more moderate positions, while at the same time re-inscribing women's roles within the traditional, culturally bound, patriarchal family, and within sexual normativity. It takes up issues that have long been a part of the

22 Thackeray, 1993.
23 Thackeray, 2002.

feminist agenda, and recasts them in ways that do not challenge prevailing sexual and cultural norms, or women's traditional roles. For example, in the area of violence against women, the women's wings of the Hindu Right have been extremely active and vocal in condemning rape, domestic violence, dowry and sexual harassment. All of these issues find mention in the government's National Policy for the Empowerment of Women (2001). In the area of obscenity, the Hindu Right has lobbied for the censorship of advertisements and film songs that they argue are derogatory to women and in violation of Indian cultural values. The concerns thus expressed often come uncomfortably close to those of feminists, who also call for censorship. Similarly, arguments in favour of a domestic violence law have been championed by the Hindu Right. The result has been particularly disastrous for a group of lawyers and feminists, drafting what was perceived as the 'perfect Bill' on domestic violence, only to have it transformed into a Bill about protecting the institution of the family and marriage, and sanctioning the right of a men to beat their wives with reasonable cause – including the circumstance of the wife making a grab for her husband's property.[24] And as already discussed, sexual harassment codes have been encouraged in an effort to exorcise sex, sexual activity and sexual expression from the workplace and from university campuses, producing a sexually sterilised environment completely consistent with the Hindu Right's moralistic agenda.

The appropriation by the Hindu Right of issues of violence against women should not be seen as a wholesale adoption of the framework within which the women's movement has understood such violence. In stark contrast to the women's movement's emphasis on women's rights and men's violence, the Hindu Right has framed the issue of violence against women within the broader political and cultural discourses of the nation-state – quite specifically a Hindu nation-state. And this discursive strategy is two-fold. It involves both: (a) the communalisation of sexual violence, through which responsibility for violence against women is seen to lie within the Muslim community, and specifically with Muslim men; and (b) the feminisation of violence against women, according to which the violence that occurs within the family is said to be the responsibility of women. This two-fold discursive strategy corresponds to the public/private distinction in the types of violence identified, and in the ways in which violence is addressed. Violence within the public sphere is associated with rape, sexual assault and sexual harassment, whereas violence in the private sphere is associated with issues such as dowry, sex selection and female infanticide. Public violence is constituted within a communalising discourse, whereas private violence is constituted through the feminisation discourse. This discursive strategy operates to reinforce the construction of the Muslim community as the dangerous Other, as well as to absolve Hindu men of any blame for violence, either inside or outside of the family. It is a move that is precisely reminiscent of the colonial move to differentiate, stigmatise or incarcerate the Other, on the grounds of the Other's 'barbarity' and 'uncivilised' behaviour.

---

24 Protection from Domestic Violence Bill 2001, s 4(2), in Lawyer's Collective Women's Rights Initiative, 2002.

The recognition of sexual violence within the public sphere is framed within a communal discourse. The perpetrators of sexual violence are constructed as the Muslim Other. Sexual violence is thus cast as that which (Hindu) women experience at the hands of Muslim men. The rape of Hindu women by Muslim men during communal riots is invariably highlighted and is also followed by a call for harsher punishments. These moves are intended to reinforce the demonisation of the Muslim community, while deflecting attention away from sexual violence within Hindu communities. The violence that women experience in the public sphere can thereby be addressed with demands for harsher penalties for the perpetrators, without threatening the authority of Hindu males. The call to harsh penalties becomes, in effect, a call for the punishment of Muslim men who have dishonoured Hindu women – and thus, by implication, the Hindu community.

Within this communalised discourse of sexual violence, the harm associated with rape becomes a harm to the community. Rape is not understood as a violation of an individual woman's right to bodily autonomy, but rather, in a more traditional discourse, as a violation of women's honour. This honour is in turn closely associated with the honour of the family and the broader Hindu community. Thus, the rape of a Hindu woman becomes symbolic of the victimisation of the entire Hindu community (Basu, 1998, pp 167–84). The communal discourse provides women within the Hindu Right with a legitimate focus for their personal and political anger about sexual violence.

Within the political rhetoric of the Hindu Right, atrocities against women located in the family – that is, issues such as dowry, sex selection and female infanticide – are rarely treated differently. These issues are constituted through a discourse of feminisation, in which responsibility for the violence is placed on women themselves. Within this private sphere, women are seen as responsible both for the atrocities themselves and for bringing them to an end. Emphasis is placed on educating women against the practices in which they are complicit. For example, the practice of sex selection is constructed as a practice engaged in by women. Eliminating this practice must therefore begin with women, who must be educated against it. It is a clever move in which the role of men in the practice of sex selection is never addressed. Even dowry and dowry deaths are seen as at least partly the responsibility of women, who must cease to agree to these practices, and who in their capacities as mothers-in-law are often seen to be involved in dowry murder.

Underlying this feminisation of violence in the Hindu Right's approach to violence against women is a heavy reliance on dominant sexual ideology, and cultural assumptions about the appropriate roles of women in the family and women's sexual conduct. The selective recognition of violence against women occurring within the family leads to a call for more education. Issues such as wife assault, marital rape and child sexual abuse, which may directly implicate men, are not raised. If they are raised, as in a recent Bill on domestic violence, it is invariably to protect men's interests. In the focus on practices such as dowry deaths, sex selection and infanticide, men's responsibility is obscured by the focus on women. It is women who are seen to have become weak – the objects of degradation and maltreatment. So women must make themselves strong in order, in turn, to make their families strong.

Within the discourse of the Hindu Right, violence against women becomes quite literally a women's issue: the responsibility for eliminating violence lies with women themselves. They are accountable not only to themselves, but also to their families and their Hindu culture. It is their duty and obligation, as mothers and wives, to make their families and their culture strong. In turn, it is this duty to the family and to the marital relationship that generates their obligation to eliminate violent practices. Women need to resist violence not as an issue of individual rights, but as an issue of family honour.

There is no doubt a difference over these issues between the secular women's movement and the Hindu Right. The former has framed the issue of sexual violence as one of women's rights – the right to equality and the right to freedom from sexual harassment. The Hindu Right, however, frames the issue quite differently, as a question of the violation of women's traditional identity: sexual misconduct and sexual violence are seen as a violation of women as sexually pure and sanctified in their roles as wives and mothers. The Hindu Right is concerned with restoring women to the position of respect and honour they enjoyed in some mythical past. The harm is to women's modesty, dignity and honour.

Yet what is distinct about present-day nationalists, as opposed to the political nationalists of the 19th-century, is that they are pursuing their agenda not by eschewing the discourse of rights, but in and through that discourse – the right to speech, the right to equality, and the right to freedom of religion. Law is a key terrain for constituting the right wing's agenda around women's rights, sexuality and culture. Women's lives have once again become a site of contest in the struggle to redefine Indian identity, and normative sexuality plays an important role in the discursive strategy employed. Indeed, many legal issues associated with the women's movement, including the issues of obscenity and indecency, are now being appropriated by the Hindu Right, whose political agenda is in many respects antithetical to that of the women's movement. The Hindu Right is seeking to redefine issues of violence, sexual morality and free speech, in pursuit of its vision of political life.

An engagement with the questions surrounding law and sexuality requires more than just appeals for more law: it requires an engagement with law as a discursive site. In the context of postcolonial India, feminists need to interrogate how issues of sexual violence against women have been taken up in a way that fails to challenge the authority or legitimacy of Hindu men, of the marital relationship, and of the patriarchal Hindu family. Hindu men are not called to account for violence against women. Rather, public violence is blamed on Muslim men, while private violence is made the responsibility of women. And women are made responsible for eradicating both public and private violence, and restoring their own place of respect within their families as loyal, chaste wives, dutiful daughters, and caring mothers. The issue is articulated within the language of restoring women to the position of respect that they once enjoyed. At one level, ending violence against women has nothing to do with women's rights to equality. However, at another level it has a great deal to do with redefining the meaning and content of equality for women. The Hindu Right, in pursuing its agenda in and through the discourse of rights, is engaging in a major battle over the meaning and content of these rights. The discourse of equality is being deployed to address issues of historic disadvantage, which are articulated primarily in terms of the oppression and degeneration of Hindu society (and thus Hindu women) at the hands of the foreign (Muslim) invaders. In the hands of the Hindu Right, the discourse of equality is based on a revivalist discourse.

This discussion touches on one of the themes that presents itself in some of the other chapters of this book. The problem is that, once we appeal for legal intervention, it becomes difficult to distinguish the different positions on issues of violence and sexuality, and on the legal responses to these issues. It is not enough, then, to understand the relationship between law and sexuality in purely formal terms, with the belief that more rights equals more empowerment. A discursive struggle lies at the heart of the issue of sexuality and the law. Law is an important site of politics and the struggle over meaning – a place where we struggle for 'temporally bound and fully contestable visions of who we are and how we ought to live' (Brown, 1991). It is neither a simple instrument of social engineering nor one of oppression; rather, it is increasingly understood as a complex and contradictory force, which does not always operate in the same way nor produce consistent results. An analysis of this issue in the context of postcolonial India demonstrates how colonial legal encounters have complicated the issues involved, and how engagements with law do not produce certain outcomes, a stable subject, or clear victories.

There is a need to re-evaluate from a postcolonial perspective the legal strategies that have been pursued by feminist and other progressive groups in their search for sexual justice. How have these strategies served to reinforce normative understandings about sex and sexuality in the law? In what ways have they upended the transformative vision that inspired such claims, and reinforced methods of domination by encouraging increased regulation and cultural surveillance? And how do these interventions, which neglect the regulatory dimensions of law and its relationship to culture, end up converting our 'swords into boomerangs' (Brown and Halley, 2002, p 4)? Legal engagements with issues of sexuality cannot be understood exclusively within a liberal feminist view of law as social engineering, or as an instrument of liberation for groups that are discriminated against. Nor can liberal internationalism address the failures that have been intrinsic to the liberal project, as discussed above. While this literature makes a significant contribution, it is important to recognise its limitations for theorising the role of law in a postcolonial context. Such positions do not capture the ambivalence that characterises engagements with rights or the discursive relevance of colonial legal histories in the postcolonial present. Law should not be viewed as a monolithic effect of social justice strategies. Rather, it is profoundly implicated in culture, colonial legal histories, and other social powers that have the effect of producing subjectivity and identity. I do not argue against law, or for abandoning a rights project; I argue in favour of evaluating legal claims from a postcolonial perspective, and engaging with law as a complex, multiple and contingent discourse whose meaning is susceptible to context, cultural histories and the legacies of the past.

Chapter 3
Erotic Disruptions: Legal Narratives of Culture, Sex and Nation in India

We always knew that the dismantling of the colonial paradigm would release strange demons from the deep, and that these monsters might come trailing all sorts of subterranean material. Still, the awkward twists and turns, leaps and reversals in the ways the argument is being conducted should alert us to the sleep of reason that is beyond or after Reason, the way desire plays across power and knowledge in the dangerous enterprise of thinking at or beyond the limit. (Hall, 1996b, p 259)

For a long time, the story goes, we supported a Victorian regime, and we continue to be dominated by it even today. Thus the image of the imperial prude is emblazoned on our sexuality, restrained, mute and hypocritical. (Foucault, 1978, p 103)

In the diasporic production called *Fire*, the film's director Deepa Mehta, an Indian based in Canada, represents the dilemma of culture and authenticity that I seek to voice through this chapter. The story involves the attraction between two rather stunningly beautiful women, Radha and Sita, who live together in a joint family household with their mute mother-in-law. Their husbands are involved in other pursuits, whether it is celibacy for the purpose of finding spiritual salvation, or a sexual relationship with another woman who happens to be Chinese. Radha and Sita are both names derived from central female characters in Indian epics. In epic form, Radha is an older, spunky, married woman who carries on a long-term erotic and spiritual relationship with Lord Krishna, while Sita epitomises the attributes of virtue, self-sacrifice and devotion to her husband – qualities that have come to represent the hallmarks of Indian womanhood. In celluloid, Radha and Sita are reimagined in the contemporary moment to transgress nearly every sexual, familial and cultural norm that constitutes India as it is imagined. The two women's appropriation of rituals such as *karva chauth*, a fast kept by wives to secure the longevity of their husbands, constitutes a celebratory moment when they trespass into an 'unacceptable' sexual space. This moment culminates in what one reviewer curiously described as 'the Indian lesbian scene'. In the film the women are not damned into the sexual exile of a 'decadent West'. Instead, they are legitimated through another cultural move, the testing of a woman's purity through the *agnipariksha*, the fire that redeemed the original Sita from the wrath and condemnation of her husband Lord Ram and her community, for her suspected adultery. Culture is invoked to counter-culture. And this is where my story begins. This chapter is located on the precipice of desire and subversion. It is a story about normative sexuality in India and the ways in which it is inbred with an exclusionary narrative about culture; a narrative that is Hindu, unitary and fixed. Yet, it is also a story about how sexual speech and the performance of the sexual subaltern in law can serve as transgressive spaces of desire and pleasure.

My key concern is to look at the multiple ways in which culture is deployed in contemporary legal controversies about sex and sexuality in India. I discuss law's role in simultaneously reinforcing an essentialist story about culture, as well as providing space for resisting this construction. I examine how culture is used to delegitimise sexual practices and activities by casting them as foreign and contaminating. I also discuss how cultural hybridity is deployed to counter this authentication of Indian cultural values, a move that is ultimately intended to expose the fluidity of culture and Indian cultural values. I look at some of the limitations cultural hybridity poses for the sexual subject, in particular the sexual subaltern in a postcolonial context.

There are several concerns that inform this chapter. The first is a political concern to create space for marginalised sexual expression and sexualities by locating them in the historical past, while simultaneously challenging and subverting dominant cultural and sexual narratives. I want to navigate the possibility of speaking about and representing sex and sexuality in a way that does not set it up in opposition to culture. I need to negotiate some complex postures to ensure that I can participate in culture in a way that challenges cultural orthodoxy, without falling over and crumbling into an essentialist heap. I attempt to create a space for a broader range of sexualities through the retelling of the past, while at the same time avoiding cast-iron representations through this retelling.

I also seek to explore why a political project of desire is important in a postcolonial context and how desire can be theorised and reclaimed in such a context. Why should we, and how can we, disrupt the script that represents women in a so called developing context as victims constantly in need of rescue and rehabilitation, and rewrite a script of women who are also interested in what lies behind Madhuri Dixit's blouse[1] (Ghosh, 1999), under Chugtai's *Lihaaf (The Quilt)*,[2] or between the sheets in the *Kama Sutra* condom ads?[3] The current literature on women in India, outside the Indian context, is largely focused on issues such as dowry murders or *satis*, poverty and population. Uma Narayan points to the need to think about '(1) the kinds of Third World women's issues that cross western borders more frequently than others; and about (2) the effects of such "editing" and the "reframing" such issues undergo when they do cross borders' (Narayan, 1997, p 100). And finally, with the ascendancy of the Hindu Right, the subject of desire has become a highly contested site.

---

1 In 1993, the hit film song and dance number, 'Choli Ke Peechey Kya Hai?' ('What Lies Behind the Blouse?'), from the Hindi commercial film *Khalnayak (Bad Man)*, was the subject of a legal challenge brought by a supporter of the Bhartiya Janata Party (BJP), on the grounds that it was obscene. The case was dismissed by the trial court and, on appeal, by the Delhi High Court.

2 Ismat Chugtai's short story, *The Quilt*, was charged in 1942 as being obscene as it depicted the erotic relationship between a Muslim housewife and her maidservant. The charges were dismissed on the grounds that no four-letter words were used in the work (Chugtai, 1990, pp 7–19).

3 Sushma Swaraj, the Information and Broadcasting Minister at the time, declared that condom ads should not be explicit and anything suggesting activity between the sheets be prohibited. *Kama Sutra* is the brand name of a condom and its advertisements have been the subject of legal and public controversy in India for a number of years (Swaraj, 2001).

Narratives of culture, sex, nation

Hysteria about culture is sweeping the country. Everywhere cries about Indian cultural values being in danger are heard. And the threat, the risk, the enemy, time and again appears to be sex and sexuality. The legal contest over the screening of *The Bandit Queen* in India, convulsions around the holding of the Miss World beauty pageant in India in November 1996, outcries over satellite broadcasting, and protests over the emerging visibility of sexual subalterns all reflect a growing unease with the increasing publicity of sex and sexuality (Kapur, 1997).

All of these reactions indicate that sex is something that threatens Indian cultural values, the Indian way of life, the very existence of the Indian nation. In order to understand these contemporary cultural controversies, it is necessary to understand something about the relationship between culture and sexuality in the story of the Indian nation – a relationship that is being disrupted by the newly emerging sexual subalterns as well as the assertion of sexual speech. The current moral paroxysms around culture must be seen in the wider context of the relationship between culture and sex negotiated in the 19th-century, which I briefly set out in Chapter 2. In the late 19th-century, Hindu nationalists and revivalists reconstituted the 'Home' – along with sex and sexuality – as a 'pure' space of Indian culture, uncontaminated by the colonial encounter.

Partha Chatterjee has argued that, as there were no public spaces or institutions available to nationalists for constructing a national culture, the modern nation was fashioned in the autonomous private domain of culture (Chatterjee, 1989, p 236). The 'official' culture of Indian middle class nationalism was elaborated in the private domain – 'the home'– which had important implications on the role of sexuality in nationalist discourse. The home, as the repository of national identity, had to be protected from colonial intrusions by women, using their virtues of 'chastity, self-sacrifice, submission, devotion, kindness, patience and the labours of love' (Chatterjee, 1989, p 287). Chatterjee links this transformation of the woman through nationalist ideology with the disappearance of social reform in the late 19th-century. The political nationalists of that period were completely opposed to social reform, as it would open the door to the colonial power to act in the domain where the nationalists regarded themselves as sovereign. Thus, the issue of female emancipation disappeared in the late 19th-century precisely because of the refusal on the part of the nationalists to allow any political negotiation of the women's question with the colonial power (Chatterjee, 1989, p 250).

But the nation, entrenched in a respectable sexuality, was not just the product of official Indian nationalism. As Tanika Sarkar has argued, the reconstitution of the norms of elite sexuality in India was also a product of the dynamics of orthodox and traditional social forces in the consolidation of elite hegemony in India (Sarkar, 1996). Sarkar argues, in contrast to Chatterjee, that the home was in fact a highly contested cultural space, and that there was considerable evidence of tension over women's roles as preservers of cultural identity. The age of consent controversies, discussed in Chapter 2, gave rise to a plethora of medical and administrative literature attesting to the extent of violence experienced by girls married off at the age of puberty, challenging the view that the home was in fact a space of honour, dignity and purity. These internal cultural contests were marginalised in the broader contests between the political nationalists and the colonial power.

Similarly, Lata Mani has examined how the *sati* debate in the early 19th-century influenced the way in which the issue was addressed later in the century, (Mani, 1998). She argues that the early 19th-century debate between social reformers and conservatives over the legitimacy of *sati* in Indian culture was not about the rights of women, but a debate over tradition. It was a debate through which social reformers tried to reform Indian culture in order to undermine the legitimacy of Britain's rule, while the nationalists took the position that the colonial power had no role to play in the sphere of tradition and culture. Women's bodies served as the primary site for the re-articulation of tradition and culture.

The works of Partha Chatterjee, Tanika Sarkar and Lata Mani on women and nationalism help us to understand the ways in which culture and sexuality were reshaped and reconstituted through the colonial encounter. Women's sexual purity, confined to and safeguarded within the home and representing in turn the purity of Indian culture, was a constituting feature in the emergence of the Indian nation. Yet the paradox is that both sexuality and nationalism as they emerged were simultaneously Western, but not. Nationalism was invoked by anti-colonial forces to draw a distinction between the East and the West, but it was a concept grounded in the typology of knowledge production of the West. While nationalism and its reliance on an active subject challenged Orientalist thought that assumed a passive native subject, this subject was caught in the trappings of modernity – of progress, autonomy and reason. Nationalism was as much a product of the Enlightenment as rights and democracy. It was embraced at the point of independence, rather than interrogated (Radhakrishnan, 1992). It was not possible to reclaim a pure and uncontaminated space prior to the colonial encounter, nor was such a project necessarily desirable. Nationalism is always contradictory. 'Its daring political agenda is always already depoliticised and recuperated by the very same representational structure that national thought seeks to put into question' (Radhakrishnan, 1992, p 87). It is only through a deconstructive and critical relationship with nationalism that the postcolonial subject can produce a subaltern history about themselves.

The second paradox is that, just as the emerging Indian nationalist bore the mark of Western conceptions of nationalism, so too did the reconstituted space of Indian sexuality bear more than a slight resemblance to Victorian sexuality. The idea of sex and sexuality as a dangerous corrupting force to be carefully contained at all costs within family and marriage, was as Victorian as it was Indian. But, within the emerging fantasy of the nation, the chastity and purity of Indian women, by which this dangerous and contaminating force was controlled, came to represent not only the purity of Indian culture but also its superiority to the culture of the Empire. The home was not an 'uncontaminated' space. It was as much a product of the colonial encounter as the public sphere. The underpinnings of the assumptions about Indian women's sexuality were both Victorian and Indian. These assumptions were absorbed through the colonial encounter into a litany of laws regulating sexual conduct, and refracted through the gaze of the colonial subject, in particular, the Indian nationalist, to construct a puritanical image of Indian women's sexuality (Nair, 1996a, p 145).

This story of nation, culture and sexuality remains as germane in the current moment as it was in the 19th-century. The suturing of culture and sexuality into the fantasy of the nation continues to set the discursive stage on which the emerging debates on sex and sexuality are erupting. New sexual images and sexual subalterns are disrupting the script. They are challenging the underlying assumptions about sex and sexuality. They are challenging what has become over the years a naturalised and universalised set of ideas about sex. The features of normative sexuality have been discussed, in the Anglo-American context, in the work of Gayle Rubin (Rubin, 1989, p 267). In her understanding of normative sexuality, sex is a natural force and something that is sinful and dangerous. And it is something that will be subjected to unduly harsh penalties unless it falls within the parameters of normative sexuality, which in its most pure form is heterosexual, marital, monogamous, reproductive and non-commercial. Normative sexuality is accorded the maximum legal and social benefits, while practices that fall outside of this dominant sexual ideology, such as sodomy or commercial sex-work, bear the greatest social and legal stigma. Border-crossings between what is described as 'good' sex and 'bad' sex take place from time to time. But the crossing of really 'bad' erotic practices into moral and legal acceptability is feared and resisted (Rubin, 1989, p 283; Valdes, 1997, p 217).

Although the idea of normative sexuality may be drawn from Anglo-American feminist legal theory, it is important not to reject the validity of this concept simply on the grounds that it is feminist or foreign. To do so would negate the rich history of feminist struggles in India as well as the contribution of feminist scholarship by Indian women that is being produced both within and outside of India. The Anglo-American bias of this concept also does not delegitimise the concept. Such concepts cannot be mechanically applied to other contexts. They must be historicised, and their relevance materially grounded in the specific context of the legal regulation of sexuality in India. Such concepts must be changed, altered or adapted according to different material and historical realities. They do not become irrelevant simply because of their western origins. Normative sexuality looks very different from the Anglo-American context when examined in the Indian context. As Brenda Cossman has argued, this difference can begin to tell us something quite interesting about the concept itself. It tells us that the flow of analysis is not just unidirectional (Cossman, 1997, p 536). The hegemonic discourses of the West are susceptible to displacement when the 'gaze' is returned, that is, when the flow is recognised as being multidirectional. Indeed, a distinct feature of postcolonial theory is the recognition of the transnational and multidirectional flows of culture, travelling theory, and the syncretism and hybridity of contemporary culture (Bhabha, 1994; Grewal and Kaplan, 1994; Said, 1989).

In India, motherhood, wifehood, domesticity, marriage, chastity, purity, and self-sacrifice constitute the primary features of normative sexuality (Chapter 2). At the same time, it is impossible to understand these features of normative sexuality outside of the colonial encounter which set the stage for legal and cultural engagements with sexuality to be deeply implicated in the constitution of the nation and national identity. Thus these features of normative sexuality were also cultural constructs used to mark the distinction between the colonial power and the colonial subject. It is this history that distinguishes normative sexuality in postcolonial India from that which has emerged from Western liberal traditions (John and Nair, 1998, p 11). Female sexuality was controlled and bounded within the institution of marriage, or it was to be subsumed to the spiritual. And normative sexuality was incorporated into the nationalist agenda, where the discourse of purity and chastity produced a sexuality that was distinct from the contaminating, corrupting, (imperial) West. It was a thoroughly modern construct. These assumptions about sexuality and culture were products of the 19th-century colonial encounter.

Today, sexual subalterns are challenging normative sexuality and in turn threatening the purity of the Indian nation. The challenge is not altogether new. In the 19th-century, the widow challenged normative sexuality; that is, she challenged the heterosexual, marital, chaste, good sex category through the assertion of her right to remarry. The contemporary sexual subaltern similarly threatens to further breach the boundary between good sex and bad sex, to speak the language of variation, and challenge the hierarchy of sexually disdainful conduct that is integral to dominant sexual ideology. Yet there is something categorically different about the new issues. The contemporary controversies pose explicit challenges to the idea that sex is a negative, contaminating and corrupting force. Part of the perceived threat to Indian cultural values is coming from the assertion of sex itself as a dynamic and affirming experience, which has led to fears that the very fabric of Indian culture and ethos is under threat of erosion, if not collapse. The unleashing of sexual speech and expression from its negative rhetoric to an assertion of sex as a right and an affirmative experience is the explicit tension that characterises the contemporary moment.

This sexual challenge is simultaneously a cultural challenge. The challenge to dominant notions of sex and sexuality is perceived as a fundamental threat to Indian cultural values. Because of the particular way in which sexuality and culture were sutured together, the new sexual subalterns and sexual images are erupting as cultural controversies. New popular Hindi film songs are being castigated for being vulgar and against Indian cultural values, and sexual subalterns, such as gays and lesbians, are being targeted as Western contaminants threatening to erode Indian culture and ethos.

The new sexual images and newly radicalised sexual subalterns are not only disrupting the cultural script, they are simultaneously attempting to rewrite the script; they are not simply abandoning the terrain of Indian cultural values, but rather trying to write themselves into the script. Both sides of the debate are draping themselves in the cultural flag. The new images and the increasing visibility of new sexualities are presenting a fundamental challenge to the nation, which has been partly constructed by the stitching together of sexuality and culture.

These challenges are taking place within a rapidly changing political and economic context. The past decade has witnessed the aggressive assertion of neo-nationalism, personified in the emergence of the Hindu Right. The contemporary contests over culture need to be addressed against the emergence of right-wing politics and an increasing nostalgia for the past in the context of contemporary globalisation. The Hindu Right, whose antecedents I discuss in Chapter 2, is producing a simplified cultural history, which is obsessed with emphasising their Hindu identity and sense of location in a more globalised world. It is necessary to understand the features of this movement, which grows out of a historical legacy of nationalist resistance to the colonial encounter, as well as being a cultural product of the postcolonial condition. The nation-state is caught between a moment when it has tried to acquire a distinct identity separate and apart from its past as free and part of the civilised family of nations, and confronting a new crisis and threat in the form of contemporary economic, cultural and political processes. These take the form of, though not exclusively, the liberalisation, privatisation, and assertion of American military power and cultural influences. Under these circumstances, the Hindu Right is constructing a monolithic and homogenous national and cultural identity to counter the impact of global economic and social restructuring and the erosion of national sovereignty. It is pursuing this nationalist project through a discursive struggle for ideological hegemony, which stretches across a broad range of discursive fields including history, politics, religion, culture and law.

In the legal arena, the contemporary contests about culture reflect different understandings of culture. Stuart Hall has discussed at least two different ways of thinking about cultural identity. According to Hall, one position on cultural identity is that it consists of 'one, shared culture, a sort of collective "one true self", hiding inside the many other, more superficial and artificially imposed "selves", which people with a shared history and ancestry hold in common' (Hall, 1996a, p 211). Cultural identity is based on a common historical experience, a sense of unity; on an idea that we are 'one people'. It is a position that assumes cultural identity is stable and unchanging. Cultural identity consists of an essence that needs to be excavated and brought to light.

The second view of cultural identity is based on the recognition that there are points of similarity within the context of a culture, but there are also points of difference, of discontinuity and dispersal. It does not entail an archaeological search, but a re-telling of the past. As Hall points out:

> [W]e cannot speak about one identity, one story without acknowledging the ruptures and discontinuities of the story we tell or re-tell. We cannot speak for very long, with any exactness, about 'one experience, one identity', without acknowledging its other side – differences and discontinuities ... Far from being grounded in a mere 'recovery' of the past, which is waiting to be found, and which, when found, will secure our sense of ourselves into eternity, identities are the names we give to the different ways we are positioned by, and position ourselves within, the narratives of the past. (Hall, 1996a, p 212)

This view recognises the hybridity of culture, that it is a fluid and shifting concept that cannot be contained.

In the legal stories I relate in this essay, I explore the different understandings of culture that characterise the current debates on culture and sexuality in the context of the emergence of the Hindu Right, as well as the increased visibility of new sexual subalterns. I expose the ways in which cultural essentialism is deployed to reaffirm sexual normativity by those in positions of power and how such an approach views culture as static and immutable. I also examine the ways in which cultural arguments are being made by those attempting to challenge this dominant narrative of culture, sex and nation. At first glance, these arguments appear to deploy the same cultural essentialism made by those in positions of power, but at a deeper level they can be seen to be based on cultural hybridity. Cultural hybridity is deployed, though in subtle ways, to counter the stagnant, fixed and unmoving approach to culture that characterises the essentialist approach. I examine the possibilities of cultural hybridity in accommodating or creating greater space for the sexual subaltern and sexual speech. These contemporary tensions are being played out in the legal domain, and law is deeply implicated in the formulation and reformulation of culture and sexuality. The results of the discursive struggles in this arena have been inconsistent and contradictory and alliances contingent upon the issues involved, often producing contradictory results for women and sexual subalterns.

Contemporary controversies

I begin with the film *The Bandit Queen* and its significance in the cultural wars being waged in the courtroom against popular representations of sex and sexuality in Hindi commercial cinema. I then talk of how 'Western' cultural contaminants are metastasising throughout Indian homes via satellite broadcasting. Programmes such as *Baywatch*, *The Bold and the Beautiful*, Fashion TV and the MTV music video channel are being condemned for denigrating women and displacing them from the position of respect and honour they enjoyed in some ancient, long lost, Hindu past. In the final section, I move to the moral panics being created by sexual subalterns, whose increasing visibility is apparently threatening to destroy the fantasy of the joint Indian family and the ancient cultural values and traditions that have cemented it together.

Sexual speech

The legal domain is providing the stage where the cultural contest over new images introduced through satellite broadcasting and commercial cinema is being fought out. Sexual speech and sexual expression, whether in the form of Hindi film songs, *Baywatch*, or even the Miss World beauty pageants, constitute zones of contest where culture is invoked by all sides to either legitimise or delegitimise sexual speech.

The controversies are informed by a cobweb of legal rules, regulations and administrative guidelines designed to regulate sexual (and other) speech. Although freedom of expression is protected by Art 19 of the Indian Constitution, the constitutional guarantee permits many exceptions. According to Art 19(2), freedom of expression is subject to 'reasonable restrictions' including those in the interests of 'morality and decency'. Thus, the court has held that the legal restrictions on obscenity constitute a reasonable restriction under Art 19(2).[4] The relevant statutory provisions which govern sexual speech in India are found in s 292 of the Indian Penal Code 1860 (IPC), the Indecent Representation of Women Act 1986 (IRWA), and section 5-B of the Cinematography Act 1952. The definition of obscenity was introduced into s 292 of the IPC in 1969. The provision states that obscenity includes any visual or written material that is 'lascivious or appeals to the prurient interest' or 'if its effect or … the effect of any one of its items, is, if taken as a whole … tend to deprave and corrupt persons' who are likely to be exposed to it (s 292(1)). The provision penalises anyone who sells, hires, distributes, exhibits or exports such material (s 292(2)).

---

4 *Ranjit Udeshi v State of Maharashtra* [1965] All India Reports 881 (SC).

The IRWA is a contemporary piece of legislation and its enactment was partly the result of lobbying by feminists and others groups intent on specifically targeting what they perceived as subordinating and indecent representations of women. The Act prohibits indecency, which it defines as the 'depiction of the figure of a woman as to have the effect of being indecent or is likely to deprave or corrupt public morality'. The Cinematography Act 1952 sets out the general principles for certifying films by the Central Board of Film Certification (Censor Board), a body appointed by the central government. It imposes restrictions on speech to preserve public order and decency, and also gives the central government power to formulate guidelines according to which the certifying authorities can grant permission for the public exhibition of films. In 1991, the censorship guidelines for the Censor Board were revised to bring more images within the censorship net. These include: the glorification or justification of 'anti-social' activities such as violence, (s 2(i)), or scenes where 'human sensibilities' are offended by 'vulgarity, obscenity or depravity' (s 2(vii)); scenes that 'degrade or denigrate women in any manner' (s 2(ix)); and scenes involving sexual violence against women, including rape, molestation, or sexual perversions, unless they are germane to the theme, in which they 'shall be reduced to the minimum and no details shown' (s 2(x) and (xi)). In 1994 these guidelines were further amended and the government elaborated on the objectionable visuals that had been specified in the 1991 guidelines.[5]

The laws which regulate sexual speech constitute the terrain on which representations are contested as legitimate or illegitimate, as within or outside legitimate public culture. It is the terrain upon which different groups and constituencies are contesting new images. Sexual speech is becoming contentious precisely at the moment when cultural nationalism is (re)emerging, finding its most visceral form in the image of the Hindu Right. In this connection, I examine two controversies: the censoring of the film *The Bandit Queen* and the call to regulate satellite broadcasting, including efforts to prevent the launch of an adult television channel in India.

---

5   Annexe II referred to in reply to parts (A) to (C) of Lok Sabha Standard Question No 445 for 25.08.94. Vulgarity was deemed to include the following types of visuals:

1   Selectively exposing [a] woman's anatomy, eg breasts, cleavage, thighs, navel, in song and dance numbers, through suggestive and flimsy dresses, movements, zooming, particularly in close shots.

2   Double-meaning dialogues referring to women's anatomy (eg breast or apple or some other fruits).

3   Simulation of sexual movements (eg by showing swinging car, cot).

4   Man and woman in close proximity to each other or one over the other and in close proximity and making below the waist jerks suggesting copulation.

5   Pelvic jerks, breast swinging, hip jerks, man and woman mounting on each other, rolling together, rubbing woman's body from breast to thighs, hitting/rubbing man with breasts, sitting on each other's thighs and waist with entwined legs, lifting and peeping inside a woman's skirt, squeezing woman's navel and waist.

6   Vulgar kissing on breasts, navel, buttocks, upper part of thighs.

7   Coins, etc being put inside blouse and other types of eve-teasing as there is invasion of privacy of women's body.

The Bandit Queen

The controversy surrounding the screening of *The Bandit Queen* in India needs to be examined in the context of broader controversies surrounding popular culture, especially with respect to Indian commercial cinema, which is bringing about a transformation of public space and public culture. Representations of sex and sexuality, whether through diasporic productions such as *The Kama Sutra* and *Fire* or through popular Indian commercial cinema, are transforming/subverting dominant sexual ideology. Several recent controversies have focused on the Hindi film industry and the allegedly vulgar and indecent representations of women within these films. 'Choli Ke Peechey Kya Hai?' ('What Lies Behind the Blouse?'), discussed above, performed by the then top female actress, Madhuri Dixit, became the focus of public controversy and a legal challenge brought by a BJP supporter. Madhuri's voluptuous hip gyrations, vampish manoeuvres with co-dancer Neera Gupta and erotic verses, led to allegations by the distraught petitioner that the sequence was 'vulgar, against public morality and decency' and against Indian culture and ethos. The case was dismissed by the trial court and on appeal by the Delhi High Court. Even though the case was not successful in legal terms, it succeeded in stirring up public opinion around the controversy. This controversy was subsequently taken up by politicians and led to a stricter approach by the Censor Board. A similar controversy followed the release of the film song 'Sexy, Sexy, Sexy' from *Khuddar* (*Old*) which triggered a debate in Parliament on the increasing 'vulgarity and obscenity' in Hindi films. The Board directed that the words 'sexy, sexy, sexy' be substituted by the words 'baby, baby, baby', which it seems were more in keeping with Indian cultural values.

The Bandit Queen tells the story of Phoolan Devi, a lower caste, poor, rural Indian woman, who after experiencing years of violence at the hands of her husband, the police and the upper caste Gujjar community, becomes an outlaw herself. Although the film had been screened in many countries around the world, its release in India was delayed by the Censor Board, which demanded a series of cuts to the film. Scenes deemed unacceptable for Indian audiences included the explicit depictions of gang rape as well as Phoolan's violent revenge against her husband and the upper caste Thakurs. The director refused to make any cuts. At the same time, Phoolan Devi, on whose life the film was based, brought a petition to prevent the film from being released in India. She alleged that the film did not accurately represent her life and, somewhat contradictorily, that the representations of the sexual violence violated her privacy. Culture was invoked at every turn in the controversy to either justify or contest the cuts to the film.

The Delhi High Court initially banned the screening of the film. The order was based in part on a cultural platform, which supported the right to privacy arguments advanced by the plaintiff, Phoolan Devi. The judge, quoting from the *Mahabharata*, an ancient brahmanical epic, stated 'a naked woman ought not to be seen and the learned ones ought to avoid seeing a naked man as well. Sex and food are to be enjoyed in a lonely place alone'.[6] Ultimately, Phoolan Devi settled her case,

---

6 Order of the Delhi High Court dated 20 December 1994, p 31, staying the screening of the film.

accepting a payment of £40,000 and the producer's agreement to make four cuts to the film. Although the High Court ban was lifted after the settlement, the struggle with the Censor Board continued until the producer finally agreed to make further cuts, against the wishes of the director. Still the controversy would not die.

A member of the Gujjar community, the caste to which the bandits in the film belong, subsequently filed a writ petition before the Delhi High Court seeking to quash the certificate granted to the film and restrain its exhibition in India. The petitioner contended that, though audiences were led to believe that the film depicted the character of 'a former queen of ravines', the depiction was 'abhorrent and unconscionable and a slur on the womanhood of India'. He further argued that his community, the Gujjars, had been depicted as morally depraved, especially in the scene involving a Gujjar rapist. He alleged that the screening would 'rupture the social fabric' and 'if that is the way we are supposed to see the abuse of a woman in a commercial movie, then it depicted a crisis of culture'.[7] The petitioner stated that the film lowered the prestige of women in general and the community of Mahallas, the community of which Phoolan Devi was a member, in particular.

The single judge of the Delhi High Court who heard the case admitted the petition and quashed the certificate granted to the film. He directed that more cuts be made to the film and, until such time as a new certificate was granted by the Censor Board, prohibited the screening of the film in India. The film's producer and distributors filed an appeal against the order to the Divisional Bench of the High Court, which upheld the decision of the single judge. The Divisional Court focused on three features of the film: a two minute frontal nude scene of Phoolan Devi being made to fetch water from a village well; one rape scene, which showed the naked 'posterior' of Baba Gujjar, the rapist; and the use of expletives throughout the film. All three representations were held to be revolting, denigrating to women and capable of 'arousing sexual or sensual or lascivious feelings in the average man'.

The court's reasoning was informed, in part, by Art 51-A of the Indian Constitution. The Article provides that 'it shall be the duty of every citizen of India to value and preserve the rich heritage of our composite culture'. In addition, the state shall endeavour to strive 'towards excellence in all spheres of individual and collective activity, so that the nation constantly rises to higher levels of endeavour and achievement'. The court also referred to the *Eighth Report of the Parliamentary Standing Committee on Communications* (1995). In response to the demand for a more liberal approach by the Censor Board, so that Indian films could compete with the foreign television network, the Committee stated that accepting such an argument 'would mean allowing competition in vulgarity'.[8] Hence, foreign television was equated with vulgarity *per se*. The court also cited with approval the Committee's view that there was:

---

7 Gujjar, 1996.
8 Central Board of Film Certification, *Eighth Report of the Parliamentary Standing Committee on Communications*, 1995, para 1.8.

[a]n erosion of traditional Indian values, folk art and culture. Basic moral values of our rich Indian traditions should not be allowed to be compromised, eroded or diluted at any cost. The question is how to guard against several Indian films, which are posing a danger to the social fabric and communal harmony. There has to be a check on films which have a baneful influence on children and adolescents. We should see that the film media is not abused. (Paragraph 1.8)

The producer and distributors appealed to the Supreme Court of India, which overturned the High Court decision, and reinstated the original findings of the Tribunal.[9] The Supreme Court reviewed the guidelines established under the Cinematography Act and the case law on obscenity. The court held the guidelines required that the individual scenes must be seen within the context of the overall theme. In applying the guidelines to *The Bandit Queen*, the court concluded that the scenes of nudity, rape and the use of expletives, 'were in aid of the theme and intended not to arouse prurient or lascivious thoughts, but revulsion against the perpetrators and pity for the victim'. The court permitted the screening of the film subject to the original conditions imposed by the Appellate Tribunal.

In the Supreme Court hearings, the arguments were primarily focused on whether the scenes in question were obscene and offended a particular community or degraded women or, if taken as a whole, had a redeeming artistic or social value. A cultural lens was deployed to determine if a part of the work, when seen in isolation to be abhorrent, had a redeeming social value. One example used by the court was the *Kama Sutra*. The justices stated: 'We may view a documentary on the erotic tableaux from our ancient temples with equanimity or read the *Kama Sutra*, but a documentary from them as a practical sexual guide would be abhorrent.'[10]

The cultural arguments were significant in *The Bandit Queen* case, as it was a film alleged to have transgressed legitimate cultural expression in India. The violence against women depicted in the film was argued by some to violate the standards of decency. However, the Supreme Court held that these representations constituted legitimate cultural expression as they were intended to expose and condemn that violence. The representation of 'social evil as evil' was no longer to be circumscribed *per se*. The cultural contest resulted in pushing at the margins of legitimate cultural expression. Freedom to express the oppressive reality of life for women in India was recognised. According to the court, the film did not insult Indian womanhood as three women members had sat on the censorship tribunal that reviewed the film and allowed it to pass.

Yet the cultural contest did not end with the Supreme Court decision. Debates over the cultural appropriateness of the film persisted in the press and in the public arena. The broader cultural controversies over the representations of sex and sexuality continued to abound. Some feminists and feminist groups regarded the film as derogatory and violating women's equality rights. Madhu Kishwar, feminist and activist, argued that the film was made from a Western gaze and 'largely to satisfy the Western palate which delights in seeing non-Western people as an exotic

---

9   *Bobby Art International v Om Pal Singh Hoon* [1996] All India Reports (SC).
10 *Ibid*, p 1851, para 50.

species very different from themselves' (Kishwar, 1994, p 35). She further argued that the film pandered to the '[s]tereotype images the West has of India, a land of female infanticide where parents are brutal in their treatment of daughters and where evil mothers-in-law torture their daughters-in-law to death' (Kishwar, 1994, p 36).

Partha Chatterjee, writing for a weekly newspaper, argued:

> Worst of all is the grading that corresponds to the aesthetics of the western eye looking at India – reducing the harsh, contrasting character of Indian light and striving for soft, luminous colours in a parody of the English water-colour tradition exemplified by the works of John S Coatman and others.[11]

Another critic, Krishna Prasad, stated that the film played up 'every recognisable cliché that the West has about India – caste, royalty, poverty, heat and lust, by his depiction of revolting and gratuitous sex' (Prasad, 1994, p 7). Prasad urged the censors to take action 'for the sake of clean cinema' and the 'greater good of the community', and 'before the floodgates of fornication open'. The tension around culture was aggravated by the very positive response that the film received in the foreign press. For example, Alexander Walker, writing for the *Evening Standard*, a London daily, stated:

> ... this film uses such brutal events to articulate an urgent argument about women's rights in an Asian society where sexist violence has never been pictured so graphically ... with the ending of apartheid in South Africa, world opinion may now focus on the sub-continent and force a reform in the apartheid of gender and caste that exists there. If so, *Bandit Queen* will have played no small part. (Walker, 1994, p 27)

A strongly criticised sequence in the film was the sex scene between Phoolan Devi and her lover, Vikram Mallah. The scene takes place in a room in a city where Phoolan takes Vikram to recover from a gunshot wound. During this sequence, Phoolan is depicted on top of Vikram Mallah having sex with him. One Indian critic, Pankaj Butalia, remarked that the representation was untenable, partly because it was unlikely that a 'rustic' woman could have made love in this manner.

Another writer stated that:

> The movie has certain scenes where Vikram Mallah and Phoolan Devi are shown making love in a room in Kanpur wherein she assumes the superior position and initiates the process. Such a scene, which Shekhar Kapur himself admits was born of 'poetic license', seems unnecessary and contrived. Another scene showing Phoolan bathing by the river, semi-nude, with Vikram Mallah playing Peeping Tom seems equally out of sync with the modesty of rural folk bathing in public places. (Choudhary, 1996, p 28)

These positions assume that the representation of a woman initiating sexual activity is in some respect indecent and outside the purview of prevailing cultural norms, representing a 'Western gaze' on India for the benefit of Western audiences. A few

---

11 Chatterjee, 1994.

groups challenged this position, arguing that the active role was in fact not alien to Indian culture. 'The inversion of traditional sexual roles is not a "modern" phenomenon. The poet Chandi Das has praised the deliberate, sensuous union of the two/the girl playing this time the active role/riding her lover's outstretched body in delight' (Kapur and Ghosh, 1995).

Culture was deployed in different ways through the case as well as in the debates surrounding it. On the one hand the representation of sexual violence was regarded as a form of titillation threatening to erode the 'rich Indian cultural heritage and ethos'. The assumption appeared to be that any representation of sex, even when it is about sexual violence is *per se* contrary to Indian cultural values. Contrary to this approach was the view that the representations of sex and sexuality have always been a part of Indian culture and heritage. Both of these approaches can be seen to represent an essential approach to culture, the former representing culture as something that has been impervious to the incursions of sex and sexuality and the latter advocating that sex and sexuality have always been a part of Indian culture. Both positions can be seen to regard culture as static and fixed, but the implications of their arguments are quite different. In the anti-*The Bandit Queen* argument, sexuality was something to be feared and kept at arm's length; whereas in the argument of those defending *The Bandit Queen*, sexuality was perfectly acceptable and integral to Indian cultural identity. In the arguments defending *The Bandit Queen*, there is an effort to complicate the cultural script in law, and disrupt the dominant narrative of culture, sex and nation.

The story of the film and its cultural moorings is a more complex story of transnational cultural flows and postcolonial paradoxes. In many ways, *The Bandit Queen* has all the hallmarks of a film 'made in India'. Director, Shekhar Kapoor and producer, Bobbi Beddi are both Indian. The film is the story of an Indian woman, Phoolan Devi, a notorious bandit, who subsequently became a politician. The film was also based on the book of the same name, written by Mala Sen, also an Indian. And *The Bandit Queen* was filmed in India. But the 'foreign hand' was also implicated in the film. Channel 4 Productions was a co-producer and its postproduction was in England. The film premiered at international film festivals, receiving considerable attention at Cannes. Phoolan Devi chased the film all the way to the Toronto International Film Festival, demanding that screening be stopped. But, when *The Bandit Queen* tried to come home, its director and producers discovered – like so many other postcolonial cultural producers – that sometimes you cannot come home again. A similar though less tangled story precedes the *Kama Sutra*, which is an ancient Indian text on sexual practices, that when made into a film by Indian director and producer Mira Nair, was also banned for a time in India. According to the Censor Board, the film contained 'serious pornographic content'. The film also opened to a more mixed acclaim than *The Bandit Queen* to audiences abroad, but when it came home, it was ultimately also subject to the censor's scissors, and the most explicit scenes of nudity were cut from the original.

The Bandit Queen and *The Kama Sutra*, are stories and cultural productions that begin in India, but end up cast as foreign/Western/Other. These cultural productions, and those who created them, are part of the postcolonial diaspora, or what Arjun Appadurai has called the 'disaporic public sphere', located neither here nor there (Appadurai, 1996, p 89). They are among the novelists, filmmakers, and other cultural producers whose works and lives are located somewhere in the transnational flow of people and images, of migration and mediation (Longfellow, 2002). Amidst these dislocations, these productions, and those who produce them, find that they have no home, or at a minimum, that any notion of home has been deterritorialised. It is neither here nor there, but at best, in the words of Homi Bhaba, somewhere in between.

These postcolonial cultural products then encounter the contradictions of a postcolonial legal regime. Works cast as 'obscene' 'indecent' and/or 'pornographic', or otherwise in violation of the Indian cultural ethos, are then prosecuted under a series of laws that have their origin in Victorian England. The Indian law of obscenity is derived from the English common law on obscenity of the mid-19th-century. And the laws governing the Indian Censor Board are in turn derived from these criminal laws of obscenity and indecency. These once colonial laws are now called upon to defend the Indian cultural ethos.

The cultural controversies around films like *The Bandit Queen* and *The Kama Sutra* symbolise many of the contradictions of the postcolonial condition. Both the cultural productions and the laws deployed against them are hybrids; products of the colonial encounter of here and there and back again. But one hybrid is deployed against the other, all in the defence of Indian cultural values. These cultural controversies have also taken many different shapes. Not all the controversies revolve around such disaporic productions. Many of the later controversies, like the failed attempt to ban the Miss World beauty pageant, or the ongoing effort to ban satellite television, music video television or fashion television, involve oppositions to the transnational flow of culture from the West to India. Beauty pageants and satellite television are opposed as violating Indian cultural values. It is an opposition to the globalisation of Western culture, and a defence of indigenous Indian culture from this destructive Western cultural influence.

Satellite broadcasting and adult television

The transmission of sexy images and images of sex through satellite broadcasting has become increasingly available to Indians and is evidently in high demand (Mankekar, 1999, pp 342–50; Skinner, Melkote and Muppidi, 1998, pp 295–315). But it has also come in for considerable disapproval from the Hindu Right, as well as many progressive, feminist, and human rights groups. Satellite broadcasting is increasingly being regarded as the vessel of contamination that transports the decadent practices of the West into the Indian anatomy, corroding and corrupting the purity of its cultural values and traditions, especially through its representations of women.

The hysteria has led to debates as well as litigation to determine what is appropriate for Indian audiences to view in their home. One women's group has filed a petition in the Delhi High Court seeking to regulate satellite broadcasting in India. It is requesting the court to instruct 'police stations not to permit the relay of any indecent, vulgar, offensive programs depicting and presenting women in an indecent manner in violation' of IRWA. The National Commission on Women (NCW) and several other women's groups have supported the petition.[12] Part of the concern stems from the fact that television was state controlled until the introduction of satellite broadcasting in the early 1990s, and hence, the images beamed into the Indian home were strictly monitored and controlled by the Information and Broadcasting Ministry.

The objection to the representation of sex on television is wrapped in a cultural loincloth. The petitioners state that sex and sexuality are imports of satellite broadcasting and are 'morally and culturally tearing [apart] the national and cultural ethos' of the country.[13] The petition questions whether 'our time tested cement, ie culture and ethos [should be allowed] to be corrupted and eroded by [the] weaponry of sex and as a consequence ... allow ourselves to be subsumed and swallowed in the Western culture resting on [the] power of sex, violence and crime'.[14] The petition goes on to state that:

> India has a different policy on sex exhibitions and sex products unlike the western world where sex shops are on display in almost every street. Sex and entertainment are regarded as an industry. Education on sex and biology is one thing, but using sex and women as weapons of sexual excitement for crass commercial gains as is done by Foreign Television Networks, is another ...[15]

The petitioners are concerned over the sensationalising of sex and its effect on the family:

> The question is whether in Indian society ... sex should be allowed to become a staple food in every home especially in joint families where in the evening members of the family from grandparents to grandchildren sit together and watch television and listen to the radio over meals. The question is whether the increasing use of sex can be allowed to tear apart our cultural ethos and cultural fibre, which is holding the vast nation state into one cohesive state.[16]

According to the petition, the threat to women's position in India is external – the contaminant resides outside of Indian cultural values; the contaminant is Western. The implicit assumption is that there is a pure space of Indian culture, untouched and uncorrupted, where women are not degraded by the decadent Western obsession with sex.

In a separate petition, the NCW has also demanded a ban of a proposed adult channel called Plus 21. Although the content of this channel remains unknown, the Commission is arguing that it is intended to be 'sexually titillating' and pornographic and can result in harm or injury to adolescents, women and other so called 'vulnerable sections' of society. The petitioners concern is to 'prevent cultural shock to the viewers'. The NCW, together with several other women's organisations

---

12 *Nirmala Sharma v Union of India*, Civil Writ Petition No 2697 of 1995.
13 *Ibid*, p 23.
14 *Ibid*, pp 43–44.
15 *Ibid*, p 23.
16 *Ibid*, p 44.

who are co-petitioners, alleges that the representations of sex and violence on the proposed channel will encourage patterns of behaviour in real life that are very harmful to women. The concern of the petitioners is once again framed through a cultural periscope. They express the view that 'Indian traditions, which have been built over centuries and are reflected in the Indian Constitution and the safeguards that it has imposed for public morality are now under threat of erosion from obscene and vulgar programs on foreign channels'.[17] The petition cites the decision of a district court judge as authority for its position:

> As regards beaming of obscene/vulgar program through the foreign channels, the government will have to initiate a clear policy to stop cultural invasion by technological and scientific means and by such other means as may be feasible. It is hoped that the government shall become live and conscious to its constitutional obligations to see that foreign TV Network [sic] do not uproot Indian Culture, traditional values and Indian laws by display of vulgar programmes for economic reasons.[18]

The petition further alleges that incest and other sexual abuses are on the rise, partly as a result of 'exposure to electronic media that [is] emphasising aspects of life that are alien to the India culture'.[19] The petitioners are seeking an injunction from the court to restrain the transmission of Plus 21 anywhere in India.

Several women's organisations have also written to the Prime Minister's office requesting that he prevent an adult channel from being created.[20] The letter states that there is a 'breakdown of social and cultural norms taking place through the invidious influences let loose in the media ...'. It further states that there is a break up of 'traditionally valued social norms in the face of "modernisation" fuelled by provocative and permissive TV programmes and advertisements in a number of channels ...'.

The broadcasters have opposed the petition seeking to ban satellite and cable television. Some feminist groups have intervened in the case, seeking to counter the position that Indian culture and ethos must be protected from cultural invasion from the West:[21]

> It is pertinent to state that India's local and indigenous cultures and traditions have enormous strengths of their own and are not likely to be undermined by foreign media. It may be recalled that the diverse cultures of India survived 200 years of colonial rule. The argument of the petitioners also rests on an assumption that 'Indian culture' is a homogenous entity, which has certain clearly identifiable ingredients, which can therefore be protected. On the contrary, India is a conglomeration of diverse traditions, races, religious groups, peoples, tribes and ideologies that cannot be defined as 'one culture'.

---

17 *National Commission of Women and Others v Union of India and Others*, Civil Writ Petition No 2697 of 1995, p 5.

18 *Ibid*, p 23.

19 *Ibid*, p 18.

20 Letter dated 21 September 1996 to the Prime Minister signed by 10 women's organisations, annexed to the petition seeking to ban satellite broadcasting.

21 Intervention application by the Centre for Feminist Legal Research and Media Storm, in the *National Commission of Women and Others v Union of India and Others*, Civil Writ Petition No 2697 of 1995.

The interveners argue that the imposition of one 'Indian culture' on the people of India is a violation of their free speech and equality rights. The forceful imposition of a homogenous Indian culture will only serve to enforce traditional notions of womanhood and family that 'are regressive and have dangerous implications for women and threaten to reinforce notions that have been challenged by the women's movement'. The interveners argue that television is providing a forum for women to challenge traditional roles and create diverse and different representations of women. Regarding sex and sexuality, the interveners contend that:

> Indian history provides countless examples of a rich and diverse heritage depicting sex and sexuality, which ought to be valued and developed rather than submerged under the assault of conservative morality. It is inconsistent to argue that sex and sexuality is not a part of India's culture considering that India's diverse cultural heritage includes the Khajuraho temples, the *Kama Sutra*, *Geet Govinda* and other such works.

The cultural arguments advanced in *The Bandit Queen*, the satellite broadcasting case, and the Plus 21 litigation represent different concerns and positions. The arguments advanced by the NCW and other women's groups in these cases are concerned with women's equality rights. Their arguments, however, are informed by an approach to culture and sexuality that is essentialist and deeply nationalistic. There is no doubt that for feminists the struggle around culture is a particularly complex one. The struggle for women's rights has emerged simultaneously with the struggle for nationalism. Nevertheless, feminism has a tenuous relationship with nationalism, and has been cast as Western and imperialist at different historical moments. For this very reason, feminists have often had to project themselves as nationalists to counter this attack. As Geraldine Heng has stated:

> Indeed, nationalism is so powerful a force in the Third World that to counter the charge of antinationalism – the assertion that feminism is of foreign origin and influence, and therefore implicitly or expressly antinational – the strategic response of a Third-World feminism under threat must be, and has sometimes been to assume the nationalist mantle itself: seeking legitimation and ideological support in local cultural history, by finding feminist or protofeminist myths, laws, customs, characters, narratives and origins in the national or communal past or in strategic interpretations of religious history or law. (Heng, 1996, p 39)

Feminism has operated within the discourse of nationalism as anti-Western and has had to position itself as anti-Western to establish its legitimacy. It has adamantly denied allegations of being Western, and sought to establish a distinctively Indian feminism with an authentic Indian feminist subject. This distinct subject has been constructed on essentialist notions of 'the West' and 'Western feminism'. This position can be a treacherous one as is revealed in the arguments presented by the NCW and other women's groups in *The Bandit Queen*, satellite broadcasting and Plus 21 cases. The anti-imperialist, anti-Western, pro-nationalist rhetoric is not necessarily progressive. As Stuart Hall argues, 'nationalism is not only not a spent force; it isn't necessarily either a reactionary or progressive force, politically' (Hall, 1993, p 353). He argues that nationalism has no sense of political belonging, that it can be progressive and reactionary simultaneously.

The use of culture is effective in countering anti-nationalist allegations, but the failure to reflect on the contradictory nature of culture leads to a host of problems. The NCW and other women's groups argue about Indian culture unreflectively and thus end up essentialising the very culture that they have sought to transform in other arenas. They have essentialised the discourse that has itself presented difficulties for women such as constructing women as mothers of the nation or the repositories of sexual purity. This position converges with the narrative of culture, sex and nation in postcolonial India with its emphasis on the purity of its women. The deployment of Indian cultural values by the NCW in the context of the satellite broadcasting case ends up being very conservative. Their arguments are constructing a pure place of authenticity, which is remarkably similar to the strategies of the religious right, whose vision for women is similarly based on restoring women to a position of respect and honour that they enjoyed in some bygone era as wives and mothers.

In contrast, the arguments advanced by the interveners in the satellite broadcasting case and others in hindsight reflect a more complex position on culture. Their primary argument is that sex and sexuality are not external contaminants, because they have always existed in Indian culture and tradition. Whether through 'Indian' poetry, literature, or sculpture, sex and sexuality have existed in Indian culture well before the introduction of the market, the Empire and the Mughals. Their effort at complicating culture is distinct. The argument rests ostensibly on an essentialist basis, but it is nevertheless challenging the dominant script in the way the story has been told and continues to be told. They are exploding the dominant authentic voice to resist the narrative of culture, sex and nation that is being told and that is being naturalised and universalised through its telling and re-telling. In challenging this voice, they are exposing the hybrid nature of culture, that there are other versions, that the story is neither stable nor fixed. The repudiation of the West and things Western within the dominant script are strategies for securing cultural and political legitimacy. The interveners are complicating the opposition of 'Western' and 'Indian' and developing a less homogenous and essentialist approach about Indian cultural values and the location of women, sex and sexuality within that culture.

The sexual subaltern

The threat to Indian cultural values, however, is not seen as coming from the celluloid screens and satellite skies alone. The cultural contaminant has also been detected in the practices of sexual subalterns, in particular, sex-workers, gays and lesbians. I use the term 'sexual subaltern' as a theoretical device derived from subaltern studies, to bring together in this instance the disparate range of sexual minorities within postcolonial India, without suggesting that it is either a homogenised or stable category. The location of the sexual subaltern in postcolonial India is complex, at times contradictory, and not invoked exclusively as an identity of resistance to dominant sexual categories.

The sexual subaltern has become the focus of increasing concern since the AIDS crisis perforated the sexual environment. The threat of a pandemic in India has posed a critical challenge to dominant cultural attitudes regarding sexuality. The concern over the pandemic has led to the harnessing of cultural arguments on both sides of the good sex/bad sex binary. In this section I address the ways in which culture is being deployed in law either to contain the practices of sexual minorities and exorcise the cultural contaminant or historically ground the existence of the sexual subaltern in an effort to recast the treatment of sexual minorities in law.

Sex-work

In the early 1980s, state officials denied that AIDS could be a problem in India because of the 'moral values' of Indian men and women. One professor of medicine at the Medical College of Trivandrum, Kerala, stated:

> Even at the end of the 20th century, the eastern culture is untinged in its tradition of high morality, monogamous marriage system and safe sex behaviour. Our younger generation and youth still practice virginity till their nuptial day. The religious customs and god-fearing living habits are a shield or protection against many social evils. It will be difficult even for HIV to penetrate this shield, except in certain metropolitan populations. (AIDS Bhedbav Virodhi Andolan, 1993, p 25)

In 2001, the UN reported that an estimated 3.97 million adults in India were infected with AIDS. The report states that with infection rates estimated at 0.7% of the population, HIV will emerge as the largest cause of adult mortality in this decade. The moral righteousness of Indian sexuality has indeed been put to a challenge and culture is being invoked to reassert this righteousness. This process is particularly evident in the legal regulation of sex-work.

The AIDS crisis has sparked a plethora of research with an emphasis on 'knowing and measuring sexual practices of "at-risk populations", such as the youth, college students, and sex-trade workers' (Puri, 1999, p 283). Moreover, the crisis has created a heightened state surveillance of sex-workers, amongst others, as the primary transmitters of the disease. The language of this surveillance is deeply imbued with assumptions about AIDS as a Western disease that has been imported into India through promiscuous Western lifestyles. The 'Western white male' is cast as a sexual conqueror tearing through the cultural hymen and leaving in his wake strews of fallen women and a fallen culture. At times the sex-worker is implicated in this cultural demise, castigated for abandoning the moral purity and sexual abstinence that constitutes the bedrock of Indian culture.

One of the state responses to the threat of cultural contamination stemming from the AIDS crisis has been to instigate law reform primarily in the area of sex-work. Currently, sex-work in India is regulated primarily by the Immoral Traffic (Prevention) Act 1956 (ITPA). 'Prostitution', which is the word used in the Act, is defined in s 2(f) as 'the sexual exploitation or abuse of persons for commercial purposes'.[22] This definition has been construed by the courts to mean 'promiscuous and indiscriminate sexual intercourse for hire'. A single act of sexual intercourse for hire, or indiscriminate sexual intercourse without payment, does not constitute

---

22 I use the terms prostitute or prostitution when referring to a text or author that explicitly deploys these terms. In all other instances I use the terms sex-worker and sex-work.

prostitution under the existing statute. The Act was enacted in pursuance of the International Convention for the Suppression in the Traffic in Persons and the Exploitation of the Prostitution (of Others) signed in New York in 1950. The primary objective of the Act is to criminalise the outward manifestations of prostitution, including soliciting, trafficking and the keeping of brothels, rather than to abolish prostitution or criminalise the prostitute *per se*.[23] However, there are specific provisions dealing with solicitation, 'living off the earnings of prostitution' (which could include any family member of the sex-worker who depends on her income), and the seizure of a sex-worker's children, which are primarily directed against the sex-worker.[24] Any demonstration of agency on the part of the sex-worker is effectively penalised through the provision against solicitation, which is the most frequently applied section of the Act. The Act also contains certain welfare measures that are directed at the rehabilitation of women in prostitution, that is, to reform those who are rescued from the industry and perceived as victims of the trade.[25] Neither construction assists women in sex-work to counter the violence and exploitation they may experience in the course of their work, nor the harassment they experience in their everyday lives, where stigma justifies abuse.

The law simultaneously reinforces a patronising and protectionist, as well as a punitive, response to the sex-worker. The sex-worker is at times regarded as a cultural contaminant. The punitive response takes the form of either incarcerating women under morality laws or criminalising the external manifestations of her work, such as soliciting. The basic logic is that if she cannot be reformed through rehabilitation, then she must be removed through incarceration. The sexually assertive woman is to be penalised by removing her from the public arena and incarcerating her so that she no longer threatens the public interest, the Indian family, or Indian culture. These strategies echo 19th-century notions about the purity of the nation being contingent on the purity of its women.

The laws regulating sex-work are based on notions of outlawed sexuality. The fact that women in sex-work are paid, perceived to be promiscuous, and regarded

---

23 Some related provisions are found in the IPC (1860) which contains general sections against the trafficking and slavery of women and children, as well as state-level police, railway, beggary, health and public order statutes. In particular, see s 365 which deals with kidnapping or abducting with intent to secretly or wrongfully confine a person; s 366A which deals with procuring minor girls; s 366B which deals with the importation of a girl from a foreign country; s 367 which deals with kidnapping or abducting a person in order to subject them to grievous hurt, slavery, etc; s 370 which deals with the buying or disposing of any person as a slave; s 371 which addresses the habitual dealing in slaves; s 372 which deals with the selling of a minor for the purposes of prostitution; s 373 which addresses the problem of buying a minor for the purposes of prostitution; s 374 which deals with unlawful compulsory labour. Other general provisions include: Art 23 of the Indian Constitution which prohibits the trafficking in human beings and all forms of forced labour; and Art 39 which provides that the state should direct its policy towards securing, among other things, a right to adequate means to livelihood for men and women equally and equal pay for equal work for men and women so that citizens are not forced by economic necessity to enter vocations unsuited to their age or strength.

24 ITPA, ss 4, 6, 7, 8, 15 and 16.

25 *Ibid*, ss 15, 16 and 19.

as carriers of contagion and disease, places them outside the framework of acceptable sexuality. Ostensibly, the law is not intended to target the women. The intention of the Act is to punish traffickers and those who exploit women for the purposes of prostitution or commercial vice. However, soliciting and 'living off the earnings of prostitution' and 'prostitution in a public place' are all punishable activities under the Act and designed to stem the cultural contagion. There is also a provision that implicates all women by placing the onus on a woman to prove that she is not a prostitute if such a complaint is made against her – otherwise she can be removed from the locality where she resides.[26] The provisions of the Act operate to deny women in sex-work rights to a residence, mobility, expression and work, and operate primarily against such women rather than those who exploit them.

The AIDS crisis has triggered an interest in the reform of the laws addressing sex-work. A number of proposals have been drafted under the auspices of various government bodies. The proposals are at times conflicting and contradictory, yet the impetus for these proposals emanates from a concern that AIDS has threatened the notion of the purity of Indian sexuality and contributed to a cultural crisis. The law reform proposals represent an attempt to respond to this crisis. Some of these proposals simply reassert the traditional cultural script against the corrupt sexual subaltern, others attempt to find ways to rescue the subaltern from her dreadful fate, and yet others attempt to radically rewrite the cultural script of sex and sex-work.

Three law reform proposals dealing with sex-work have been drafted by the National Law School of India University, at the behest of the Ministry for Women and Child Development. One of the proposals recommends mandatory testing of sex-workers, while also conferring rights on the woman to take legal action against pimps, brothel owners and clients. The Prevention of Immoral Traffic and Rehabilitation of Prostituted Persons Bill 1993 seeks to prohibit immoral trafficking, especially in women and children, and mitigate the suffering of 'victims of prostitution'. It provides 'victims of forced prostitution' the right to take legal action against brothel keepers, pimps and customers alike. Women are also given the right to demand special damages for harm resulting from sexual abuse or the intentional transmission of diseases acquired through the refusal of a customer to practise safe sex. A proposal to mitigate the suffering of women and children in prostitution through community-based rehabilitation, vocational training and health schemes, which includes mandatory testing of prostitute women for HIV, is also suggested. In addition, a welfare fund, made up of fines and grants from the government and other bodies is to be set up to support the rehabilitation of women 'rescued from prostitution' and HIV prevention programmes, and meet the educational and medical expenses of the children of these women.

In contrast, the second proposal focuses on the AIDS crisis, recommending that 'in order for prostitutes to protect themselves from HIV infection, AIDS and other sexually transmitted diseases, they must have safe working conditions'. The Prohibition of Immoral Traffic and Empowerment of Sexual Workers Bill 1993 is intended to 'prohibit immoral trafficking especially in women and children and to confer rights on sexual workers with a view to prevent sexual exploitation and

26 *Ibid*, s 20.

protect health and hygiene in sexual work'. It provides for severe punishment of people involved in immoral trafficking and child prostitution. The Bill also proposes the decriminalisation of voluntary sex-work, equating it with other kinds of labour and the establishment of a rehabilitation regime to be maintained by a welfare fund set up by state governments. It further recommends the decriminalisation of sex-work, but the criminalisation of all other individuals who are connected to the trade, and emphasises rehabilitation of the sex-worker.

A third proposal was also drafted by the school, but not submitted to the government for consideration. The Sex Worker (Legalisation for Empowerment) Bill 1993 recognises that sex-work is a legitimate exercise of the right to work and that the right to work includes the right to solicit. It sets out a number of non-discrimination measures that need to be implemented to help remove the stigma which sex-workers experience. The Bill provides that a sex-worker cannot be deprived of her personal liberty or the right to retain custody of her child because she is a sex-worker. It prohibits sexual abuse of a sex-worker and provides for criminal and civil remedies for such abuse. A sex-worker is entitled to exercise her right to health care and anyone who prevents her from doing so can be charged under the provisions of the IPC. There is a recommendation for minimum pay for sexual services, the creation of a welfare fund to pay for medical expenses and old age support. This draft also recommends guidelines for the formation of sex-workers collectives, which will determine the conditions of work including the maximum number of customers that a woman will entertain as well as the minimum wage to be received. The collective can also have its own fund to which members of the collective can contribute. The funds may be used to set up childcare facilities, education for their children, the purchase of prophylactics and any other purpose that is beneficial to them.

Some of these proposals have been considered by the NCW. In 1996, the NCW submitted its *Report on Societal Violence on Women and Children in Prostitution, 1995–96* to the government, recommending reforms to healthcare, education, childcare and housing for women in prostitution and their children. The overall focus of the recommendations was to mitigate the harshest impact of prostitution on sex-workers and their children, and in so doing, the NCW attempted to take the concerns of women in prostitution into account. In terms of specific legal reforms, the NCW recommended several amendments to the ITPA, including the elimination of imprisonment of sex-workers, referring cases involving sex-workers to civil rather than criminal courts, and repealing s 4 of the Act, which prohibits living off the earnings of prostitution. Other recommendations included reforms to law enforcement intended to reduce police harassment and violence. Beyond these legal reforms, the stated objectives of the NCW included preventing the entry of women into prostitution, and an effort to reduce the demand for prostitution.

The report of the NCW concludes with a brief discussion of the place of prostitution in Indian culture:

> Many historical visions contain the germ of the desirable response from the mainstream society towards women in prostitution. Legend says one jealous group of persons, envious of the growing fame of Sri Ramakrishna Paramahansa, took him to Sonagachi, sure that he would be seduced and subsequently exposed. As a pre-plan, some women surrounded Sri Ramakrishna. He was moved and fell at their feet saying he could see

'ma' in them .... Lord Buddha's famous disciple Amrapali was a famous courtesan. Women in prostitution in our society have traditionally been held in high esteem and their rights ensured and protected by Chanakya in the Arthashastra. (1996, p 55)

The report thus concluded by wrapping its recommendations in a culturally appropriate bow. Overall, the recommendations of the NCW sought to address the real concerns of sex-workers, without condoning sex-work itself. It was for the rights of sex-workers, without being in favour of sex-work. The NCW report indicates a slight shift in the thinking about the rights of women in sex-work. At the same time, it must be evaluated against the overall stand of the NCW on the issue of culture and the role of women in Indian society. The Commission endorsed the recommendations proposed in the draft National Cultural Policy (1992), which emphasised that 'women in India were a great sustaining and preserving force of culture ... the cultural fabric in India continues to be enriched by women's contribution and ... women must be assigned an important role in all programs of creativity or preservation'.[27] Any position deviating from this stand is deemed to be anti-Indian culture and womanhood.

Although some of the legislative proposals discussed seek to recognise the rights of sex-workers and move away from a moralising and culturally conservative approach to the issue, recent indications are that the government has little interest in addressing the human rights of sex-workers and is proposing even more repressive measures to deal with this sexual subgroup. One example is the 1998 *Report of the Committee on Prostitution, Child Prostitutes and Children of Prostitutes and Plan of Action to Combat Trafficking and Commercial Sexual Exploitation of Women and Children* (hereinafter 'The Report'), submitted by the Department of Women and Child Development to the government. The plan is intended to help the children of sex-workers, yet its underlying interest remains public morality and protecting the normative family. The Department recommends that children above the age of six be removed from their mothers and placed in institutional care. It adds that resort to coercive measures to remove children is permissible as it is in the best interests of the child. These measures remain concerned with the spread of HIV and also with the 'weakening of the family structure, (and the) changing social and family scenario' (The Report, p 1). The recommendations are largely punitive and also directed at strengthening the surveillance powers of the police, immigration officers, and border authorities. The Report suggests that strict instructions 'be issued to immigration officers, border police authorities and local police in the transit areas for the purpose of keeping a vigil on the entry of young girls under suspicious or unexplained circumstances into the country from neighbouring countries' (p 16). To check internal trafficking, the Committee proposes that '(p)olice, railway police and transport authorities would ensure surprise checking and inspection of persons taking young girls and women under suspicious circumstances for the purposes of trafficking in buses and trains and in bus and railway stations'. The Report also recommends a strengthening of the existing laws governing sex-work, and encourages raids on 'red light areas', cabaret shows and live band performances as an effective method for deterring 'exploiters' of women and children.

---

27 *National Commission for Women's Annual Report of 1992–93*, p 55. The Commission was asked to comment on the draft National Cultural Policy proposed by the Department of Culture.

The AIDS crisis, and its rupturing of the cultural script of the purity of Indian sexuality, has led to a heightened concern and surveillance of so called 'at risk populations', including sex-workers. The language of this surveillance is deeply imbued with assumptions about AIDS as a Western disease that has been imported into India through promiscuous Western lifestyles. The state's interest in sex-work is impelled by international concern over the spread of the AIDS virus through the subcontinent. At the same time, the more conservative ideological component of the Hindu Right seeks to counter the impression that India is a nation of 'rampant promiscuity', perpetuating the myth that AIDS is associated with promiscuous lifestyles. A report in *The Organizer*, the ideological mouth piece of the Hindu Right, states that '(m)any foreign based companies along with a number of NGOs have in the name of social service literally turned on an AIDS scare to earn thousands of dollars. Huge grants allotted for AIDS and the lure for this money has spawned many a [sic] aficionado of the anti-AIDS campaign'.[28] In addition:

[c]ertain NGOs, foreign development agencies, syringe and condom manufacturers wants [sic] to paint India as a country of promiscuous sinners, while just the opposite is true. This is done by independent NGOs with dollar aid by various means including conducting spurious surveys that 'show' increased sexual activity among unmarried women in India.[29]

Although the state is motivated by public health concerns to promote an AIDS awareness campaign, it simultaneously places sex-workers under strict surveillance and reinforces their status as communicators of the virus. The state protects the nation's image of 'cultural purity' by casting the virus as a Western contaminant and a capitalist ploy. Government interventions and assertions of cultural purity are producing contradictory results for women. While sex-workers are blamed for the spread of the disease, the stigma against them is reinforced, and in legal terms nothing has been done to endow them with rights to help in fighting the disease and securing access to health services that are responsive to their needs.

Ironically, some women's groups in India are accusing the government of promoting 'prostitution' through its commitment to address the problem of AIDS in the country. Their position is framed as a cultural defence argument.[30] In a letter to Prime Minister Atal Bihari Vajpayee, over 50 women's groups alleged that the government had violated constitutional and legal norms by directing World Bank money and other bilateral aid to intervene in the behaviour of 'high risk groups' and promote condom use. The letter states that:

[w]e write to communicate our anguish and horror at recent state-led developments. Instead of strong measures to remedy age-old malpractices and curb trends derogatory to the dignity of women, we are witnessing in this, the 51st year of our Independence, State acquiescence to the gross violation of the Constitution and the laws of the land aimed at prevention of Immoral Traffic [sic] ... There is now the beginning of State co-

---

28 Thackeray, 2000. Bal Thackeray is the leader of the Shiv Sena.
29 *Ibid*, p 52.
30 Letter from the Joint Action Forum to the Prime Minister of India, dated 11 November 2000.

operation for a *permissive environment* within which there is acceptance of the woman's body as a commodity for sale together with abdication of State responsibility to rescue and rehabilitate the poor women caught in a vicious vice trap as non-feasible/not-cost effective! This will perpetuate sexual abuse and exploitation; and, *constitutes degradation of the dignity and human rights of Indian womanhood itself.* (Emphasis added)

The victim status conferred on the sex-worker is essential to the survival and the purity of the nation and the preservation of Indian womanhood. This statement is at some level even more restricting of the rights of sex-workers as it seeks to deny them information on how to practise safe sex. The signatories seek 'culturally sound' and 'legally correct efforts' to address the problem, including a stringent application of existing laws.

Some feminist groups are trying to shift the explanation for legal reform away from a moral argument more clearly onto an economic exploitation argument. Notwithstanding this effort, the cultural arguments slip in via the back door and end up reinforcing the cultural essentialism that informs the state's discourse. Their approach is to characterise sex-workers in India as victims, whose work is determined by economic hardship. This approach is located on an East/West binary and assumes that choice is possible in the West, while economic oppression in Asia is so all-encompassing that the very possibility of choice or agency is negated. For example, Jean D'Cunha, states that even if it were to be assumed that in the North prostitution should be a woman's occupational choice:

> [I]t cannot be considered so in the socio-cultural milieu of Asia where it is at best a 'survival strategy' for the large majority of women. Choice can exist only when a certain amount of freedom or option is available in decision-making. This is conspicuously absent in most cases at least in India where either physical force or socio-economic coercion lead women to a life in prostitution.[31]

The discourse of feminists and the state in the context of the legal regulation of sex-work is embedded in a tension over culture and the construction of the sex-worker as either a victim of the Western male and market or a cultural contaminant (Solanki and Gangoli, 1996, p 3,299).

The intensification of the repressive move to further regulate the lives of sex-workers has been challenged by the sex-workers themselves. AIDS intervention strategies have intensified mobilisation among sex-workers to lobby for their basic human rights, as well as to articulate their concerns in related areas such as the rights of their children, support in their old age, and better working conditions. They are contesting the underlying assumption that economic necessity drives women into prostitution. In 1995, the Durbar Mahila Samanwaya Committee (DMSC) (the Unstoppable Movement for Women's Equality) was formed as a

---

31 Revised Draft Bills with Explanatory Notes on The Immoral Traffic (Prevention) Act 1956, prepared by Dr NR Madhava Menon, National Law School of India University in association with students, faculty, and task force experts from Calcutta, Lucknow, Bangalore, Bombay and Madras, December 1993, sponsored by the Department of Women and Child Development, Government of India, New Delhi, p 2.

forum exclusively consisting of sex-workers and their children.[32] In 1995, DMSC organised the First National Conference of Sex Workers, which issued a statement asserting that sex is primarily for pleasure and intimacy. The statement also challenged dominant sexual ideology, which allows 'for sexual expression only between men and women within the strict boundaries of marital relations within the institution of family'.[33] Another group of sex-workers, *Sangram* (Struggle), based in the western state of Maharashtra, similarly stated:

> We believe that a woman's sexuality is an integral part of her as a woman, as varied as her mothering, domestic and such other skills. We do not believe that sex has a sacred space and women who have sex for reasons other than its reproductive importance are violating this space. Or if they chose to make money from the transaction they are immoral or debauched.[34]

These emerging voices of the sexual subaltern are posing a frontal challenge to the nationalist narrative of sex and culture. These sex-workers are directly challenging the idea that sex in general, and commercial sex in particular, are inherently negative, corrosive or otherwise dangerous. They are boldly asserting the rightful place of sex. And in so doing, they risk being cast as an even more dangerous affront to Indian culture and the nation.

The extent to which increasingly outspoken sex-workers represent a challenge to the dominant narrative of culture, sex and nation may help explain the lack of willingness to promote the rights of women in sex-work and the continued emphasis on regulation and moral surveillance. Supporting the rights of sex-workers runs the risk of being cast as foreign, Western and corrosive to Indian cultural values. It thus becomes safer to address some of the problems within the existing law on a terrain that does not condone the practice of commercial sex, but rather, simply attempts to mitigate its harsher impacts. Even groups like the NCW, which have begun to recognise some limited rights for sex-workers, also continue to condemn the practice of sex-work and go to some length to ensure that this pro-sex-worker/anti-sex-work position is given some cultural justification. Moreover, the nationalist narrative aligns with a particular feminist approach, which similarly views sex and sexuality from a lens of danger. The merging of these two discourses is such that the politics of positive sexuality and pleasure advocated by the sex-workers remains virtually inaudible.

As a result of the alliance between cultural nationalist and feminist discourses, the sex-workers who advocate a pro-rights, pro-work stand may be unlikely to succeed on their own discursive terms. It may be that they will need to address the issue of culture and formulate their own arguments in more explicitly cultural terms. Some writers and feminist groups have begun to draw attention to the need

---

32 *Tales of the Night Fairies*, 2002, a documentary directed by Shohini Ghosh, represents the struggles and aspirations of thousands of sex-workers who constitute the Durbar Mahila Samanwaya Committee (DMSC), an initiative that emerged from the Shonagachi HIV/AIDS Intervention Project in Calcutta. It is a collective of men, women and transgendered sex-workers. DMSC demands decriminalisation of adult sex-work and the right to form a trade union.

33 DMSC, *Sex Worker's Manifesto*, presented at First National Conference of Sex Workers, 14–16 November 1997.

34 Sangram, 1997, p 2.

to address the cultural arguments when advocating the rights of sex-workers. They are attempting to develop a more complicated analysis of the cultural location of the sex-worker in India and counter the cultural essentialism that has informed the legal debates (Nair, 1996b). Prabha Kotiswaran, for example, sees the need 'to uncover, document and rescue from patriarchal and colonial discourses, the successes and struggles of prostitute women in India over the ages contained in tales and epics' (Kotiswaran, 2001).

She reviews the existing literature on the treatment of sex-work in ancient literature to reveal the existence of sex-workers in the Indian cultural context, as well as the manner in which sex was celebrated in ancient texts and social life in contrast to the stigma that surrounds the subject of sex in the contemporary moment. Kotiswaran states that her argument is not intended to be revivalist or regressive. She is not calling for a return to any glorious past, much less to state-sponsored and regulated sex-work. Her purpose is to challenge the stereotypical images of the third world woman, in particular the sex-worker, at a time when India is seriously rethinking the legislative policy on this issue.

Similarly, Sumanta Banerjee has reviewed the history of the sex-worker in 19th-century Bengal. He provides a brief account of the sex-worker's shifting position from pre-colonial to colonial times. He uncovers a vast literature stretching back to the 4th-century BC that lays down rules of conduct between sex-workers and their clients and the punitive measures to be imposed on clients who harmed the sex-worker and cheated her of her earnings. Sex-work came to be regarded as a crime during colonial times, when the British sought to penalise it through the enactment of the Cantonment Act 1864 and the Contagious Diseases Act 1868 (Banerjee, 1998, p 146). Banerjee's work reveals the complex relationship between sex-workers, their clients and the colonial regime. His work challenges the assumption of the sex-worker as a recent 'import' from the West, as well as the assumption that the category of sex-work was homogenous and uniformly regarded as sinful or bad. The literature he draws upon reveals the diverse composition of the sex-workers' community, as well as their presence and popularity in popular culture (Nair, 1996b; Oldenburg, 1990).

Banerjee's and Kotiswaran's work historicise the contemporary debates on sex-work by locating the role of the sex-worker in the construction of the nation, countering imperialism and consolidating Indian national culture. They further complicate the cultural essentialism inherent in the state's discourse and some feminist discourse, which is based on static models of Western or Indian cultural differences. A more complicated notion of culture is developed to counter the assumption that the sex-worker is either an external contaminant infecting the native population through promiscuity and disease or a victim stripped of the mantle of chastity and sexual purity that are the markers of Indian culture for women. It is used to recuperate a position of pleasure and desire for the sex-worker within the framework of Indian culture, thus refuting the challenge that she is an external contaminant. It is deployed to counter the cultural move that erases the existence of the Indian sex-worker, as well as to challenge dominant sexual ideology through the lubricant of pleasure and agency of the sexual subaltern. In challenging dominant sexual ideology, the excavation of culture simultaneously creates a space for arguing for the sexual rights of women in sex-work.

Homosexuality

The issue of sexual identity has been dragged into the public debate on sex and sexuality partly as a result of AIDS, but also through the increasing visibility of gay men and lesbian women. The holding of gay and lesbian conferences and national retreats, publications by members of the gay and lesbian community, and the tentative, but significant engagement with this issue by academics from different disciplines is a new phenomenon. The controversy that exploded over the screening of *Fire* in India propelled the issue of homosexuality into the forefront of public debate.

Homosexuality is not directly targeted by law. However, it is indirectly regulated by s 377 of the IPC which makes it an offence to have voluntary 'carnal intercourse against the order of nature with any man, woman or animal'. Such carnal knowledge includes buggery, sodomy and bestiality. The punishment for such acts can extend to life imprisonment. Although it is neutral on its face in terms of sexual identity, the provision is used primarily to harass gay men (Bhaskaran, 2002, pp 15–28; Khanna, 1992, p 4).[35]

(a) The cultural out-law

A cultural contest over the existence of homosexuality in the Indian tradition has emerged in the legal domain. Between February and April 1994, there were several reports in national newspapers about the existence of 'rampant homosexuality' in New Delhi's Tihar jail, which is India's largest jail block for convicted criminals and under-trials (people on remand). A report by a team of doctors who visited the facility and interviewed the inmates revealed that 90% of them engaged in 'homosexual activity'.[36] The doctors expressed concern over the possibility that many of the men could be carriers of the HIV virus. They recommended that condoms be provided to prisoners in order to protect them from the virus or the further spread of the virus. However, the Inspector General of Prisons at the time, Kiran Bedi, was opposed to the distribution of condoms on the grounds that it would encourage homosexuality and also that it would amount to an admission that homosexuality existed in the prison. She stated that homosexuality was a punishable crime under the IPC, and that the distribution of condoms would amount to the acceptance of the crime.

There was considerable debate about the issue in both the print and visual media. Bedi held the view that Indian society was not ready to amend the existing law, implying that homosexuality had never been a part of Indian culture. She also stated that she was personally not reconciled 'to accept homosexuality as a normal human practice' (Prakash, 1994, p 2). Others disagreed, arguing that s 377 of the IPC, which criminalised the act of sodomy, was an obsolete law, that had been enacted by the British and had since been repealed in Britain, and that India should follow suit (Prakash, 1994; Sen, 1994, p 8). They simultaneously argued that homosexuality had always constituted a part of Indian culture as was evident from passages in the *Kama Sutra*. Once again the cultural move that denies the existence

---

35 See also *Asian Age*, 1998b, p 4.
36 Jain, 1994, p 83.

of homosexuality in India is challenged through a counter-cultural move which argues that homosexuality has always existed in Indian culture.

In a related case, Janak Raj Rai, a lawyer and chairman of the Family Conciliation Service Centre, an organisation working for the welfare of families in trouble, filed a petition in 1994 in the Delhi High Court objecting to the suggestion to distribute condoms to the inmates in Tihar jail. He argued, amongst other things, that the proposal violated s 377 and would 'turn the jail into a brothel'.[37] He requested the court to prohibit the Delhi administration from supplying condoms to the inmates of Tihar Jail, and conduct an investigation into the practices taking place in the jail. He also argued that the Delhi administration be directed to medically examine each of the inmates and segregate those suffering from the AIDS virus. In order to prevent sexual activity from taking place between the inmates, he recommended that neon lights be used in the wards during the night and night patrols be conducted by the wardens. He defended his position on the ground that 'homosexuality [is] against the dignity, honour and religious sentiments of the citizens of the country' and defended s 377 as a part of 'Indian tradition'. Interestingly, a law deeply embedded in Christianity, Victorian morality and the colonial project, comes to be equated by Rai with Indian tradition and evidence that homosexuality is inimical to this tradition.

A more recent controversy concerned the harassment of outreach workers in the MSM (men seeking sex with men) community involving the arrest of HIV/AIDS workers from the Bharosa Trust and Naz Foundation International in Lucknow, a northern Indian city, in 2001. Both of these organisations have been involved in HIV/AIDS education and sexual health initiatives. The Bharosa Trust has been functioning in the state for almost three years, working on 'targeted interventions' in the area of HIV/AIDS. Such interventions include disseminating information about safe sexual practices among the MSM community, and their materials are in line with the government's guidelines on prevention. A complaint was made against both groups by a local individual who alleged that they were running a gay club racket. The police raided the offices of the Trust in July 2001, seizing videos and magazines, as well as material used for safe sex demonstrations. The police alleged that this material was pornographic and charged the office members under the respective obscenity and indecency provisions of the IPC and IRWA. The group argued that the materials were purely educational. The bail applications of those arrested were rejected by the lower courts, one magistrate stating that 'the work of the accused is like a curse on society'. The Sessions judge also denied bail, upholding the arguments of the prosecution that the defendants were 'a group of persons indulging in these activities and ... polluting the entire society by encouraging young persons and abetting them for committing [sic] the offence of sodomy'.[38] The prosecutor specifically stated that homosexuality was being encouraged by the defendants and that it was 'against Indian culture' (Human

---

37 Rai, 1994, p 2.
38 Rajalakshmi, 2001, pp 113–14.

Rights Watch, 2002a, p 20). There was also an attempt to link one of the accused, Arif Jafar, a Muslim, with Pakistani intelligence and Kashmiri militants, and therefore cast him as a threat to the security of the nation. Jafar, in a subsequent interview, stated that the police told him that he was 'trying to destroy our country by promoting homosexuality' and that 'Hindus don't have these practices – these are all perversions of the Muslims' (Human Rights Watch, 2002a, p 20). The four members were granted bail after an appeal to the Lucknow High Court. They were also subjected to a medical examination to determine if they had committed an offence under s 377 of the IPC.

The cultural arguments in this case were displaced onto both a sexual and religious Other. Homosexuality was not a part of Indian cultural values, and the Muslims in particular were indulging in these activities in order to undermine the Indian state and Indian culture. The equation of homosexuality as not just anti-cultural, but also as anti-national, is a recurrent feature in the literature of the Hindu Right ideologues. The Hindu male must not be effeminate but must be virile and masculine. However, the Muslim who is hypersexual is a threat to the nation. His intentions are maligning. As I discuss in Chapter 2, the Muslim is represented as a perpetrator of sexual violence, lustful with evil intentions towards Hindu women, and determined to undermine the Indian nation. The move to communalise any 'deviant sexuality' and equate it with the malevolent intentions of the Muslim reinforces the worst kind of stereotype of Muslims. The harm associated with homosexuality comes to be associated with harm to the community and to the nation, and perpetrated by the outsider, or externalised enemy, that is, the Muslim.

The representation of HIV, homosexuality and other sexual practices as 'foreign' cultural contaminants and a security threat also played out in a separate controversy involving an AIDS research project. Several members of Sahyog, an NGO working in the field of women's health and empowerment in Almora, a district in the northern Indian state of Uttar Pradesh, were arrested under the National Securities Act 1980 for threatening to undermine the culture and traditions of the region through their work (Human Rights Watch, 2002a, pp 4–5). The specific target was a report released in September 1999, entitled *AIDS and Us*, which was a field study on the prevalence of AIDS/HIV in five villages in the district of Uttarkhand (Das and Das, 1999). The report, based on interviews, questionnaires and discussions with local villagers, documented how multiple sexual relations, prostitution, and sexual relations within the family, were all prevalent in several of the villages. There were also several sexually explicit quotes from the villagers in their description of the activities taking place within their villages. The report did not purport to be a status report for the entire region, nor did it come to any general conclusions. Six months after the release of the report, the offices of Sahyog were ransacked by protestors led by BJP *sainiks* (foot soldiers), who regarded the report as an insult to the community's morals and honour. For some of the local community, the report also constituted an insult to the people of the region and was obscene. Four of the eleven activists who were arrested were detained under the National Security Act 1980. The Act gives the government wide powers of detention to prevent persons from 'acting in any manner prejudicial to the security of the state'. The Act allows persons to be detained for up to 12 months in the interests of national security or the maintenance of public order. The notice of arrest stated that:

The book has upset the sentiments of the peoples as expressed through demonstrations, *Dharnas* (protests) etc. People in the region, civilians, *sainiks*, are outraged. Jasodhara Dasgupta (one of the heads of the organisation) is a mischievous woman and is anti-Uttarakhand and anti-Indian men. The activities of the NGO are against society and disturb law and order. If released on bail they will frighten and terrorise the people. People will get angry. Foreign funding agencies, through Sahyog, have hurt the sentiments of the people through indecent literature.

The outreach workers were publicly accused by the police of being 'threats to national security' and spreading ideas said to be 'against Indian culture' (Human Rights Watch, 2002a, p 5). The two co-authors of the report subsequently apologised for the sexually explicit language and the suggestions of incest that they made in the report. On appeal to the Allahabad High Court they were released on bail, though their organisation was banned from conducting any further activities in the region. The national security charges were ultimately dropped and the last of the defendants released from prison after 40 days (Human Rights Watch, 2002a, p 21).

The non-governmental organisations, the left, the major opposition parties, and the BJP-led coalition at the centre all unanimously condemned the report for its cultural insensitivity. There was a sense that the women and men of the region had been exposed through what should have been confidential research, and that their strong and independent culture had been reduced to nothing more than immorality and their women represented as merely promiscuous. Although leading intellectuals, media persons and lawyers issued a statement condemning the arrests under the security laws, they also specifically challenged what they perceived as the government's culturally insensitive policy around AIDS. The statement levelled a specific criticism against the 'World Bank-funded' HIV control programme, and blamed the adoption of an 'alien' AIDS education approach for creating tensions in a 'tradition-bound' society. According to the statement, the Sahyog incident highlighted 'the alienated nature of policies being adopted not only in AIDS control but also in other spheres of development whether it is health, education, forestry or water management'. The responses had an almost 'you deserve it' feel, highlighting just how difficult it is to articulate sexual issues in opposition to or without a grounding in a cultural framework. It also suggested the extent to which culture had come to be equated with sexual explicitness. What was lost sight of, or marginalised, was the fact that the Sahyog report was released during a period of intense agitation within the district for the establishment of a separate state based on the area's distinct cultural and ethnic identity. The report came to be associated with moral corruptness, which would in turn adversely affect the move for a separate cultural identity and the statehood claims of the local population. The authors were cast as outsiders, cultural invaders whose project was to threaten the cultural identity and integrity of the region, and the possibility of statehood and regional autonomy within India, and hence as a threat to the security of the imagined, local 'nation'.

In this case the cultural arguments were simply asserted to challenge efforts to raise issues of sexuality outside of a cultural framework. At one level the report was merely a report about unsafe sexual practices that could increase the risk of HIV transmission. However, given the fact that culture and sexuality have been sutured together within postcolonial India, the report came to be cast as an attack on the cultural integrity of the region and a challenge to the morality of the local population, which was seeking to establish a separate state. It threatened the region to the point that the issue was no longer articulated within the discourse of speech and obscenity, but the very survival and security of the local community identity. It went beyond issues of obscenity and was implicated in the very security of the incipient nationalism in the region.

Alongside such controversies, there has also been an increase in the mobilisation of AIDS groups, gays and lesbians, which has been met with considerable resistance. Petitions have been filed by the AIDS Bhedbav Virodhi Andolan (the Movement Fighting Against AIDS Discrimination) (ABVA), and the Naz Foundation, an HIV and sexual health agency working in South Asia, against the Union of India, challenging the constitutional validity of s 377 of the IPC. The ABVA petition, filed shortly after the Tihar jail incident discussed above, counters the indignation of those who view homosexuality as a 'foreign contaminant' by locating the emergence and visibility of gay, lesbian and bisexual identities within the narrative of an ancient Indian cultural tradition. The petitioners argue that 'ancient Indian art and sculpture in India testifies to the prevalence of homosexuality in this country to a greater or lesser extent'. This strategy is intended to refute the idea that homosexuality is a perverted Western import by demonstrating that it is materially inscribed in the historical context of India.

The petition is replete with references to homosexuality within the texts of the *Kama Sutra*. Quoting references from its own report, *Less than Gay*, on the existence of homosexuality in India, the petitioners allege that the *Kama Sutra*, which was compiled as early as the 4th-century AD, contains an entire chapter on homosexual sex as well as on lesbian sex. One example that has been translated from the original verses states:

> Young masseurs usually wearing hair ornaments do allow their friends as well as some men to have mutual oral congress. Sometimes young actors or dandies allow undersexed or older men to have sex with them. It is also practised by young men who know each other well. Sometimes men who are effeminate indulge in oral sex with each other simultaneously by lying alongside one another inversely. When a man and a woman lie down in an inverted position with the head of the one towards the feet of the other and carry on oral sex with each other, it is called Kakila; this term is also applicable to oral congress between two males as also two girls or women.[39]

The petition also refers to passages which explicitly describe the sexual acts performed by transvestites and eunuchs. The petitioners called upon the court to declare s 377 as unconstitutional, and also made several other prayers relating to the treatment of HIV infected prisoners in Tihar jail and the provision of condoms in the jail.

---

39 *AIDS Bedbhav Virodhi Andolan v Union of India*, Civil Writ Petition 1993, p 142.

In a more recent case, the Naz Foundation has also argued that s 377 of the IPC is inconsistent with Indian tradition which does not treat sodomy as a crime. The petition quotes from a recent publication on same sex love in India, which states, 'The texts we have compiled thus far indicate a set of generally tolerant traditions in pre-colonial India. As far as we know, not a single person has ever been executed for homosexual behaviour in India' (Vanita and Kidwai, 2000, p 194). The petition goes on to state that the introduction of s 377 was a form of cultural imperialism imposed by the colonial power, which resulted in a shift in Indian cultural conceptions of sexual relations, including tolerating homosexuality. Once again they quote from Vanita and Kidwai who argue, 'Although we are aware of the limitations of an analysis that blames all modern ills on colonialism, the evidence available to us forces us personally to conclude that homophobia of virulent proportions came into being in India in the late 19th- and early 20th-century and continues to flourish today' (Vanita and Kidwai, 2000, p 200). The High Court dismissed the petition without dealing with the merits of the case, holding that as there was no cause of action, a petition could not be filed just to test the validity of the legislation.

The mobilisation of AIDS groups, gays and lesbians has been strongly opposed, especially by the Hindu Right. They have been condemned, for example, by Shiv Sena, the militant wing of the Hindu Right. Navalkar warned that any attempt to propagate 'perverted sexual values' would not be tolerated. The previous BJP-led government opposed the constitutional challenge to s 377 which criminalises sodomy, arguing that the deletion of the section could 'open the flood gates of delinquent behaviour and be construed as providing unbridled license' for homosexuality. It further argued that Indian society on the whole disapproved of homosexuality and that the disapproval was strong enough to treat the activity as a criminal offence, even if it took place between consenting adults. Similarly, the women's wing of the BJP, the more moderate voice of the Hindu Right, has stated that 'the demand for legal sanction of lesbianism is too vulgar and irrelevant in the Indian context'.[40] The opposition to the sexual subaltern is also contrasted with the hypermasculinity of the Hindu male (Chari, 2001). As Paola Bachetta has argued, the unacceptable Hindu male is sexually promiscuous, materialist, Westernised and effeminate (Bachetta, 1999, p 150). In the context of Hindu nationalism, the Hindu male is cast as virile and militaristic. He can be celibate in order to commit himself to the nation, but he is always heterosexual (Bachetta, 1999, p 143). All other sexual identities within the nation are categorised as non-Hindu, primarily as Muslim, or as foreign (namely Western) contaminants.

The cultural arguments presented by ABVA and the Naz Foundation highlight how the existence of homosexuality, which is legitimated partly through the tracing of its historical and cultural origins in Indian tradition, is informed by cultural essentialism at one level. The legal arguments deploy tradition and culture in much the same way as those who oppose homosexuality. Yet once again, the position on culture being advocated by the litigants can be read as an attempt to counter the dominant story being told about homosexuality. Their story is not an intransigent archaeological rendition of the past attempting to unearth the 'true' cultural history. Rather, it is an approach that is attempting to capture the complexity of culture and

---

40 BJP, 1991.

sexual identity within the context of Indian history. Cultural essentialism is, at one level, being used to argue that lesbian and gay sexuality has always been a part of Indian culture and that such practices have been buried under the legal debris of colonialism. Their arguments are evidence of the fact that gay and lesbian sexuality is not a contemporary phenomenon of Western pollutants that are destroying Indian culture. The cultural story that insists that lesbians and gays do not exist in Indian culture is being countered by a story that they do exist. The strategy of the litigants constituted an attempt to complicate the story, to challenge the dominant heterosexist overtures of the dominant cultural script, with one that challenged the story line as well as the storytellers.

Locating gay and lesbian sexual identity in a golden past performs several strategic functions. Jyoti Puri has argued:

> First, to locate the emergence and visibility of gay/lesbian/bisexual identities within the narrative of an ancient, albeit discontinuous, sexually liberal national cultural tradition; second, to assert contemporary gay/lesbian/bisexual identities against the manifestations of homophobia and heterosexism through representations of this history. This strategy also serves to refute pervasive heterosexist attitudes that dismiss gay/lesbian/bisexual women and men as the embodied imperfections of westernisation or Islamisation. (Puri, 1999, pp 263–64)

The fact that homosexuality is materially inscribed in the historical context of India refutes the argument that sexual identity is Western and alien to Indian culture. In an interesting turn, sexual subalterns argue it is sexual repression rather than sexual licence that is a Western import. The arguments simultaneously serve to subvert dominant sexual ideology and the heterosexist assumptions on which sexuality is based in the contemporary context.

(b) The cultural politics of Fire

In November 1998, Deepa Mehta's diasporic film *Fire* was released in India and became the subject of yet another moral and cultural panic (as discussed above). The henchmen of the Hindu Right, including the Mahila Agadhi (Women's Front), the women's wing of the militant and virulently anti-Muslim Shiv Sena, and the Bajrang Dal, a faction of the Right that has become the moral policeman of Indian culture, directed their ire towards the screening of *Fire*. Despite the fact that the film cleared the Censor Board without any cuts, mobs disrupted screenings in a number of major cities in India, including Mumbai, Delhi, Meerut, Surat and Pune. These protests took the form of an alarming destruction to the property of cinema houses as well as attacks against members of the viewing audiences.

Several film personalities, including the director, filed a petition against the government of Maharashtra, where most of the vandalism had taken place, in the Supreme Court of India. They submitted that the attack on the cinemas violated the directors' freedom of expression and requested the court to direct the state to take action to stop the vandalism and safeguard the rule of law. By the time the case came up for decision, the circumstances had altered.[41] The Shiv Sena had lost in the state elections, and the government had taken steps in filing criminal charges

---

41 *Yusuf Khan v Manohar Joshi* [2000] All India Reports 1121 (SC).

against the vandals. During the course of these proceedings, the central government directed that the film be sent back to the Censor Board for a further review. The Board once again cleared the film without any further cuts. However, many cinemas did not screen the film for a second time for fear of further destruction to their property or harm to the patrons.

Prior to the release of the film, Deepa Mehta anticipated an aggressive response to its cultural content and agreed to change the name of one of the protagonists, from Sita to Neeta. The move was an attempt to slip into a less confrontational and compliant position on culture. This alteration reflects fears about the offence that the film could cause to Indian audiences because of its representation of an intimate and sexual bond between Sita and her sister-in-law, Radha. Mehta's compromise is a move that stands out as a stark example of the ways in which Indian society is being held to ransom to one version, one story and one truth about Indian culture. The change is nevertheless a curious one given that so much of the film is transgressive, and to tinker with names merely draws attention to its subversive possibilities rather than mitigating a potentially violent reaction to the film.

The controversy over the film involved a contest over the meaning of Indian culture as well as the place and status of homosexual identity in Indian culture. Opponents argued that the representation of the sisters-in-law in a lesbian relationship and the appropriation of cultural rituals such as *karva chauth* (a fast kept by wives to ensure the longevity of their husbands) celebrated a perverse bond. Shiv Sena threatened to continue disrupting the screening of the film in Maharashtra unless it was banned, alleging that it was 'not a part of Indian culture'.[42] They read the film as an attempt to convert women to lesbianism, which would lead to the demise of the Hindu family.

These groups represented Indian culture as a museum piece – something that was static and immutable, that could be excavated and restored to its pristine purity. This view was seriously challenged during the course of the controversy. Gay and lesbian groups, among others, contested the position of the various segments of the Hindu Right, and defended the film as an important statement of lesbian identity in India. In Delhi, gays and lesbians came into the public space for the first time to defend the screening and challenge the stark declaration that lesbians do not exist in Indian culture. They asserted that 'Lesbianism is not alien to Indian culture'.[43] Lesbian rights supporters also argued that homosexuality had always been a part of Indian culture. 'Why do we pretend it doesn't exist? Homosexuality has always been there.'[44] The suggestion here seems to be that lesbians have been inscribed into Indian culture, rather than merely existed in India (Vanita, 2002). Fora such as the New Delhi-based 'Campaign for Lesbian Rights', which formed as a result of the controversy, lobbied for the film to be a means for recognising the rights to sexual identity and a catalyst to repeal legislation that discriminated against such preferences. Their arguments were also in part based on

42 Jain and Raval, 1998, p 78.
43 *Asian Age*, 1998a, p 9.
44 Subramanyam, 1998, p 10.

the position that homosexuality had always been a part of Indian cultural values. In contrast to the position of the Hindu Right, proponents argued that lesbians had always been included in the story of Indian culture. Their arguments can be read as complicating the notion of culture, treating it as something that is constantly negotiated and constructed. And it is this process that has been used to create space for the subaltern, including, in this instance, the sexual subaltern: the lesbian subject. Throughout the film, traditional rituals and stories are invoked to counter the dominant cultural view of Indian families, and create space for the lesbian relationship in and through these cultural moves.

There can be no return to a pristine, unalloyed Indian culture. This is not to argue that there is no such thing as Indian culture. Rather, it is to argue that the production of culture is a historical process, constantly changing and altering. It is to argue that the shape-shifting of culture and an inquiry into its construction are legitimate processes. The cultural argument provides the legitimacy tool for sexual subalterns. However, the cultural argument has serious limitations, which I address in the following section.

The culture conundrum

> We need to move away from a picture of national and cultural contexts as sealed rooms, impervious to change, with a homogenous space 'inside' them, inhabited by 'authentic insiders' who all share a uniform and consistent account of their institutions and values. (Narayan, 1997, p 33)

These controversies over sexual speech and sexual subalterns reflect the growing unease and discomfort over the 'cultural transformations' taking place in India. Law has served as a site of contest over the meaning and construction of Indian culture in the context of sex and sexuality. In this section, I elaborate on the different ways in which culture is being deployed in these legal debates.

The longing for a strong cultural identity has been an important desire and symptom of postcolonialism in the contemporary Indian context. However, the way in which culture is deployed can lead to substantially different results. Cultural essentialism, that is, a stagnant, exclusive understanding of culture, is being deployed by those in a position of power and dominance to legitimate dominant sexual ideology. And it is simultaneously used to delegitimise those who are attempting to challenge dominant sexual ideology and cultural authenticity. Cultural essentialism weaves a cultural tale based on a notion of oneness, of one culture that is fixed and timeless. In the hands of dominant conservative groups, it is based on the idea of a substantive or real essentialism, and becomes reactionary. It becomes an exclusionary discourse – a tale shaped in the image of intolerance and disapproval of difference. Cultural essentialism has been used in the legal stories I have discussed to resist the challenges posed by the defenders of sexual speech and the sexual subalterns who are perceived as threatening to Indian cultural values and the dominant sexual ideology on which such values are based. The theme of contagion and contamination is constantly invoked in each of these areas. The airwaves are contaminating Indian cultural values through the sexual representations they beam into the pure and sexually sanitised homes of Indian families. Similarly, sex-work is contaminating in a physical way in so far as it is spreading HIV through the respectable population. And the gay issue has also been perceived as something that is contaminating the Indian family with its proselytising agenda.

This theme of contamination is also deployed to counter the threat of 'Western imperialism'. The contaminant which is corroding Indian culture comes from the West, from outside of Indian culture. Satellite broadcasting is regarded as contaminating Indian culture. Gay sexual identity is similarly cast as a Western import that is targeting Indian youth and stripping them of the secure mantle of Indian cultural values, which reside in the institution of heterosexuality. AIDS is also posited as an import from a decadent and promiscuous Western culture that is setting adrift Indian cultural moorings. It is a step short of arguing that sex as a whole is a contaminating and corrosive import of Western cultural values.

At the same time, cultural arguments are being deployed by disempowered and marginalised groups to challenge the dominant narratives of culture, sex and nation. The effects of these arguments are rather different. By complicating the cultural script, they are challenging the homogenous and essentialist approach to Indian cultural values and the location of women, sexual subalterns, sex, and sexuality within that culture. These arguments expose the hybridity of culture and challenge the search for a real, original culture as a narrow essentialist telling of the story of Indian culture in relation to sexuality. It is based on the idea that culture is never stagnant and fixed, but is constantly shifting and fluid. Cultural hybridity exposes the limits of cultural essentialism by revealing that culture is and continues to be in a process of construction. And this process creates space for the possibility of alternative sexual practices and behaviour that both challenge and subvert dominant sexual ideology. Cultural hybridity represents the postcolonial moment, which Stuart Hall describes as the point of recognition that a return to a set of uncontaminated values is impossible (Hall, 1996b, p 247).

Thus, the focal question is: by engaging with Indian cultural values, do all sides of the debate not run the risk of also essentialising and authenticating Indian cultural values? Cultural arguments can be a powerful and creative force for hitherto disempowered and excluded people. The unearthing of some buried past has been, and continues to be, an important exercise for marginalised and disadvantaged groups, including women, racial, caste and religious minorities. It can be an empowering and important form of resistance. In the context of the three issues discussed, cultural essentialism is at times being used to argue that sex and sexuality, sex-work and homosexuality have always existed in Indian culture. In the hands of marginalised groups, cultural essentialism can be strategic, rather than based on a substantive or real essentialism. As Annie Bunting argues, 'essentialism from a dominant position can perpetuate oppression while, as a means of challenging dominant ideologies, it can be necessary and persuasive' (Bunting, 1993, p 12).

But there is a need to ensure that the cultural move, which is used to challenge the dominant narrative of culture, sex and nation, does not in turn become its own unifying, essentialist and exclusionary discourse. The use of culture in this exclusionary way can be detected in the legal stories I have related in this essay. In the ABVA petition challenging the constitutional validity of s 377, the deployment of culture presents this very problem. The petitioners' rendition of the cultural past is overwhelmingly a Hindu rendition. Their story for the inclusion of gays and lesbians can be said to be at the cost of the exclusion of another minority – a religious minority, namely the Muslims. The problem of exclusion is starkly manifested in the work of Giti Tandani. Her story of the exclusion of lesbian identity is told explicitly within a Hindu nationalist framework. The Muslims are among those who obliterated the glorious (Hindu) lesbian past through conquest and imposition of their alien cultural norms and values (Tandani, 1996). The dangers of such an argument are all too obvious within the context of communalism and right-wing politics. The Hindu nationalists are unlikely to take on the issue of sexual identity as a serious cause. However, as has been demonstrated in other situations where they purported to champion women's rights, their motivating concern was to use this strategy as a way in which to attack the Muslim Other as intolerant and barbaric (Kapur and Cossman, 1996, p 232).

Similarly, the position of Kidwai and Vanita, referred to in the ABVA petition, that homophobia in its 'virulent' form only arrived into India in the late 19th-century with the colonial power, requires deeper interrogation. The colonial response to Indian sexuality needs to be located within a much broader context of Empire and the imperial enterprise, which was partly constructed on assumptions about the sexual deviance and decadence of the Other. It was a 'hypermasculinist' enterprise, which established stereotypes of the Englishman as powerful and superior, as against the effeminate, impotent and weak masculinity of the 'native' subject (Chatterjee, 1991, p 61). The flawed native male came to be associated with a host of sexual practices, including homosexuality, which both fascinated and repelled the oriental scholar and fiction writers. Homophobia operated alongside homoeroticism and homosocial assumptions. The complex responses and engagements with sexuality cannot be caught within an uncomplicated assertion about homophobia, but need to be read within the context of the broader political, cultural and economic contexts in which they are located. These complex circuits have operated in different historical moments within India to categorise certain sexual practices as deviant, irrelevant or subordinate. For example, the *Kama Sutra*, composed or compiled between the 2nd and 4th-centuries AD is cited by the ABVA to prove the existence of homosexuality in ancient India. However, the text actually locates sexual desire primarily within the framework of the 'heterosexual desires of upper class men vis-à-vis all women (directly) and lower class men (indirectly)' (Roy, 1998, p 56). Assumptions about desire were informed by relations of power, the growth of regional politics and urban centres during this period, and mediated by class, caste and gender. Responses to sexuality are thus neither linear nor one-dimensional and arguments that erase these complexities are likely to fall into the traps of cultural essentialism and reproduce binaries.

This brings me back to *Fire* and the point where my story began. The celluloid Radha (not Sita) is forced to undergo the test of purity through fire. Unlike the epic version where the *agnipariksha* is a public event, and Sita voluntarily sits in the middle of a burning wood fire (to prove her fidelity to her husband and divine consort, Ram), Mehta's *Fire* takes a different cultural turn. Radha's sari catches fire from a burning gas stove. We have no idea if she survives until the camera brings us to the closing sequence in the setting of the famous Nizamuddin tomb, the burial place of a Sufi Muslim saint – Sufism being a belief system that accommodates different sexual practices. The camera encircles the two women, Radha and Sita, embracing one another with a beloved's gaze. Radha survives the test of purity, but unlike the epic version of Sita, this time the test is not for the sake of cultural purification and sexual recuperation. Rather, it is for validating her love for Sita through the represented cultural space that they inhabit. Mehta's counter cultural move does not leave us in the end with an uncomplicated authenticated subject. The two women strategically invoke culture throughout the film and their relationship is continuously reconstituted through these moves. In the end, their temporary occupation of a Muslim spiritual space, the space of a persecuted religious minority, the space of another Other, brings us to the brink of a new level of complexity and challenge.

But I am pulled away from the brink by my recurring dilemma. The risk of strategic cultural essentialism is that we do essentialise culture, albeit momentarily. *Fire* can be subject to another interpretation – namely one of a totally essentialised culture – the mythologisation of a culture from the point of view of an Asian immigrant in Canada. Deepa Mehta's subsequent disavowal of *Fire* as a lesbian film, thus refuting that which is most subversive of Indian culture, unmasks her project as one of securing legitimacy. Strategic essentialism can be deployed to mobilise people to do political work, yet it can still fall into the trap of some irreducible essentialism. In deciding 'when our essentialising strategies have become traps, as opposed to having strategic and necessary positive effects', Gayatri Spivak argues that a strategic use of essentialism must be subject to persistent critique, 'otherwise the strategy freezes into something like what you call an essentialist position' (Spivak and Rooney, 1994, p 153). She also emphasises how the position of the strategist is important. 'So, to an extent, we have to look at where the group – the person, the persons, or the movement – is situated when we make claims for or against essentialism. A strategy suits a situation; a strategy is not a theory' (Spivak and Rooney, 1994, p 154). She has argued that her own remarks about strategic essentialism have been taken up in discourses that are influenced from sites of power, and 'that the marking of the critical moment, which is the strategic moment, has been erased'.

The fact remains that cultural essentialism used for either dismissing or validating issues of sexuality takes us only so far (Narayan, 1997, p 111). The use of culture to argue against the existence of female sex and sexuality or against the existence of the sexual subalterns reinforces dominant sexual ideology and the idea that there is just 'one way to do it' and 'live it'. Similarly, cultural explanations that try to prove the existence of these 'contaminants' within Indian culture can become their own exclusionary discourses, as I have already discussed. The arguments around culture are to some extent arguments about authenticity, more specifically about who constitutes the authentic Indian subject. The desire to produce a purified, authentic subject slides into cast-iron representations of identity and culture. In the sexuality debates, the sexual subject is a site of cultural contest, where cultural legitimacy entails making a claim of authenticity. And these claims rest, albeit momentarily, on cultural essentialism.

There is a need to push the intellectual inquiry further in order to move beyond the impasse that results from the opposition between cultural essentialism and anti-essentialism. I suggest a foregrounding of two aspects that persist in the arguments of the cultural dissenters – erotic desire and exclusion. Focusing on the erotic desire of the sexual subaltern subject challenges both the cultural and sexual articulations which cast sex as dirty and a negative force. Next there is a need to inquire into how the legitimate sexual subject, or normative sexuality, comes to be bounded and constituted by that which it excludes.

I focus on the erotic desire as well as the complex location of the sexual subject who is simultaneously excluded by dominant cultural and sexual norms. Foregrounding the complexity of her location as well as her eroticism can assist in moving beyond the cultural essentialist/anti-essentialist divide. It provides a trajectory into the debates on sexuality and culture that ensures the instability of sex and sexuality, as well as culture as a category that is fluid and shifting. More specifically, the erotic desire of this subject can challenge the dominant cultural and sexual norms that perpetuate the notion that sex is dirty and corrupting, that it needs to be curtailed, confined, and restricted (Gabriel, 2002). It also challenges the ways in which cultural essentialism is used in law to reinforce a negative representation of sex, and casting it as something that is alien to Indian culture and ethos. The pursuit of erotic desire, at least as a heuristic device, is both positive and empowering. Erotic desire also recognises the subjectivity of the sexual subject, challenging representations of her exclusively through the lens of victimisation. It creates space for the articulation of a notion of partial agency, a space somewhere in between the victim subject and the autonomous ahistorical liberal subject (Abrams, 1995).

We also need to foreground the exclusionary implications of the legitimate, rights-bearing sexual subject. The existence of the legitimate sexual subject is only possible through the process of exclusion and cultural illegitimacy, an issue I discuss in Chapter 2. That which is excluded is inchoate, abject, existing in the exclusion zones, and culturally alien. This excluded site haunts the boundaries of the legitimately constituted sexual subject, its threatening presence exposing the grounding of the legitimate subject as based on erasures and exclusions, and preventing foreclosure on the issue of cultural authenticity. This excluded site challenges the legitimate sexual subject, the stability of sex, and produces a crisis in any claim to a universal sexual and cultural truth or story. It challenges the ways in which cultural essentialism can be used to reinforce and reinscribe normative sexuality and a creeping cultural hegemony around sex as something that is alien to Indian culture and ethos.

The focus on erotic desire as well as exclusion is not intended to correspond to a sexual libertarian politics which exalts the subject and her agency. It is a subject that challenges the notion of sex as dirty, as monolithic, and the subject as victimised. It also forces a re-articulation of culture through her constant presence at the boundaries of law. Her exclusions, erasure, abjection and her constant disruptive return impel a reconstitution of both the legitimate sexual subject and the cultural space which the legitimate subject inhabits. Focusing on the subjectivity of the excluded subject and her erotic desire helps to untangle at least some of the dilemmas surrounding cultural essentialism and enables us to remain committed to the project of cultural hybridity This re-articulation exposes claims of cultural authenticity and sexual normativity as forms of power, rather than reflecting a universal, natural order. There is a need to continue to understand the fluidity of culture as a concept that is constantly shifting, changing and malleable, constituted differently in different specific historical moments (Grewal and Kaplan, 1994). My use of hybridity is not intended to reflect the position of an uncritical native informant or an uncritical position on the history of imperialism. Hybridity, as useful as it is in these cultural and sexual debates, does not mean that I want the deployment of hybridity to amount to a celebration of the imperialism that helped produce it. It is important to remember that postcolonialism is about a critique of the imperialism that produced hybridity, not simply about its production. Hybridity is a confused, at times alienated, and displaced concept. My intention is to use it to disrupt the purity of Indian cultural values and the surety of knowledge on which the sexual subject is based.

Yet several questions remain. How can this erotic subject be articulated in law? Law is not a celebratory space. It is a space we go to when things go wrong – when the rules are broken. However, as a discursive process, law plays a role in the construction of the subject and culture. Law is constantly engaged in re-inventing and re-interpreting the subject, including the sexual subject, and the cultural story woven around this subject. In the legal stories I have related, law is a space where a cultural story is told about sexuality, often a cultural story that is rooted in a dominant cultural script. When the erotic subject comes to law, whether to claim rights or challenge a punitive regime that bounds her off as someone who is stigmatised, inauthentic or foreign and to be excluded, she counters the weight of sexual and cultural normativity as she transgresses the boundaries of both. In challenging these normative boundaries, she creates the possibility of disrupting the cultural and sexually normative content of law, and of the recognition of multiple sexual identities or sexual practices.[45] She constantly threatens a disruptive return, forcing a radical re-articulation of sexual subjects that matter and the cultural context from which she speaks (Butler, 1993, pp 10–12). More concretely, erotic desire and exclusion force our attention to the disruptive possibilities that the sexual subject can bring to law and creates space for legal arguments that recognise that culture is not fixed and static. The sexual subject speaks from within a contested cultural framework, forcing courts and law to engage with the fluidity of culture and its contested histories.

In this essay, I begin to complicate the picture of Indian cultural values and its relationship to sex and sexuality in law. In exploring this relationship in the context of contemporary debates on sexual speech, and the rights of the sexual subaltern subject, I seek to destabilise the dominant narrative of culture, sex and nation that keeps sex stigmatised and the sexual subaltern marginalised and silent. The dilemma that remains is how to strategically deploy culture without falling into the essentialist and universalising trap of that orthodoxy. I challenge cultural and sexual hegemony by reframing the inquiry and focusing on the erotic desire of the sexual

---

45 Eg, Lisa Bower discusses the disruptive possibilities of the queer subject in the legal arena in the US. She examines how the articulation of a queer notion of 'non-identity' within the legal field has created the possibility of destabilising certain legal classifications (Bower, 1994, p 1,014).

subject, as well as the role of the exclusionary zone which she inhabits in partly constituting the legitimate sexual subject in law. There is potential for this subject to bring about a crisis in the bounded subject and threaten its constant disruption through claims to sexual rights, or sexual speech within a specific cultural context. The inquiry into erasures and exclusions avoids the traps of essentialism, and exposes how the sexual subject in law is constituted partly in and through such exclusions. The disruptive possibility posed by these exclusionary zones, their existence and persistence at the boundaries of law, denaturalises claims to cultural originality and the naturalness of sex.

The erotic subject can recuperate a space for sexuality within the cultural text, which has been stigmatised and treated as incoherent and unnatural in the contemporary culture wars. It is a device that is not merely asserting the eroticism and agency of those who participate in normative sexuality. Rather, this subject can create heterogeneous ways in which to speak about sex (in and outside of law) from an excluded subaltern location and shift the stigma associated with this location. At the same time, there is a need to remain attentive to problems and risks associated with the space from which she is speaking. The 'eroticism' of the sex-worker is not intended to negate her struggle against exploitation or hardship, but it can challenge the prejudice and the cultural straitjacket that attempts to silence her through an exclusive discourse of victimisation, pain and moral contamination. Similarly, the homosexual, and other sexual subalterns, can assert and are in fact asserting their agency through claims of pride and erotic desire that are no longer entombed in cultural crypts, yet are at the same time located in the very complex story of Indian culture and Indian sexuality. They simultaneously risk familial and social rebuke and even violence for expressing their subalterneity. The erotic subject challenges the inviolability of the linear narrative that law tells about sex and culture in India, and continuously ruptures and redraws the boundaries of both. Its disruptive potential creates the possibility of telling more complex stories and to speak from a space 'somewhere in between'.

Chapter 4
The Tragedy of Victimisation Rhetoric: Resurrecting the 'Native' Subject in International/ Postcolonial Feminist Legal Politics

Through travelling to other people's 'worlds' we discover that there are 'worlds' in which those who are the victims of arrogant perception are really subjects, lively beings, constructors of vision even though in the mainstream construction they are animated only by the arrogant perceiver and are pliable, foldable, file-awayable, classifiable. (Lugones, 1990)

To have a right as a woman is not to be free of being designated and subordinated by gender. (Brown, 2002)

[E]ven while it is important to critique an ahistorical category of 'woman' it is just as problematic to seek authentic versions of women's locations within societies. The erection against the modernist discourse of 'woman' is not to revert to its other 'traditional roles' but to delineate the problematics of both these forms of female gender construction and the complex ways in which they intersect. (Grewal, 1994)

In postcolonial India, the subject of sex and desire play out in a multitude of cultural spaces: in celluloid fantasy; 'radio *mirchi*' (chilli) chartbuster numbers; and erotic dance sequences both on screen in the cinema halls and off screen in the cacophony of Indian weddings. Women do dance in the postcolonial world, though this image is largely absent from the imagination and scholarship of the international women's rights movement. It is at one level hardly surprising given the representations of the third world subject – in particular, the female subject – that dominate news items in the Western hemisphere and the developed world. Indeed, that look of starvation, helplessness and victimisation is remarkably familiar to our imaginations, irrespective of the reality.

The victim subject is a transnational phenomenon. It appears, at least within legal discourse, in both the West and the postcolonial world. However, the postcolonial or third world victim subject has come to represent the more victimised subject; that is, the real or authentic victim subject. Feminist politics in the international human rights arena, as well as in parts of the postcolonial world, have promoted this image of the authentic victim subject while advocating for women's human rights.

In this essay, I examine how the international women's rights movement has reinforced the image of the woman as a victim subject, primarily through its focus on violence against women (VAW). I examine how this subject has been replicated in the postcolonial context, using the example of India, and the more general implications this kind of move has on women's rights. My main argument is that the focus on the victim subject in the VAW campaign reinforces gender and cultural essentialism in the international women's human rights arena. It also reinforces some feminist positions in India that do not produce an emancipatory politics for women. This focus fails to take advantage of the liberating potential of important feminist insights that have challenged the public/private distinction along which human rights have operated, and of traditional understandings of power as emanating exclusively from a sovereign state.

In the first part of this chapter, I examine how the victim subject has become the dominant focus of the international women's human rights movement. I examine this move specifically within the context of VAW campaigns and then look at the broader implications it has for women's rights. I argue that the victim subject has reinforced gender essentialism and cultural essentialism. These have been further displaced onto a third world and first world divide. I discuss how this displacement resurrects the 'native subject' and justifies imperialist interventions. In the second part of this essay I demonstrate how the victim subject has been central to feminist legal politics in India, especially in relation to nationalism, and how this focus in turn is a symptom of the postcolonial condition (Anderson, 1991; Jayaprasad, 1991; Pandey, 1990). In the final section, I argue in favour of transcending the victim subject and disrupting the cultural and gender essentialism that have come to characterise feminist legal politics. I discuss the political and emancipatory value of focusing on the peripheral subject and identifying her locations of resistance when addressing women's human rights.

The hegemonic victim subject

The 1993 Vienna World Conference on Human Rights marked the culmination of a long struggle to secure international recognition of women's rights as human rights. It was a turning point for both the international women's rights movement and the human rights movement. State parties participating in the conference acknowledged that women too were entitled to enjoy fundamental rights. These included full and equal participation in political, civil, economic, social and cultural life at the national, regional, and international level. Article 18 of the declaration provides that:

> The human rights of women and of the girl-child are an inalienable, integral and indivisible part of universal human rights. The full and equal participation of women in political, civil, economic, social and cultural life, at the national, regional and international levels, and the eradication of all forms of discrimination on grounds of sex are priority objectives of the international community.[1]

Article 39 of the Vienna Declaration also urges states to withdraw reservations to the Convention on the Elimination of All Forms of Discrimination Against Women (CEDAW). The final document that emerged from Vienna also acknowledged that, partly as a result of the artificial line drawn between the public and private sphere, certain gender-specific issues had been left out of the human rights arena

---

1 *Vienna Declaration and Programme of Action*, United Nations World Conference on Human Rights, UN GAOR, at 25, UN Doc A/CONF/157/23 (1993) Part I, Art 18. See Otto, 1993, p 371 for an analysis of how the public/private distinction continues to inform international law and its exclusionary impact on women.

(Charlesworth, Chinkin and Wright, 1991; Engle, 1993; MacKinnon, 1992; Romany, 1993; Schneider, 1991). The document provided that a broader spectrum of harms experienced by women in the family be subjected to human rights scrutiny. Article 38 of the Vienna Declaration provides:

> [t]he World Conference on Human Rights stresses the importance of working towards the elimination of violence against women in public and private life, the elimination of all forms of sexual harassment, exploitation and trafficking in women, the elimination of gender bias in the administration of justice and the eradication of any conflicts which may arise between the rights of women and the harmful effects of certain traditional or customary practices, cultural prejudices and religious extremism.

The demand to include violence against women as a human rights issue was reiterated at the Women's Conference in Beijing in 1995 (Bunch, 1990). The Beijing document challenged the public/private distinction along which human rights have traditionally operated and increased awareness of the fact that power operates in multiple arenas. Since that time, the international and regional women's rights movements, alongside the official recognition of women's human rights, have continued to focus primarily on the issue of violence against women and victimisation of women. Immediately after the Vienna conference, the UN General Assembly passed a Declaration on Violence Against Women (The Declaration).[2] The Declaration was adopted to strengthen and complement the process of effective implementation of CEDAW. It recognised that violence against women 'is a manifestation of historically unequal power relations between men and women, which have led to domination over and discrimination against women' (The Declaration, Preamble). It reiterates the consensus reached at Vienna, that violence against women covers 'gender-based violence ... whether occurring in public or in private life' (Vienna Declaration, p 217). Under Art 2 of the Declaration, violence against women specifically includes violence in the family, marital rape, female genital mutilation, and other 'traditional' practices that are harmful to women. It also covers similar violence in the community, including harassment at work and violence perpetrated or condoned by the state, wherever it occurs. The Declaration also set the basis for the appointment of a UN Special Rapporteur on Violence Against Women to cover aspects of violence against women, including its causes and consequences. In 1994, Radhika Coomaraswamy from Sri Lanka was appointed as the UN Special Rapporteur on Violence Against Women. During her tenure, she

---

2   Declaration on the Elimination of Violence Against Women, GA Res 104, UN GAOR, 48th Sess, 85th plen mtg, Supp No 49, at 217–19, UN Doc A/48/49 (1993). The United Nations Economic and Social Council endorsed the resolution of the UN Commission on Human Rights to appoint a special rapporteur on violence against women, its causes and consequences, for a three-year term: UN ESCOR, 42d plen mtg, UN Doc E/DEC/1994/254 (1994).

submitted a series of annual reports to the UN General Assembly addressing the issue of violence against women.[3] Even Recommendation 19 of the CEDAW, which deals with violence against women and is not binding, has achieved greater visibility after the Human Rights World Conference in 1993.[4]

The focus on VAW has had some extremely important and beneficial consequences for women. The women's human rights movement has drawn attention to the lack of domestic governmental responses to women's demands for more effective rape laws, laws against child sexual abuse, and domestic violence laws. The VAW campaign has been overwhelmingly successful in translating very specific violations experienced by individual women into human rights discourse.[5] VAW discourse has succeeded partly because of its appeal to the victim subject. In the context of law and human rights, it is invariably the abject victim subject who seeks rights, primarily because she is the one who has had the worst happen to her. The victim subject has allowed women to speak out about abuses that have remained hidden or invisible in human rights discourse. Moreover, the Vienna World Conference and subsequent women's conferences have enabled women to speak out to the international community. A powerful form of this presentation has been through personal testimonials in public tribunals, as at Vienna, or through international video links.[6] These accounts are usually very graphic and horrifying,

---

3 See Reports of UN ESCOR the Special Rapporteur on Violence Against Women, Its Causes and Consequences, 1997 to 2003, including Report of the Special Rapporteur on Violence Against Women, Its Causes and Consequences, UN ESCOR Hum Rts Comm, 53d Sess, Provisional Agenda Item 9(a), E/CN 4/1997/47 (1997) (concerning violence in the community); Report of the Special Rapporteur on Violence Against Women, Its Causes and Consequences, UN ESCOR Hum Rts Comm, 54th Sess, Provisional Agenda Item 9(a), E/CN 4/1998/54 (1998) (concerning violence against women as perpetrated and/or condoned by the state); Report of the Special Rapporteur on Violence Against Women, Its Causes and Consequences, UN ESCOR Hum Rts Comm, 55th Sess, Provisional Agenda Item 12(a), E/CN 4/1999/68 (1999) (concerning violence against women in the family); Report of the Special Rapporteur on Violence Against Women, Its Causes and Consequences, UN ESCOR Hum Rts Comm, 56th Sess, Provisional Agenda Item 12(a), E/CN 4/2000/68 (2000) (concerning trafficking in women, women's migration, and violence against women); Report of the Special Rapporteur on Violence Against Women, Its Causes and Consequences, UN ESCOR Hum Rts Comm, 57th Sess, E/CN 4/2001/73 (2001) (concerning violence against women perpetrated and/or condoned by the state during times of armed conflict); Report of the Special Rapporteur on Violence Against Women, Its Causes and Consequences, UN ESCOR Hum Rts Comm, 58th Sess, E/CN 4/2002/84 (2002) (on cultural practices in the family that are violent towards women); Report of the Special Rapporteur on Violence Against Women, Its Causes and Consequences, UN ESCOR Hum Rts Comm, 59th Sess, E/CN 4/2003 (concerning developments in the area of violence against women from 1994–2002).

4 UN General Recommendation No 19, Violence Against Women, UN CEDAW Comm, 11th Sess, UN Doc A/47/38 (1992) provides that discrimination against women includes gender-based violence; that is, violence directed against a woman because she is a woman, or violence that affects women disproportionately. It further states that gender-based violence is a form of discrimination that inhibits a woman's ability to enjoy rights and freedoms on an equal basis.

5 The campaign on reproductive rights has also acquired a certain degree of visibility. However, it has not translated into effective policies or actions by state parties. See UN Report of the International Conference on Population and Development, UN GAOR, 49th Sess, UN Doc A/CONF/171/13 (1994). Furthermore, the failure of the governments participating in this meeting to incorporate sexual rights into their programme leaves women's roles as mothers and procreators undisturbed. Their identities as sexual beings entitled to sexual rights, rather than exclusively as victims of sexual wrongs, remains unaddressed (Lai and Ralphy, 1995).

6 See, for example, UN Global Videoconference, A World Free of Violence Against Women (8 March 1999) at http://webevents.broadcast.com/unifem/women (last visited 28 December 2003).

and are told through the location of the victim subject. 'Victim talk' has an appeal at the level of popular discourse that must not be underestimated (Minow, 1993).

The victim subject also provides a shared location from which women from different cultural and social contexts can speak. It provides women with a subject that repudiates the atomised, decontextualised and ahistorical subject of liberal rights discourse, while at the same time furnishing a unitary subject that enables women to continue to make claims based on a commonality of experience. Any further fragmentation of the subject raises fears that the absence of a common subject will leave feminists divided and women even more disempowered. The idea of multiple or fractured subjectivities threatens to deprive women of a foundation from which to make claims for rights and for broader global recognition (Benhabib, 1989; Brown, 1995, p 77; Fineman, 1990, pp 34–43). If women's experiences are represented as fragmented, they may lose power and undermine certain 'truth claims' about women's lives.

However, an exclusive reliance on the victim subject to make claims for rights and for women's empowerment has some serious limitations. The articulation of the victim subject is based on gender essentialism; that is, overgeneralised claims about women (Harris, 1990; Kline, 1989). As Chandra Mohanty points out, essentialism assumes that 'women have a coherent group identity within different cultures ... prior to their entry into social relations' (Mohanty, 1991, p 70). Such generalisations are hegemonic in that they represent the problems of privileged women who are often (though not exclusively) white, Western, middle class, heterosexual women. These generalisations, based on some abstract notion of strategic sisterhood, efface the problems, perspectives, and political concerns of women marginalised because of their class, race, religion, ethnicity, and/or sexual orientation (Ong, 1996). The victim subject ultimately relies on a universal subject: a subject that resembles the uncomplicated subject of liberal discourse. It is a subject that cannot accommodate a multi-layered experience.

The second problem with a reliance on the victim subject, particularly in the context of violence against women, is that it presents a position based on cultural essentialism. Women in the postcolonial world are portrayed as victims of their culture, which reinforces stereotyped and racist representations of that culture and privileges the culture of the West. In the end, the focus on the victim subject reinforces the depiction of women in the postcolonial world as perpetually marginalised and underprivileged, and has serious implications for the strategies subsequently adopted to remedy the harms that women experience. It encourages some feminists in the international arena to propose strategies which are reminiscent of imperial interventions in the lives of the native subject and which represent the 'Eastern' woman as a victim of a 'backward' and 'uncivilised' culture.

Thirdly, the victim subject and the focus on violence invites remedies and responses from states that have little to do with promoting women's rights. Thus, a related concern is that the victim subject position has invited protectionist, and even conservative, responses from states. The construction of women exclusively through the lens of violence has triggered a spate of domestic and international reforms focused on the criminal law, which are used to justify state restrictions on women's rights – for the protection of women. The anti-trafficking campaign, with its focus on violence and victimisation, is but one example. It has spawned initiatives by some states that impose minimum age limits for women workers going abroad for employment. In 1998, Bangladesh banned women from going abroad as domestic workers. Although Bangladesh is reconsidering the ban, it still remains in effect. In a similar vein, although not entirely prohibiting migration by women, the Nepal Foreign Employment Act 1985 prohibits issuing women with employment licences to work overseas without the consent of the woman's husband or male guardian (Sanghera and Kapur, 2001, p 24). Similarly, the government of Burma, reacting to a publication of a report by Human Rights Watch about the trafficking of Burmese women and girls into Thailand's sex industry from the eastern Shan State, imposed rules prohibiting all women in this area between the ages of 16 and 25 from travelling without a legal guardian (Belak, 2003). The UN Protocol on Trafficking 2001 and the South Asian Convention on Trafficking 2002 regard the consent of the women who move or are moved across borders as largely irrelevant.[7] Such measures conflate women's movement or migration with trafficking, where even women moving (legally or illegally) to seek higher-wage work are suspected of being trafficked.[8] At the same time, there is no mandatory requirement to provide any services or protect the rights of the victim under these documents, as states are reluctant to provide support for non-nationals. Such interventions reinforce women's victim status and resort to a protectionist and conservative discourse that early feminist interventions struggled to move away from through anti-discrimination discourse.

Gender essentialism

Gender essentialism refers to the fixing of certain attributes to women. These attributes may be natural, biological or psychological, or may refer to activities and procedures that are not necessarily dictated by biology. These essential attributes are considered to be shared by all women and hence are also universal. 'Essentialism thus refers to the existence of fixed characteristics, given attributes, and ahistorical functions that limit the possibilities of change and thus social reorganisation' (Grosz, 1994, p 84). It is 'a belief in the real, true essence of things, the invariable and fixed properties, which define the "whatness" of a given reality' (Fuss, 1989, p xi). The limits of gender essentialism are not new to feminist legal thinking, and in recent years there has been considerable critique of the hegemonic generalisations

---

7   Article 3(b), United Nations Protocol to Prevent, Suppress, and Punish Trafficking in Persons, Especially in Women and Children (GA Res 55/25, UN GAOR, Annexe II, Supp No 49, at 60, UN Doc A/45/49 (2001)) which came into force 25 September 2003; and South Asian Association for Regional Co-operation Convention on Preventing and Combating Trafficking in Women and Children for Prostitution (2002), Art 1(3).

8   US Act 2001, s 102(b)(4).

about women that result from essentialism (Spelman, 1998). In the postcolonial context, Spivak has addressed some of the problems of essentialism in the work of the subaltern historians, who are attempting to recuperate the voice of the marginalised subject. She has argued that the 'subaltern cannot speak' and that subaltern historians are erecting a native subject with an authentic voice (Spivak, 1988, p 296; Spivak and Rooney, 1994, p 151). She challenges the essentialism that is inherent in such a position.

Anti-essentialists argue that the claims of essentialists represent primarily the problems of privileged women and result in the production of theoretical agendas and perspectives that efface the problems of more marginalised women. In the US, gender essentialism has been challenged by black, Latina/o and lesbian feminists as being exclusive and failing to recognise that women experience various forms of oppression simultaneously (Anzaldua, 1999; Cain, 1989–90; Collins, 2000; Crenshaw, 1989; hooks, 2000). Black, Latina/o, Asian American, Native American and Muslim women experience the complex intersection of sexism, racism and/or religious identity. Their experiences of gender oppression cannot be extricated from their experiences of racial oppression because they occur simultaneously. They come to the law not just as women, but as black women, and/or Latina/o women and/or Muslim women, negotiating with the dominant and stable discourses on race, ethnicity, culture, sexuality, religion and/or family (Butler, 1993, pp 223–42). For those who do not experience such intersecting oppressions, the focus on gender remains less complicated. As Marlee Kline explains, the focus on gender as the primary variable of oppression conceals the way in which privilege may be operating simultaneously. Kline argues that white women 'are able to ignore the experience of our race because it does not in any way correlate with an experience of oppression and contradiction' (Kline, 1989, p 123). Arguments that focus on sex discrimination do not reflect the fact that women do not experience discrimination exclusively on the basis of sex. Rather, they may also experience discrimination on the basis of race, religions, ethnicity, caste, physical ability and/or sexual identity. To focus only on the category of gender is to obscure the ways in which women – particularly women in minority and disadvantaged communities – experience multiple forms of subordination. To focus on gender as the exclusive or primary site of oppression, reflects only the experience of those women who do not experience other forms of subordination, such as religious, ethnic or caste subordination. These various forms of subordination are not separate and discrete, but rather intricately connected.

Some scholars such as Catherine MacKinnon have nevertheless focused on the commonality of women's experiences. She states, 'what [women] have in common is not that our conditions have particularity in ways that matter. But we are all measured by a male standard for women, a standard that is not ours' (MacKinnon, 1987, p 76). In her analysis, sexuality and sexual relations remain central to women's oppression. 'If sexuality is central to women's definition and forced sex is central to sexuality, rape is indigenous, not exceptional, to women's social condition' (MacKinnon, 1989, p 172). MacKinnon argues that, as sexual exploitation and sexual violence are experiences women share in common, these commonalities are more important than any differences between women. In her view, all women experience oppression at the hands of patriarchal power, and she argues that power is invariably male (MacKinnon, 1989, pp 157–70). In law, it is expressed through 'male laws' and 'male' systems of justice (MacKinnon, 1982; MacKinnon, 1983). The fact that women do not come from a shared social position (and hence may not prioritise issues of sexuality or sexual violence) is not addressed in MacKinnon's work. For MacKinnon, the centrality of sexuality is inherent regardless of whether women consciously consider it as such.

MacKinnon's analysis is based on the assumption that regardless of a woman's material situation, her sexual subordination is intrinsic to gender relations. Rape, sexual harassment and other forms of sexual violence are used to generate gender and the distinction between men as superior and women as subordinate or inferior (Halley, 2002, p 83; MacKinnon, 1982). Heterosexuality has institutionalised the construction of male sexual dominance and female sexual submission. Thus, sexuality becomes the lynchpin of gender inequality (MacKinnon, 1987). Janet Halley points out how MacKinnon, in her early US work, was of the view that recourse to the law in situations of rape would not necessarily provide the solution to women's concerns because the law was male and based on male experiences. A mere reforming of the laws governing rape or other forms of sexual violence would not address the male dominance which informs the legal regulation of sexuality. However, Halley identifies a distinct shift in MacKinnon's later work, where she argues that it is possible to produce a feminist jurisprudence based on a *women's point of view* and women's claims of sexual violence, that exposes how male dominance informs the law and subordinates all women (Halley, 2002, p 86; MacKinnon, 1989). This position marks a radical departure from MacKinnon's complex analysis of sex in terms of power and the relations of male dominance and gender subordination produced in law, to a more liberal one that views the law as a site for solving these problems through the assertion of a women's point of view (Halley, 2002, pp 84–85).

Although there has been a substantive critique of MacKinnon in her own domestic arena, she has succeeded in bringing her analysis into the international arena, largely unmodified (Smart, 1989, pp 76–85). We can find at least three aspects of MacKinnon's domestic scholarship present in her subsequent work on women's human rights. The first is her claim that sexuality – erotic or genital relations – constitutes the basis of inequality between men and women. This argument permits no distinction between 'normal' heterosexual sex and rape either in times of war or peace. Secondly, even though human rights have been a tool of male dominance, there is a possibility for individual women's claims to expose this inequality and write women's voices into human rights discourse. One concrete proposal she makes in this regard is to address issues of sexual violence as questions of equality. Finally, examples of women's rights claims can be understood as a form of resistance, and the claim of one woman can represent the experience of all women. As Halley has pointed out in her discussion of the transformation of MacKinnon's position on the issue of sexual harassment in the domestic context, '[a]s long as her legal cause of action for sex harassment performs the perspective produced by *women's point of view*, it will allow her to interrupt the ontological seamlessness joining male superordination with the law, enabling her to make not only her injury but the injury of all women visible, audible, and interruptible' (Halley, 2002, p 86; emphasis added). Thus, one woman can act on behalf of all women, even if she has not personally suffered any injury, provided her claim is informed by a *women's point of view*.

While MacKinnon acknowledges the multiplicity of women's experience in her work on women's human rights and sexual violence, she remains reluctant to interrogate the extent to which this multiplicity displaces gender as the central category of analysis. She focuses on that which is shared amongst women rather than on their differences. She discusses how the experiences of rape, prostitution and pornography are the primary ways in which women experience a violation of their human rights. In her work on rape in war in Bosnia, she argues that sexual violence is a weapon of war (MacKinnon, 1993a; MacKinnon, 1994). She made similar arguments as lead counsel in a case filed under the US Alien Tort Claims Act 1993 and Torture Victim Protection Act 1991, in which Bosnian Muslim and Croat survivors of Serbian sexual atrocities sought international justice for genocide.[9] She argues that pornography is a tool of genocide and tries to make a direct causal link between pornography in Bosnia and the rapes of Muslim women (MacKinnon, 1993b). She also argues that torture on the basis of sex in the form of rape, domestic battering and pornography should be seen as a violation of the human rights of women (MacKinnon, 1992, p 21).

MacKinnon's analysis of women's rights in the area of human rights is based on the idea that women have been treated as less than human and hence denied their human rights. She argues that a human is not understood as someone who has been sexually and reproductively violated, but is defined as a 'man'. She states that when someone's human rights are deemed to be violated 'he is probably a man' (MacKinnon, 1993a, p 91). This assumption is produced by the fact that rights have been and continue to be based on exclusions, based on difference, and gender has been a basis for excluding women on the grounds that they are naturally inferior, weak and stupid. They need protection rather than recognition of their subjectivity or capacity to choose and make decisions. MacKinnon argues that human rights are therefore intrinsically male defined and that the male reality has become the human rights principle. Using this rationale it is possible for men to take or deny women their liberties and not have this act recognised as a human rights violation. When the rights of men are denied or withdrawn, there is little debate over whether such actions constitute human rights violations. The entire paradigm of human rights has therefore been based on the experiences of men. Although MacKinnon has taken up the issue of women's rights in the context of wartime and specifically within the context of the sexual atrocities inflicted by the Serbs on the Bosnian and Croatian women, she argues that 'men do in war what they do in peace, only more so' (MacKinnon, 1993a, p 94). She suggests that the casualties women endure in times of war are similar to the ones they endure in times of peace. She thus collapses any distinctions made between violence against women in times of war or peace. Pornography, for example, proliferates in times of peace, and in times of war is officially mobilised to commit atrocities against women that men are already conditioned to enjoy. The only difference is that the acts are officially sanctioned. 'It does help that men did these acts in declared military groups, instead of one on one everywhere at once and all the time, or in small packs, murdering, raping, pimping, and breeding, but not recognised as an army of occupation' (MacKinnon, 1993a, p 109). In both times of war and peace, these violations are met with complacency regardless of the laws enacted.

---

9   *Doe v Karadzic*, 866 F Supp 734, SDNY, 1994, rev'd, *Kadic v Karadzic*, 70 F 3d 232, 2d Cir, 1995.

MacKinnon supports the emergence of a women's human rights movement in the international arena, which scrutinises and publicises the sexual violence and atrocities that women endure. And this movement, according to MacKinnon, finds its best articulation in the form of the equality law advocated by blacks in the US and the women's movement in Canada in the 1980s and 1990s. They envision equality as moving beyond the Aristotelian understanding of treating likes alike and unlikes unalike, to a more substantive vision of equality which calls for relief against state inaction as well as action, to redress the discrimination to which these groups have been historically subjected. She advocates this more attenuated understanding of equality to address and redress the violence women have experienced at the hands of men globally. Despite their diversity, women everywhere are subjugated to men, primarily in and through some form of sexual violence such as rape, wife battering, prostitution or pornography. She lists a range of diverse countries in which such atrocities continue to take place, in times of peace and war, and argues that equality guarantees should be used in both of these situations to address the problem of violence against women.

The focus on commonality of women's experience places her analysis on a slippery slope where it can easily slide into the essentialist and prioritising category of gender; it can blunt rather than sharpen our analysis of oppression. MacKinnon does not consider the way in which legal systems have been shaped by social, economic or historical forces, such as colonialism, enslavement of non-white populations (including both men and women), or the role of the Christian church. The class, cultural, religious and racial differences between women are collapsed under the category of gender through women's common experience of sexual violence and objectification by men. Differences between women are simply understood as cultural, without exploring or elaborating on how the cultural context was shaped and influenced in and through the colonial encounter – an encounter between the West and 'the Rest'. To miss this part of the argument is to present a narrative of women's exploitation and subordination that does not implicate the ways in which race, religion and imperial ambition constituted the vortex of knowledge that affords us a historically grounded and contextualised understanding of that experience. MacKinnon is one of several scholars, including Martha Nussbaum, Andrea Dworkin, Kathleen Mahoney and Kathleen Barry, who resort to metanarratives in addressing women's rights issues. This approach has a broad appeal – an appeal that lies in the ability to tell a grand story in modernist terms which counters the dominant narratives and creates the possibility for some common basis on which to speak about women's rights (Brown, 1995, pp 41–43).

Despite the appeal of such grand metanarratives, gender essentialism produces a theory that effaces the differences between women. The exclusive focus on violence against women does not reveal the complexity of women's lives, but only the different ways in which they may experience violence. Thus, culture is invoked primarily to explain the different ways in which women experience violence, in the process often reinforcing essentialist understandings of culture and representing particular cultures as brutal and barbaric. This response has not been a liberating one. The tension between accounting for women's multiple experiences of race, gender, culture and class on the one hand, and violence against women as a universal phenomenon on the other, is resolved through the victim subject.

Difference is acknowledged through the different experiences of violence that the victim is exposed to in diverse economic, social and cultural settings. While VAW operates as something of an equaliser, it also sets up a subject who is thoroughly disempowered and helpless. This subject, in turn, becomes the universal subject of human rights discourse for women. VAW either erases diversity or constructs diversities as aggravating experiences of oppression, whereas in reality, the aspects of a woman's life that differ from the essentialised concept may serve to alleviate oppression. As Tracy Higgins says: 'In short, when feminists aspire to account for women's oppression through claims of cross-cultural commonality, they construct the feminist subject through exclusions, narrowing her down to her essence' (Higgins, 1996, p 102).

MacKinnon's account of violence against women and how to address it at the international level coincides with the VAW campaigns. The feminist legal agenda, despite its international complexion, has not sufficiently taken on board the critiques of gender essentialism in formulating the women's human rights project. The VAW campaign has not translated into a complex understanding of the ways in which women's lives and experiences are mediated by race, religion, class, gender and a history of the colonial encounter. Although the issue of violence against women is a critical human rights concern, the analysis of MacKinnon and others is not necessarily contributing to an alleviation or elimination of such violence. Indeed, it may be missing the point altogether. In examining women's human rights, it is not enough to illuminate the ways in which women have been subordinated by men through sexual subordination. Although MacKinnon's theory of power was indeed radical for its time, it has been subsequently translated by her into an exclusively liberal endeavour (Halley, 2002, p 85). Indeed, her analysis of how liberal rights, in particular its focus on formal equality, has justified the exclusion of women is not used as a starting point for challenging the premises of liberalism and its understanding of the subject. Rather, MacKinnon's analysis merely seeks to provide ways in which to *include* women within the discourse of equality without disrupting or challenging the metaphysical foundations and ontological limitations of rights discourse to women's empowerment struggles. My critique is not intended to suggest that rights are not useful. As I set out in Chapters 1 and 2 of this book, my argument is that we need to engage with the discourse of rights differently, in ways that are constantly disruptive. The intention is not to create more uncertainty, nervousness or anxiety, but to ensure that complacency or a surrender to liberalism's lofty and false claims do not become the substitute for a transformative politics and an alternative political vision.

There is no question that women have struggled as victims to subvert power; yet that power has not emanated from a single source – men. In the context of India, resistance to the colonial encounter was central to the experience of subordination for women on the Asian subcontinent. This history cannot be understood simply in terms of the history of gender subordination or sexual violence perpetrated by men against women. It was also about the broader economic and political subordination and expropriation of another nation's labour, resources, land, raw materials and market, and the exclusion of the native – both men and women – from sovereignty and legal entitlements. Resistance therefore had to be understood in terms of resistance to the imperial project and the processes of Empire and not just opposition to men. Similarly, we need to understand how English women were implicated in the imperial project, deriving their power partly from their status as part of the white race and ruling or colonial power (Stoler, 2002, pp 41–42). They participated in the subordination of the native subject, including men, while simultaneously experiencing a sense of liberation on visits to the subcontinent, an experience not necessarily available to them in the metropolis.

What history tells us is more – it speaks to the construction of the agency of victims through the mechanisms of social, political, cultural and colonial control. We cannot speak of women through a history of common victimisation, nor exclusively in terms of women's lived experiences of violence and subordination. We need to unpack how that victimisation has come to be constructed in different contexts and historical moments, and also how this construction erases the complexity of gender subordination. This construction is a manifestation of the pervasive discourse-power complex. By not focusing exclusively on women's lived experiences, I am not suggesting that the subject simply does not exist. My intention is to highlight what has been missing from the victim-centred politics – the power/knowledge complexes that materially constitute the self, quite specifically from a postcolonial location.

Gender essentialism may be used for a strategic purpose, but the way in which it is being deployed in the international women's human rights arena has had a reactionary effect. The danger of essentialism lies in the way it is deployed in dominant discourses. By not remaining sufficiently attentive to cultural and historical specificities, gender essentialism constructed through a VAW discourse has prompted state actors, non-state actors and donors to embrace universalising strategies in responding to human rights violations against women. It has further obscured differences between women located in very different power relationships. Religion, for example, is of acute significance in many parts of the postcolonial/third world, especially for women located within minority communities (Kapur, 1999a). In postcolonial India, for example, the relationship between gender and religion remains very complex due to the considerable relevance and influence of the Hindu Right's political agenda emphasising the assimilation of religious minorities. Muslim women are caught in the tension between their demands for gender equality within their religious community and their dependence upon and support for the community as a site of cultural and political resistance to Hindu majoritarianism (Kapur, 2002b; Kapur and Cossman, 2001). Religion is also of significance in different Western countries, though its presence remains unaddressed. Religion and culture are frequently cast in the non-Western world as fundamentalist, present and pervasive. However, the religious right in Western (and non-Western) democracies have successfully deployed liberal rights discourse (especially the rights to free speech and equality) to capture the public imagination (Kapur, 1999b). Unfortunately, the VAW agenda has taken up issues of culture and religion in ways that have not only reinforced gender essentialism, but have also essentialised certain features of culture and reinforced racial and cultural stereotypes.

Cultural essentialism

One response to the critique of gender essentialism's failure to pay sufficient attention to third world women and to the diversity of women's lives has been the reiteration of the need to take account of national and cultural differences among women. Culture and cultural diversity have entered into the women's human rights discourse primarily through VAW campaigns. However, in an effort to avoid the critique of exclusivity and gender essentialism, the move to address violence across difference has sometimes resulted in the reification of culture. I discuss the ways in which cultural essentialism is reproduced through the VAW agenda.

I examine how the issue of culture is often displaced onto a first world and third world divide with the result that colonial assumptions about cultural differences between the West and the Rest, and the women who inhabit these spaces, are replicated. Some cultural practices have come to occupy our imaginations in ways that are totalising of a culture and its treatment of women, and are nearly always overly simplistic or a misrepresentation of the practice. For example, the veil is assumed to be an oppressive and subordinating practice that typifies Islam and its degrading treatment of women. The veil may not be a modern practice, yet the multiple meanings of the veil, through different cultural and historical contexts, get subsumed in rhetoric that focuses almost exclusively on veiling as an oppressive and subordinating practice. It is read in a uniform, linear manner as an oppressive practice because it erases women's physical and sexual identity and is symbolic of the subjugation of women in Islam. Yet, there is no universal opinion as to its function amongst those who wear the veil. For some, it does represent honour, and an effective mechanism to avoid tempting men. More significantly, the veil has also been a very empowering symbol for Muslim women in some countries. In Iran, it was the sign of rebellion and rejection of the Shah and Western imperialism. Amongst immigrant communities in the West, it is the symbol of an exclusive cultural space and a rejection of assimilation. In other contexts, the veil is considered a private space: one in which no one can intrude. The veil also disrupts the public space, where women are often marginalised. The sheer symbolism of the veil brings the woman very visibly into the public sphere – she simply cannot walk by unnoticed (Mernissi, 1994, pp 112–22). However, in the assumptions about the veil that inform refugee cases and opinions outside of Islamic contexts, the multiple readings and functions of the veil are erased and only one stands out: the veil as a tool of oppression and barbarism against women.

Another example is female circumcision, which has been represented as a brutal procedure that is practised by all Africans and receives cultural sanction – a representation that reinforces the inferiority of the African people (Gunning, 1992; Kim, 1993). In the context of postcolonial India, a common image that resides in popular imagination or perceptions about India is the image of the female body in flames.[10] Women are burned to death, and this act apparently has some kind of

---

10 Early feminist writings had a considerable influence on the development of this perception. Such writings continue to inform contemporary feminist politics, especially the women's human rights movement: Bumiller, 1990, pp 44–74; Daly, 1978, pp 113–33. Bumiller became a bestseller in the US and has also been included in college curricula. For a critique of these two works, see Lourde, 1984, pp 66–71; Narayan, 1997, pp 105–07.

cultural sanction. The body in flames is invariably associated with ancient Indian cultural practices, without any regard to more obvious political, economic and social explanations. For example, in some texts, the practice of *sati* is collapsed with dowry murders, two practices that are completely unrelated. As Narayan explains, the practice of *sati*, which relates to the immolation of a widow on her husband's funeral pyre, was a traditional practice in *some* communities in India, and exceptional rather than a routine practice (Narayan, 1997, p 106). To attribute the practice to 'Hindu tradition' generally is both inaccurate and misleading. It has been a contested practice and has had a tenuous status as part of 'Hindu tradition' (Narayan, 1997, p 107; Sangari and Vaid, 2001). Dowry murders, as I discuss later in this essay, have no relationship with *sati*, and have never been a part of, nor sanctioned by any tradition in the Indian context. Accounts of these practices are often inaccurate and misleading, and have been frequently essentialised and set up in opposition to liberal rights discourse. Such a binary is more of an obstacle than an aid in providing an understanding of how rights campaigns often serve as a conduit for entrenching cultural stereotypes. What is frequently lost sight of is how the subject in different cultural contexts comes to be constituted through such oppositions, which end up erasing the very subjectivity of the woman whose rights are being denied or implicated. We need to look at how these oppositions contribute to the discursive constitution of the subject and accounts about the cultural atrocities to which she is exposed. The VAW campaign, though constantly asserting that it is dealing with the 'real lives' of women, furnishes accounts of the lives of these victims from the perspective of others, and the victim herself loses control of her own existence. Merely prioritising the victim's voice as a response to this critique risks being equated with 'the truth' and producing an experiential politics that has taken us down the road to identity politics, which have surrendered any commitment to a transformative vision of the world and women's lives in that world. What is missing from the VAW position and the writings of scholars such as MacKinnon who endorse it, is an analysis of how the mechanisms of discursive engagement produce the victim subject and the accounts of violence to which she may subjected. In other words, an account of the reality of women's lives, though important, cannot adequately explain the social construction of violence and resistance to such violence. These must be examined through an understanding of how women's subjectivity and experiences of violence are partly constituted and constructed, at least in the arena of women's human rights, in and through the discourse of the VAW campaign and the foregrounding of the victim subject.

'Death by culture'[11]

The invocation of culture as a way in which to explain the different forms and shapes that violence against women takes has resulted in a reification of culture, especially the culture of people in the postcolonial/third world. In this section, I discuss, by way of example, how dowry murders have been used in the international VAW campaign as an example of the cultural form that violence against women in India/South Asia assumes. I choose the issue of dowry murder primarily because of the vast amount of research that has been conducted and the innumerable international conferences that have been held on this issue. These conferences and research efforts continue to describe dowry murder as an ancient Hindu practice and fail to reflect how this 'practice' is a thoroughly modern and contemporary phenomenon. The VAW discourse bears some responsibility for setting up dowry as a tradition that has been in existence since time immemorial and for reinforcing inaccurate and often racist cultural stereotypes.

Dowry murders in India frequently have been explained through appeals to broad assumptions about Indian women and fire, and the assertion that the burning of women is sanctioned by some kind of Indian cultural or religious tradition (Bumiller, 1990, pp 44–45). The act is cast as a cultural practice, and in turn represents the entire culture as barbaric and uncivilised in its treatment of women. Yet, as Uma Narayan explains, dowry murders are thoroughly modern in their origin (Narayan, 1997, p 85). Dowry was a practice that took place in some communities, such as Punjab, and itself was an economic transaction rather than something cultural which was sequestered in the home or private sphere (Oldenburg, 2002, pp 19–39). It has been characterised at times as a gift, at times as compensation (to the groom's family for taking on the responsibility of providing for a wife), and at times as pre-mortem inheritance, reflecting a daughter's rights to a share in the family property (Narayan, 1997, p 109). However, these explanations do not account for the expectations that the groom's family has some share in the dowry. Narayan explains that this part of the phenomenon is connected to the setting up of a market economy in India since the 1970s and the growth of a consumer-oriented culture. In some communities, this phenomenon has produced a practice known as dowry bargaining, where the groom's family has come to expect certain consumer items at the time of (and indeed for many years after) his marriage (Narayan, 1997, p 111). This expectation is compounded by demands on families to provide large dowries for their own daughters. If a woman and her parents are unable to meet these demands, which can at times take the form of threats, intimidation and even violence, then the woman is deemed expendable. As Narayan points out, there is a failure to understand that dowry violence is a part of domestic violence and that dowry murders are the most extreme form of violence that a situation of domestic violence can take in India (where the method of killing

---

11 I borrow this term from Uma Narayan who uses it in her discussion of how dowry murders are cast in first world scholarship as an age-old Indian/Hindu cultural practice, and contrasts it with research on domestic violence murders in the US, which are not similarly cast as practices of 'American culture' through references to Christianity. She argues that the 'death by culture' arguments used to explain the phenomenon of dowry murders are neither accurate nor helpful because they offer very little understanding about the nature and causes of such practices (Narayan, 1997, p 82).

more often than not is by fire). There is also an extraordinary lack of common sense displayed by some writers who attempt to understand violence against women through a cultural spectrum. For example, there is, in the literature, a curious connection made between violence and Hindu women's relationship to fire. Narayan clarifies that fire has the forensic advantage of simply getting rid of any evidence in a society where guns are not as easily available as in the US. According this mode of murder some kind of spiritual significance misses the most simple, practical explanations that are available. Narayan discusses the conflation between Sita, *sati* and dowry, and how this misrepresentation of 'Hindu culture' has created an exotic representation (Narayan, 1997, p 102). As Narayan has indicated, the cultural explanations offered both by Western and Indian scholars are of little value. She states:

> I can therefore only note with irritation the tendency of many discussions of dowry murders, both by westerners and Indians, to be sprinkled with such 'religio-cultural explanations' even when they go on to also provide the sorts of social and economic explanations I have sketched. There seems to be a fairly widespread tendency in discussions of 'Third-World issues' to engage in what I increasingly think of as a 'schizophrenic analysis', where religious and mythological 'explanations' must be woven in willy-nilly, even if they do no real 'explanatory work'. (Narayan, 1997, p 111)

The gratuitous connection between culture and violence is almost invariably brought up in relation to the third world (Jethmalani, 1995). In particular, culture is frequently invoked to explain the kind of violence experienced by women in the third world, though it is not invoked in a similar way when discussing violence against women in various Western contexts.

This perception has been continuously reinforced and reiterated by the women's human rights movement, specifically in the context of VAW campaigns. For example, Charlotte Bunch, a co-organiser of the 1993 Vienna Tribunal on Violence Against Women, stated:

> In India, more than 5,000 women are killed each year because their in-laws consider their dowries inadequate. A tiny percentage of the murderers are brought to justice ... Traditions also feed the practice of 'dowry death', in which a woman is killed because she is unable to meet her in-laws' demands for dowry. In India, over a dozen women a day die as a result of such disputes, mostly in kitchen fires designed to look like accidents. (Bunch, 1997, p 41)[12]

---

12 It is beyond the scope of this article to provide a comprehensive understanding of the problem of dowry. The simple point I wish to make is that dowry has existed in some Indian (as well as in some non-Indian) communities and is not a helpful lens through which to understand domestic violence and domestic violence fatalities in India. Such a lens obscures more than it reveals and reinforces discriminatory and racist representations of culture, especially in the global arena. Dowry murders are a new phenomenon and cannot be explained as an outcome of religious belief or practices. Accounts, other than those readily available and unexamined assumptions about culture, need to be explored to provide more adequate explanations about the cause of dowry murders and the reasons they have emerged as a relatively recent phenomenon in Indian society.

Such statements add nothing useful to the understanding of domestic violence or female fatalities in India, and they perpetuate inaccurate understandings of culture, dowry and dowry murders. The VAW campaigns are not the only international arenas in which the influential but inaccurate understandings of dowry murder are reinforced. There have been at least four Harvard University-sponsored conferences on bride-burning and dowry deaths in India.[13] The narrative about dowry murder at these conferences typically runs as follows:

> the problem of bride-burning stems from the ancient custom of giving a dowry. In India, the dowry is given to the groom's family to ensure the bride gets a good husband. The amount given as a dowry has increased over the centuries ... to the point where today the bride's family often goes into debt, sometimes for generations, in order to put together the dowry ... In some cases, the bride can become something of a hostage as the groom's family demands more and more, sometimes exceeding the original agreed upon dowry. If more money isn't forthcoming, the bride can suffer an 'accident' in the kitchen, where kerosene used for cooking can be spilled on her and lit. (Powell, 1998)

Yet these narrow cultural explanations further skew our understandings of the causes of domestic violence fatalities in India.[14] Dowry murders continue to receive attention from researchers because of their connection with the Other and their misplaced cultural association with fire, which exoticises the practice. This understanding translates into the broader public space in ways that are almost Kafkaesque. For example, *The New York Times*, which has published innumerable articles on dowry murders in India over the past few years, ran a feature titled 'Kerosene weapon of choice for attacks on wives in India'. The article provides an account of 'bride-burning' that conflates culture and domestic violence as an unquestioned fact. Dugger states:

> Typically, these women and thousands like them have been depicted as victims of disputes over the ancient social custom of dowry and as symbols of the otherness of India, a place where lovely young brides are doused with kerosene and set ablaze for

---

13 See First International Conference on Dowry and Bride-Burning in India, Harvard University, 30 September–2 October 1995; Second International Conference on Dowry and Bride-burning in India, Harvard University, November 1996; Third International Conference on Dowry and Bride-burning in India, London University, November 1997; Fourth International Conference on Dowry and Bride-burning in India, Harvard University, 5 December 1998. A similar international conference was held in New Delhi in January 2001 at the Fifth International Conference on Dowry, Bride-Burning and Son-Preference, 27–30 January 2001.

The contributors to these conferences make the common mistake of collapsing the practice of dowry with *sati*. See also Narayan, 1997, p 41 for a critique on how *sati* has also been cast as an ancient cultural practice, embedded in the notion of a good Indian wife. For an excellent historically grounded explanation and understanding of *sati*, see Sangari and Vaid, 2001, pp 383–440; Sunder Rajan, 1995, pp 15–63.

14 See Daga, AS, Jejeebhoy, S and Rajgopal, S, 'Domestic violence against women: an investigation of hospital casualty records, Mumbai', presented at the International Conference on Preventing Violence, Caring for Survivors: Role of Health Profession and Services in Violence, SNDT Women's University, Churchgate, Mumbai, India, 28–30 November 1998, www.hsph.harvard.edu/Organizations/healthnet/SAsia/suchana/0929/rh370.html (last visited 28 December 2003). This study of victims of domestic violence reveals that most of the women who were victims of domestic violence were kicked, beaten, punched, bitten, choked or strangled. Only 4% had been deliberately burned. The study and statistics suggest that a large percentage of women are beaten or abused for failing to perform domestic tasks such as cleaning or cooking adequately.

failing to satisfy the demands of their husbands' families for gold, cars and consumer goods that come as part of the marriage arrangement.[15]

The exoticism move serves to exonerate the researcher from any responsibility to investigate the issue at a deeper level, by inquiring whether there are more complex stories to tell about dowry, and about domestic violence generally, that elaborate on the material, social and institutional explanations for dowry (Oldenburg, 2002, pp 217–25). Although the author refers to studies conducted by the International Centre for Research on Women in 1999 and 2000, which point to the fact that there has been an overemphasis on dowry as a cause of abuse, and that such emphasis has distorted understandings of the problem of domestic violence, she does not use this information to dispel the myths and assumptions that surround the issue of dowry and culture in India. She simply proceeds to provide more details about kerosene deaths and the importance of dowry in a marriage arrangement in India. She does this by focusing on the account of her main protagonist Geetha, who lies ravaged from burns received from a kerosene attack by her husband and mother-in-law.

Cultural explanations ultimately neither challenge nor arrest the problem of dowry murders. They also deflect attention from the broader and more prevalent crime of domestic violence and the many other reasons why women are beaten, abused or killed in family violence situations. In fact, such explanations reproduce the native subject of colonial discourse, leaving in place the distorted image of the Indian woman in flames and of the practice as something that is both exotic and barbaric. It is necessary to explode the mystery often set up by cultural arguments that obscures the real issues concerning women's human rights. There is a need for economic, social and institutional analysis in order to make certain kinds of politics and strategies feasible in various national settings. Researchers, scholars and women's rights activists must take responsibility for understanding and informing themselves about the complexity of debates that surround issues of women's rights in the postcolonial world. They need to put to rest the search for the native subject and the essential cultural explanations that are used to exoticise the Other. A deeper and more rigorous kind of contextual analysis is essential to protect against simple, unreflective and naive strategies that invariably harm more than help those who are victims of rights violations.

At the same time there is a need to critique the narratives about culture and the native subject produced in and through the VAW discourse. These narratives produce stories about women's experiences of violence globally, and seek to incorporate these experiences into an argument that recognises such violence in terms of human rights. Yet it does not attend to the ways in which violence and subjectivity come to be constituted by the VAW discourse. Women's agency is found in their resistance to violence through rights claims. As MacKinnon has stated:

---

15 Dugger, 2000.

It [resistance] is not based on being the same as men, but on resistance to violation and abuse and second-class citizenship because one is a woman. It starts close to home. African women oppose genital mutilation. Philippine, Thai, Japanese and Swedish women organise against the sex trade. Women in Papua New Guinea and the US and workers at the United Nations resist sexual harassment. Brazilian and Italian women protest domestic battery and 'honour' as a male excuse for killing them. Indian women protest 'dowry' and 'suttee' [sic] as a male excuse for killing them ... Women everywhere rise up against rape, even in cultures where women have recently been regarded as chattel. Women in the US, Scandinavia and the Philippines resist pornography. Forced motherhood is opposed from Ireland to Germany to Bangladesh. Female infanticide and objectifying advertising are legislated against in India. (MacKinnon, 1993a, pp 101–02)

Agency is articulated as part of the will of the victim subject, rather than as a discursive effect. I do not intend to argue that women's subjectivity can only be understood in terms of discourse analysis. My argument is that in the area of women's human rights and law, subject constitution has not been sufficiently analysed in terms of how rights discourse has produced a particular understanding of the subject which is a manifestation of the pervasive discourse – power relationship. This relationship cannot be understood in terms of women's rights claims. Rather, it is a relationship that locates these struggles within broader and more complex paradigms of competing discourses. To understand women's human rights claims within this broader normative canvas assists in moving beyond the simple goal of persuading governments to recognise women as humans and sexual violence as a human rights violation. It enables us to understand the human rights terrain as a discursive terrain where competing visions and understandings of women as cultural subjects, moral subjects, wives and mothers, sexual victims and agents, are played out. Acquiring a right to fight rape is important. But a more complex analysis is required if we are concerned with women's rights victories that are based on normative assumptions about women as passive, chaste and upholders of cultural values. For example, in 1999, six years after the VAW campaign was launched in Vienna, the Indian Supreme Court issued a ruling in a rape case that reversed the decision of the High Court of Mumbai and reinstated the conviction of the accused.[16] The bench included Justice Fatima Beevi, the first woman to sit on the bench of the Indian Supreme Court. The decision was in favour of the victim, but I want to draw attention to the reasoning in this case. The court held that corroborative evidence was not required in a case of rape, except in the 'rarest of rare case'. In rape cases, a woman must be believed partly because, according to the justices, 'an Indian woman attaches the maximum importance to her chastity' and hence it follows that she would not lie about rape. The VAW campaign may have helped in securing her victory (though that is not at all clear from the decision), yet the victory did nothing to disrupt the normative assumptions about gender, sexuality and culture in India. The court stated:

---

16 *State of Maharashta v Chandraprakash Kewalchand Jain* [1990] All India Reports 658 (SC) (as discussed in Chapter 2).

Ours is not a permissive society as in some of the western and European countries. Our standard of decency and morality in public life is not the same as in those countries. It is, however, unfortunate that respect for womanhood in our country is on the decline and cases of molestation and rape are steadily growing. An Indian woman is now required to suffer indignities in different forms, from lewd remarks to eve-teasing (a form of sexual harassment), from molestation to rape. Decency and morality in public life can be promoted and protected only if we deal strictly with those who violate the societal norms. The standard of proof to be expected by the court in such cases must take into account the fact that such crimes are generally committed on the sly and very rarely direct evidence of a person other than the prosecutrix is available. Courts must also realise that ordinarily a woman, more so a young girl, will not stake her reputation by levelling a false charge concerning her chastity. (Paragraph 17)

Such reasoning prompts the question, what exactly was gained as a result of the conviction in this instance, and what exactly was lost? Women's rights claims based on sexual violence are forcing women into a regulatory apparatus that simply reinforces assumptions of gender, sexuality and culture. There is no challenge to the normative underpinnings about gender, culture and sexuality, and the historical genealogy of the relationship between culture and sexuality that inform the decision. These can only be understood when read against the impact of the colonial encounter in the 19th-century and how women's sexuality and culture were sites of contest in law between the imperial power and the political nationalists. The relationship is as complex today in the postcolonial present. Such insights and understandings provide the possibility of producing strategies that are not simply confined to formal rights violations. They also challenge the normative dimensions of the law that constitute the subject, frame our understandings of the violence to which she has been subjected, and the colonial power/knowledge complex that have implications on the constitution of the subject and culture.

The imperialist move and reproducing the 'native'

The VAW agenda is contingent on the victim subject. It is a subject that provides the common foundation on which to build a shared movement and vision. But it is also a subject that is ahistorical, invoked by scholars and activists alike to analyse issues concerning women from the lens of a universal, unemancipated subject. It has invited, at times, imperialist responses towards women in the developing world, by accentuating the difference between first world and third world women. I examine how victimisation rhetoric has reinforced an imperialist response towards women in the developing world whereby the third world subject is represented as the real, or most authentic, victim subject.

There are a large number of 'cultural' practices that have been held out as practices of violence and oppression against women – the veil, female sexual surgeries, and more recently, honour killings. Several scholars have complicated our understandings of these 'cultural' practices (Abu-Odeh, 1997; Gunning, 1992; Koso-Thomas, 1997; Lewis, 1995; Lewis and Gunning, 1998). Honour killings have become the latest item on the women's human rights agenda. There is a considerable amount of donor funding being made available to address this issue, which is being represented as a 'cultural artifact' of different societies and misrepresented in ways that are similar to dowry murders. Although it is beyond the scope of this chapter to address this issue in any detail, it is an area that deserves to be scrutinised, not exclusively from the perspective of cultural practices that discriminate against women, but also by considering how this issue has become such a popular item on feminist airwaves and conferences, in the same way that female sexual surgeries/genital mutilations were a few years ago. I emphasise that my critique does not endorse these practices nor deny that they take place. My argument is that to cast them as 'cultural' fails to provide us with the insights and information required in order to formulate effective human rights strategies. Cultural explanations are deemed sufficient even though they add little to our understanding of what is going on and why (Volpp, 1994, pp 91–93; Volpp, 1996).

The move to integrate cultural diversity into a gender analysis was intended to counter the gender essentialism that has characterised the women's human rights campaign. However, this move has been approached through the spectrum of violence, which has reinforced cultural essentialism and the construction of the Other as backward and uncivilised. The result is that international feminist legal politics has reinforced the representation of the third world woman as thoroughly disempowered, brutalised and victimised: a representation that is far from liberating for women. Moreover, in some respects it recreates the imperialist move that views the native subject as different and civilisationally backward.

The image that is produced is that of a truncated third world woman who is sexually constrained, tradition-bound, incarcerated in the home, illiterate and poor. It is an image that is strikingly reminiscent of the colonial construction of the eastern woman (Chaudhuri and Strobel, 1992; Mani, 1990). Current scholarship on trafficking and sex-work that takes place in the postcolonial world evokes such imagery. Kathleen Barry's work on trafficking, which has been extremely influential in this debate, recreates this colonial imagery (Barry, 1990). She argues that prostitution (to use her term) is violence against women and that it reduces all women to sex. She states that prostitution is *per se* a violation of women's human rights. Any woman who migrates for prostitution or to work in the sex trade is also a victim of human rights violations. Barry is a co-founder of the Coalition Against the Trafficking of Women (CATW), which exerts considerable influence on the strategies against trafficking being developed at the international level. Her work, and that of CATW, has been subjected, however, to a considerable amount of critique for their colonialist representation of women in the developing world and the imperialist character of the interventions they recommend, especially rescue and rehabilitation (Kempadoo, 1998, pp 11–12; Kempadoo, 2001; Kotiswaran, 2001, p 188).

Barry locates trafficking of women in preindustrial and feudal societies, where women are excluded from the public sphere, and contrasts them with postindustrial, developed societies, where women have been economically independent and prostitution is normalised. The consequence of this kind of argument is that women in the third world and non-Western world are represented as ignorant, illiterate, tradition-bound, domesticated and victimised. As Kamla Kempadoo states, Barry's representation of the third world woman leaves her not yet a 'whole or developed' person; instead, she resembles a minor needing guidance, assistance and help (Kempadoo, 1998, p 11). In striking contrast to this emaciated image stands the image of the emancipated Western woman; she has 'control over her income, her body and her sexuality'. The analysis is structured along the contours of colonial thought: the assumption being that women in the third world are infantile, civilisationally backward and incapable of self-determination or autonomy.

Similar assumptions justified incursions into the lives of the native and the colony. Empire would assist in the development of the civilisation until it reached a point at which it was capable of self-determination (Mehta, 1999). For example, in Chapter 2, I discuss Mehta's analysis of the relationship between 18th- and 19th-century liberal theory and liberal practice, and how this theory was used to justify colonialism – what he calls the 'inclusionary pretensions of liberal theory and the exclusionary effects of liberal practices' (Mehta, 1999, p 46). A society's treatment of women was itself used as an index of civilisational development. He discusses the work of 19th-century British liberal thinkers, including James Mill and JS Mill, who argued, albeit in markedly different ways, that political institutions such as representative democracy depended on a society having a certain state of development or maturation. The mechanism of Empire operating through colonialism was one way in which to rectify the deficiencies of the past – what has frequently been described as the civilising mission of Empire – in societies that have been stunted by history. Civilisational achievement was a necessary pre-condition for realising progress, and the stage of civilisation was the marker for determining if progressive possibilities would be within the reach of a community at any given point of time. Infantilising women in the third world reproduces the colonialist rationale for intervening in the lives of the native subject (to save those incapable of self-determination) in order to justify the rescue operations advocated by Barry and others.

Even human rights groups and pro-sex-work groups in the first world at times perpetuate this representation of the third world sex-worker as dependent and incapable of making choices. Some human rights groups are also responsible for reinforcing these divisions and feeding into the moralistic and patronising responses of governments to the issue of sex-work. Human Rights Watch has recommended that the South Asian Association for Regional Co-operation should co-operate with Interpol to stem the increase in trafficking in women between India and Nepal (Human Rights Watch, 1995, p 90). Many of the recommendations in the report are directed towards the curtailment and restriction of rights rather than their facilitation. For example, the report criticises the open border policy, which permits people to pass freely between the two countries without a passport, visa or residential permit. Instead of contextualising the strengths and limits of an open border policy in a region closed and isolated from its neighbours, Human Rights Watch states that the policy 'makes it extremely difficult for border police to check illegal activity. Traffickers and their victims move easily across the border and the onus is on individual police officers to stop and question suspicious-looking travellers' (Human Rights Watch, 1995, p 12). The report thus recommends that Nepal and India should establish a system for strictly monitoring the border to 'guard against the trafficking in women and girls, including the inspection of vehicles'. The suggestion to tighten borders as a way to control trafficking has been enthusiastically adopted by many governments around the world, especially first world governments that fear the spectre of the immigrant.

Although Human Rights Watch claims not to take a stand on prostitution or sex-work in the report, it favours the criminalisation and punishment of owners of brothels, pimps and traffickers (Human Rights Watch Women's Rights Project, 1995, p 86). It also strongly condemns 'laws and official policies and practices that fail to distinguish between "prostitutes" and victims of forced trafficking, treating the latter as criminals rather than as persons who deserve "temporary care and maintenance" in accordance with international human rights standards' and oppose 'laws and policies that punish women who engage in prostitution, but not the men who operate and profit from prostitution rings and who patronise prostitutes: such policies are discriminatory on the basis of sex' (Human Rights Watch Women's Rights Project, 1995, p 198). This statement demonstrates a concern for the human rights of victims of forced trafficking, while refusing to advocate in favour of the human rights of those engaged in prostitution or sex-work. In making a distinction between the two categories of women, Human Rights Watch makes human rights contingent on the subject's victim status.

In a similar report on cross-border trafficking between Burma and Thailand, Human Rights Watch requests donors to ensure that loans for the construction of roads and other infrastructure projects near the border take into consideration the effect of such a project on the trafficking in women (Thomas and Jones, 1993, p 159). The extraordinary assumption implicit in this recommendation is that withholding assistance for the construction of basic infrastructure will help stop cross-border traffic. Indeed, it will curtail, if not entirely stop, border-crossings, both legal and illegal.

The debate on 'voluntary prostitution' and 'coerced prostitution' is frequently displaced onto a first world and third world divide, where the sex-workers in the latter are deemed to be the primary targets of coercion, while those in the first world are deemed to have some rights as well as choices. This dichotomy denies women in the third world the right to self-determination. As Kempadoo argues, the struggle for sex-workers' rights in the postcolonial world is not essentially Western. Sex-workers have historically struggled for rights and against discrimination in the postcolonial world, and they have been involved in insurgent activities outside of their own needs and demands. Veena Oldenburg's work on the Lucknow Courtesans provides an important example of how these women occupied multiple spaces of resistance and power simultaneously (Oldenburg, 1990). In 1976, Oldenburg was examining the civic tax ledgers of 1857–77 and related records in the Municipal Corporation Office in Lucknow, a large city in northern India. Much to her surprise, she discovered in these ledgers the presence of the Lucknow Courtesans, the famous dancing and singing girls of the city who also performed sexual services. She was not only surprised to find them present in the tax records, but they were in the highest tax bracket, with the largest individual incomes of any in the city. Their names were also on lists of property confiscated by the British from these women for their involvement with the rebellion against the British in 1857. Apparently they were penalised for instigating, as well as providing, pecuniary assistance to the rebels. Their struggle was anti-colonial as much as it was pro-courtesans' rights. As Kempadoo states, '[s]ex workers struggles are thus neither a creation of a Western prostitutes' rights movement or the privilege of the past three decades' (Kempadoo, 1998, p 21).

The discourse of women in the postcolonial world as being in a state of perpetual victimisation, partly informs the artificial divide and assumption that the struggle for rights and self-determination is a first world phenomenon. This divide and the assumptions on which it is based are in part due to the fact that anti-trafficking has operated along a forced versus voluntary nexus (Doezema, 1998). As Doezema argues, the recognition of the human rights of sex-workers would entail the recognition of voluntary prostitution, and there is a discomfort in taking a position on voluntary prostitution which neither governments nor many feminists are prepared to accept. Doezema observes: 'It is not only governments who prefer saving innocent women to giving rights to guilty ones. Most feminist discourse on trafficking limits itself to the fight against "forced prostitution", the "voluntary" prostitute is condemned – she is ignored' (Doezema, 1998, p 45). The abuse that sex-workers experience at the hands of law enforcement authorities or even in the context of rehabilitation homes or in protective care remains unaddressed. Those who are already in sex-work, regardless of how they got there, are endowed with an agency and choice that remains stigmatised. If a woman continues to choose to remain in sex-work, then she deserves what she gets. It is frighteningly reminiscent of the requirement in rape laws where the victim must prove her chaste history in order to retain her credibility. The division created between forced and voluntary sex-work is further displaced onto the representation of women in the first world and third world. One way in which force is understood is through its association with poverty. The idea that women in the third world, who have no options available to them given their grinding experience of poverty, are 'forced' to go into sex-work is a pervasive one. By equating choice with wealth, and coercion with poverty, no space remains to recognise and validate the choices that women make when confronted with limited economic opportunities.

The consequence of this approach has been that international actors and state and non-state actors condemn forced sex-work in the name of promoting women's human rights. Simultaneously, these actors do nothing about promoting the human rights of sex-workers. The focus on forced sex-work as a violation of human rights leaves voluntary sex-work, or the rights of those who exist and continue to exist in sex-work, unaddressed. There is a greater possibility of securing support for the victims of trafficking than for influencing structures to respond to the human rights of sex-workers. This dichotomy has reinforced the representations of sex-work in the third world as purely exploitative and of the women as abused and victimised. As Doezema states, the 'concern for rights loses out to hysteria over victims' (Doezema, 1998, p 42). The situation of women who engage in sex-work, regardless of how they entered into this work, remains completely unaddressed by a politics that simply states that they should not be there, or that they should not do such work, and if they do choose to remain, regardless of the reasons, they deserve to be abused and violated and denied their basic human rights.

Contemporary international feminist legal politics has reproduced the subject of colonial discourse in its articulation of the exploited sex-worker in the postcolonial world. The victimised subject is based on the assumptions of the Other as incapable of self-determination, justifying rescue and rehabilitation operations, which are strikingly reminiscent of the British justification for colonisation and the establishment of the Empire. The victimised subject completely ignores the lived reality of the lives of sex-workers in these other parts of the world. As Kempadoo points out, African and Caribbean countries, 'where one can speak of a continuum of sexual relations from monogamy to multiple sexual partners, and where sex may be considered as a valuable asset for woman to trade', are completely ignored in this analysis 'in favour of specific Western ideologies and moralities regarding sexual relations' (Kempadoo, 1998, p 12). And the victimised subject has consequences on the legal strategies being formulated in the international arena and first world countries that have little to do with the rights of 'victims'.

The strategy espoused by Barry and others has invited legal interventions on issues of trafficking in the international arena that reinforce the victim status of women. These proposals fail to draw a clear distinction between consent and lack of consent when it comes to trafficking.[17] For example, the Protocol to Prevent, Suppress and Punish Trafficking in Persons, Especially Women and Children (2000), which sets out the services that governments should provide to trafficked persons, is not mandatory. This serious gap in the Protocol is partly due to government reluctance to make any commitment to provide services and protections to undocumented migrants, even if they are victims of horrific crime. Protection and assistance are provided under the terms of the Protocol primarily to advance prosecution rather than as part of a state's obligation. Numerous governments expressed the view that trafficked persons are valuable as witnesses, and therefore deserving of protection during trials, but that they should be deported immediately after the trial. This approach has implications for all women, whether they are forcefully trafficked or migrate voluntarily (even if primarily for economic need), and has specific implications for women in the third world. I elaborate on some of these implications in Chapter 5. The issue is linked to organised crime, an understanding that encourages a punitive approach to human trafficking for sexual exploitation. The emphasis is on the purpose of the movement, rather than on the violence experienced by women in the course of being transported, migrating or moving (Chuang, 1998).[18] While women are increasingly encouraged to avail

---

17 Protocol to Prevent, Suppress and Punish Trafficking in Persons, Especially Women and Children, supplementing the United Nations Convention Against Transnational Organised Crime, GA Res 55/25, UN GAOR, 55th Sess, Supp No 49, at 60, UN Doc A/55/49 (2000), contains strong law enforcement provisions and the first ever international definition of 'trafficking in persons'. Note especially Art 3, which deals with the issue of consent in relation to trafficking: '(b) the consent of a victim of trafficking in persons to the intended exploitation set forth in subparagraph (a) of this article shall be irrelevant where any of the means set forth in subparagraph (a) have been used.'

18 Recommendation of Comm of Ministers, Eur Consult Ass, 710th Meeting, Doc No R (2000) 11, urging action by member states against trafficking in human beings for the purpose of sexual exploitation.

themselves of opportunities outside the confining domestic familial arrangement, these new approaches send a strong message: women who move are invariably regarded as 'victims' of trafficking, conflating migration (legal or illegal) with trafficking, lending to the notion that the solution lay, in part, in directing governments to draft legislation to keep their people at home.[19]

As demonstrated in the context of anti-trafficking, these representations invite state responses, primarily in the area of criminal law, that perpetuate gender and cultural stereotypes. Moreover, foregrounding the state neither addresses nor accounts for the myriad of actors that have entered the international arena and become contenders in the play for power, or the impact their activities have had on women's lives (Sassen, 1996; Symposium, 1996; White, 1998). Globalisation is challenging the traditional structures of sovereignty and of state power as it simultaneously alters domestic and familial arrangements. What are the implications of these shifting alignments on women's rights, on the rights of third world women, and on feminist legal politics? These questions cannot be adequately addressed within the exclusive matrix of a state/VAW/victim-centred analysis.

The authentic victim subject and postcolonial feminist constructions

The imperialist responses and victimised representations of women in the third world have been aided by certain aspects of the politics of feminists in the postcolonial world. I discuss specifically the example of India, where feminism has set itself up as anti-Western in order to meet the charge of anti-nationalism. This authenticity move, which is a symptom of postcolonialism, has been played out partly through the victim subject. Ironically, this move feeds into the representation of third world women and the victim subject that dominates feminist legal politics in the international arena.

The prerequisite of authenticity has been integral to the way in which feminism has operated during the modern period in India. This feature is partly the result of the fact that women's issues were integral to the nationalist struggle. In late 19th-century India, women did not play an obvious role in the independence struggle or resistance to colonial rule, but they were the sites of contestations between political nationalists, social reformers and the colonial power. Law was one site at which the meaning and place of certain cultural practices performed by or pertaining to women in the Hindu tradition were fought out (Chatterjee, 1993; Mani, 1998; Sarkar, 1996). The British colonial power used the position of women to legitimise colonial rule by pointing to extreme cultural practices as evidence of the 'barbarity' of Indian society and of its resulting need for colonial intervention. Social reformers sought legal changes by the colonial administration to improve the status of Indian women,

---

19 Eg, the US Act 2000, 22 USC ss 7101–7110, noting especially ss 7106 and 7107.

in particular to eliminate social practices such as *sati*, the prohibition on widow remarriage and child marriages (as discussed in Chapter 3). Their interventions were by no means progressive, that is, they were not based on an assumption that women ought to be equal to men. The interventions were protectionist and promoted the image of the ideal Hindu woman as the ideal wife and mother (Kosambi, 2000). The political nationalists opposed these moves by social reformers. They challenged the authority of the law, regarding it as a colonial tool that should not be used to intervene in the domestic sphere. This place was projected as the pure space of 'Indian culture', and had to be protected from colonial intervention. They were not only challenging the legitimacy of engaging with the colonial state through law reform, but were also challenging the colonial power's authority to define Hindu culture and tradition.

In the early part of the 20th-century, women began to participate in the struggle for independence. The turn of the century also witnessed the 'resurgence of Hinduism' and marked a 'clear ideological shift' from the social reform debates of the 19th-century. The Western and 'alien' ideas of the social reformers actually came into disrepute as the political nationalists sought to resurrect the ideals of the Hindu past. Indian womanhood gradually became the embodiment of nationalism, as the nation came to be constructed as a divine mother and as mother India, and women became 'the mothers of the realm'.

Nationalism and feminism in the postcolonial moment

In the postcolonial period, both nationalism and feminism took on a different meaning. Nationalism was a crucial mobilising discourse at the time of Independence and had a liberatory and emancipatory potential in so far as it was directed against colonial rule. In postcolonial India, however, the state retains its anti-imperialist stance, but this has not necessarily operated in a liberating fashion (Chatterjee, 1993). The nation-state has come into existence, but today nationalism is playing a conservative rather than a progressive role. The negative dimensions of nationalism are baring themselves. The exclusive focus of Indian nationalism a half century ago was the British colonial power. The sub-continent was otherwise characterised by a vast amount of difference and diversity. Today, these differences are asserting themselves in the forms of separatist movements, regional movements and other cleavages along the lines of gender, caste and religion. It is becoming increasingly difficult for a nationalist ideology to keep all of these fragments together.

Religion emerged in the struggle for Independence as the site for the creation of two independent nations. Religion is re-emerging in the postcolonial present as a central attribute of nationalism and national identity. It is not possible to speak about nationalism today without speaking about religious identity and religious community. Hindu nationalism is emerging as the new nationalism of the Indian state, and the most vociferous exponent of this new nationalism is the Hindu Right. In the contemporary period, this new nationalism is a complex phenomenon. As discussed in Chapter 2, the Hindu Right is establishing its ideology at one level through liberal rights discourse, that is, through the discourse of secularism, free speech, and equality. Their strategy at another level involves an emphasis on religion as the real basis of national identity and is therefore quite reactionary. Religion is being deployed as the overarching category to create one people and one nation, and to create a common enemy: the Muslim. The new Hindu nationalism is not concerned with the rights of women. Its agenda for women fits into its overall ideology of creating a Hindu Raj (Hindu rule) or the establishment of a Hindu state in India.

The emergence of the Hindu Right provides the backdrop for the contemporary women's movement in India. The contemporary movement has shifted its focus from women as mothers of the nation to women's individual rights. It has once again sought a redefinition of tradition and gender, this time by revealing and challenging the violence and oppression that women experience. These efforts, like those of the social reformers of the 19th-century, have met with considerable resistance from powerful discourses (Kapur and Cossman, 1996, p 71). The primacy of women's roles as wives and mothers is strongly asserted, and any challenge to these traditional roles within the family are met with cries of 'religion in danger' and of 'the family under attack'. Feminists have had to contend with the fact that the Hindu Right has been appropriating its issues and strategies, as I illustrate later in this section using the examples of beauty pageants and sex-work.

Feminism in India continues to have a tenuous relationship with nationalism and has been cast as Western and imperialist at several historical moments (Radhakrishnan, 1992). Indeed, feminism has been charged with being a product of decadent Western capitalism; [and] that it is based on a foreign culture of no relevance to women in the third world (Jayawardena, 1986, p 2). For this reason, feminists have had to project themselves as nationalist and anti-Western (as discussed in Chapter 3). They have adamantly denied allegations of being Western, and sought to establish a distinctively Indian feminism: the 'authentic Indian feminist subject'. This distinct subject has been constructed on essentialist notions of the West and Western feminism. The search for the authentic subject has been a cornerstone of feminist politics search for legitimacy in the contemporary Indian context. The unreflective embrace of nationalism, by at least some significant sections of the feminist movement, has led to troubling and contradictory results. On several issues that have been characterised as women's rights issues, Indian feminists have sought to distinguish their position from Western feminism – not only in the hope of being heard, but also because of a genuine belief that these issues are different. Two recent examples where this position has been very starkly presented are beauty contests and sex-work.

Beauty pageants and fashion shows have emerged as zones of cultural contests over the past few years. In November 1996, when the Miss World beauty contest was held in the southern city of Bangalore in India, many women's groups opposed the holding of the pageant on the grounds that it degraded and commodified women and was vulgar. Some of them countered the pageant space by proposing to hold a 'Miss Dowry Victim' pageant that would represent the true plight of Indian women in the country. According to one pamphlet circulated by a large number of women's groups in Delhi that opposed the staging of the pageant, 'Beauty contests foster a false notion of "free choice" which obscures the reality of violence against women' (Kapur and Ghosh, 1996, pp 11–12). The Indian woman as victim came to be equated with recognising the distinctness of the Indian nation – the idea that women in India were different from Western women. The 'real Miss India' was represented as someone totally different from the beauty queen. 'Every four minutes a crime is committed against women in India. Every 47 minutes a woman is raped. Every 44 minutes a woman is abducted. Every 17 minutes women are killed for dowry' (Kapur and Ghosh, 1996). In contrast to the agency implicitly ascribed to the Western woman, the Indian woman was represented as a suffering subject, impoverished and violated. The victim image was the message conveyed to women in India, as well as to international audiences, in order to secure legitimacy for Indian feminists.

These groups came to share an uncomfortable platform with different segments of the Hindu Right, who opposed the pageant on the grounds that it was against Indian cultural values (especially the swimsuit competition). The Hindu Right regarded the swimsuit competition as extremely offensive as it revealed women's bodies in a fashion that was alien to 'our culture'. Similarly, in denouncing the Miss World beauty pageant, the chairperson of the National Commission of Women invoked Indian cultural values. The Commission also focused cultural indignation on the swimsuit competition. This part of the pageant was ultimately flown out of India and held in Mauritius (where ostensibly it was not against Mauritian cultural values). The most extreme form of protest came from women members of the Hindu Right who threatened to crash the pageant and immolate themselves should the pageant be held.

Between 1996 and 2000, Indian women have been crowned beauty queens of the Miss World pageant, Miss Universe pageant and Miss Asia-Pacific pageant. The response from some feminists continues to be to deride these victories as further examples of the commodification of women and of the impact of Westernisation and globalisation. These statements constantly converge with those of the Hindu Right. In April 1998, Hindu-Right-supported student groups took control of the University of Lucknow, located in the northern state of Uttar Pradesh, to declare a blanket ban on fashion shows and beauty pageants on campus. The government also banned the screening of the Miss Universe beauty pageant, at a time when Sushma Swaraj, the 'moral police woman' of the previous BJP-led government at the centre, was the Information and Broadcasting Minister. It was contended that such contests were not in keeping with the profile of India's national image. Shortly after Priyanka Chopra won the title of Miss World 2000, Rajnath Singh, the Chief Minister of her home state, Uttar Pradesh, banned the holding of beauty pageants and fashion shows in the state. He condemned them as a form of Western imperialism that was eroding Indian cultural values and degrading Indian womanhood. According to Singh, beauty contests were part of a 'larger game plan to build a massive cosmetics market in India'. He further stated: 'Beauty contests are nothing more than exhibition of the female body and this is extremely unfortunate. Real beauty lies in one's intellect. I believe that beauty is God's gift and there is no need to put it up for public display.'[20]

---

20 Pradhan, 2000.

Sex-work has been another area in which Indian feminists have tried to distinguish themselves from Western feminism. The arguments of some feminist groups have assumed that sex-work in the North or West is an occupational choice (emphasising thereby the agency of Western women, albeit in a disapproving, not supportive manner), but that in India women enter the trade as a consequence of poverty. In March 2001, some groups called for a ban of the first International Sex Workers Carnival held in Calcutta to celebrate the lives and struggles of sex-workers in Asia, and to demand that their basic human rights to mobility, family and work be respected. Opponents of the carnival argued that sex-work in South Asia was a form of exploitation and largely a condition of poverty, and that those who were participating were simply promoting sex tourism.[21] This position has been supported by a large number of feminists and women's groups in India and South Asia.

For example, Ruchira Gupta, who produced the film *Selling of Innocence*, on trafficking in India and Nepal, argues that in America, pro-choice arguments are used by feminists to make pro-sex-work arguments. However, she states that in rich countries 'they understand and manage globalisation differently from people in poor countries'. In poor countries, 'when people do choose to be trafficked or get into prostitution, they're choosing it as a survival strategy for a very limited period of time, under tremendous pressure – economic pressure, pressure from the family, from children crying for food, husbands beating up wives, and no income in the village' (Shifman, 2003, p 128). As Donna Fernandes, activist with a Bangalore-based women's group, has argued: 'Hence ... western women may opt for prostitution as an occupational choice ... On the other hand, most Asian women are compelled into prostitution by poverty and deception (in the form of marriage or promises of finding her employment)' (Kotiswaran, 2001, pp 188–89).

Such critiques are located on an East/West binary (as discussed in Chapter 3). The West is set up as revolving around the needs of the individual. In contrast, Asia or the East is community based. The critique assumes that, although choice is possible in the West, economic oppression in Asia is so all- encompassing that the very possibility of choice or agency is negated. Secondly, the critiques are also based on certain cultural assumptions. The culture of Asia is said to be more communitarian, as opposed to the culture of the West, which is more individualistic. Asian women are set up in opposition to Western women: the Asian woman is cast as chaste and vulnerable to exploitation, in contrast to the promiscuous Western woman who is ruled by the (im)morality of the market. The discourse of feminists in this instance is embedded in the idea of an authentic Indian subject and the construction of the woman in sex-work as a victim of the (Western) market. The victim status conferred on women by some postcolonial feminist positions becomes almost indistinguishable from the discourse of the purity of the nation and the

---

21 *Hindustan Times*, 2001; Mukherjee, 2001.

preservation of Indian womanhood that characterised the nationalist discourse in the late 19th- and early 20th-centuries. It is a status that invites the state to resort to the criminal law to address women's issues and, more significantly, coincides with the agenda of the Hindu Right, whose position on women's rights is very different.

The Hindu Right's official position on women is filled with commitments to equality and pledges to restore women to a position of equality with men which is accepted as part of the Indian tradition. Their discourse of equality is fused with a more specifically revivalist discourse that seeks to reclaim a glorious and ancient past. The objective of equality of the more moderate voice in the Hindu Right that is the BJP, is the restoration of women to the position they ostensibly enjoyed in a 'golden age'. It is critical to understand the Hindu Right's approach to equality in order to understand its approach to women's rights. According to the BJP, men and women are equal but not necessarily the same. Since women and men are not the same, then according to the logic of formal equality, they do not have to be treated equally. Thus, the Hindu Right is able to invoke the discourse of equality while at the same time undermine any real entitlement to equality by stating that women are different. The question remains of what equality means in the discourse of the Hindu Right. The answer lies in the BJP's policies and statements on women.

The BJP policy on women often focuses on the roles in the family that have traditionally been allocated to women according to the sexual division on labour. For example, healthcare, particularly maternal and natal care, is taken up, as are sanitation facilities for poor, rural and slum women. Policies that reinforce women's role in the family as mothers and wives are supported as part of women's equality rights. In so doing, the Hindu Right reinforces the assumption of natural and essential differences between women and men. Women are mothers and wives – they are different – and these differences must be honoured and protected. Women are self-sacrificing and dutiful and in turn they are to be protected from any indignity, harm or violence.

The focus on the authentic victim subject triggered a host of law reform proposals by the previous BJP-led government that were consistent with its policies towards women. The government declared the year 2001 to be the 'Year of Women's Empowerment'. They proposed to reform a number of laws in order to promote women's empowerment. However, a close analysis of this policy reveals that most of the proposed law reforms concerned the criminal law. These included strengthening the punishment for giving dowry; the prevention of *sati*, trafficking in women, prostitution and obscenity; and the introduction of a law on domestic violence.[22] Even the proposed sexual harassment law was to be brought within the framework of the criminal law. Although many of these proposals touched on issues that concerned women, there were no corresponding proposals to promote women's civil rights, mobility, freedom, bodily integrity or substantive equality. While there are some tentative proposals to reform some of the laws of religious minority communities that discriminated against women, these strategies were not

---

22 Department of Women and Child Development, 2001b; *The Indian Express*, 2001.

designed to foreground women's rights and interests. Rather, they reinforced the law and order agenda of the Hindu Right, their paternalistic approach to women's issues, and their communalising agenda.

The treachery of 'authenticity'

By entering onto the terrain of authenticity, feminists have headed down a treacherous path. Indian feminists' adoption of this anti-Western rhetoric, although often a dictate of political realities, is not necessarily progressive. Moreover, the idea of an 'authentic victim subject' in India operates along two assumptions: that Indian women are a monolithic victim group who are all similarly oppressed, and that there is an essentialised Indian culture and Indian woman. The result is that Indian feminism has essentialised the very category of gender that it, along with others, critiqued Western/first world/white feminists for producing. The position of Indian feminists has resulted in the exclusion of other subjugated identities. Some Indian feminists have also essentialised culture by setting up 'Western culture' against 'non-Western culture' (Narayan, 1998). The essentialising of discourses that have presented such difficulties for the women's movement during the colonial period has produced contradictory results for feminists in postcolonial India. The fact that feminists have come to inhabit a highly contradictory space is not in and of itself problematic, since many spaces feminism inhabits are contradictory. The problem arises when that space is inhabited unreflectively.

The failure to reflect on the contradictory nature of nationalism has led to a host of problems. First, the denial of agency, as illustrated by the responses to the beauty pageant and the issue of sex-work, has been articulated by feminists in and through the discourses of nationalism and authenticity. A consequence of such arguments is the construction of a pure place of authenticity. This is remarkably similar to the strategies of the religious right. The contemporary discourse of the Hindu Right around women's rights is based on the idea of 'modern but not Western'. This idea relies heavily on the language of tradition: of returning women to their rightful place of honour and respect that they enjoyed as wives and mothers in some long-lost ancient Hindu past. Their discourse of tradition is a selective and thoroughly modern reinterpretation of the past.

The legitimisation of the Indian feminist position has also demanded a repudiation of the West (in particular the Western feminist), the polarisation of Western versus Indian feminism, and the search for the authentic subject. This is troubling because it falls all too easily within the more traditional relationship between women and nationalism, and is not clearly distinguishable from the contemporary discourse of the Hindu Right on women's rights. The construction of the authentic victim subject position, constantly in opposition to imperialism or the West, seems to be critical to the legitimacy of Indian feminism. As illustrated by the beauty pageant and sex-work examples, the subject is distinguished from the West and the Western feminist subject through her position of victimisation. The closer the association between the Indian feminist and this victim subject (who is projected as the *real* Indian woman or the authentic subject), the greater the legitimacy for feminists and feminism to operate in India. Yet, this subject has not produced a liberatory politics for women. Indeed, its existence has reinforced both a protectionist position of the state towards women and the women's rights agenda of the Hindu Right. The denunciation of beauty queens or sex-workers does not create a space for a more complex politics; it simply eliminates such experiences and prioritises the victim as the true symbol of Indian feminism and Indian womanhood. In negating women's agency, the complex negotiations and the multiple subjectivities of women are also eradicated. How can we articulate a space for women's multiple subjectivities? What is to be done with Malleswari, who won the bronze medal (the only medal for India) at the Sydney Olympics in 2000 in women's weightlifting?[23] Or with Lara Datta, who won the Miss Universe pageant in 2000, and has no reluctance to speak explicitly about sex, safe sexual practices, and the issue of AIDS? Or the sex-workers who state, 'We want bread. We also want roses!'[24] Where do we locate these women in a politics that operates along the strict binaries of victim/agent, East/West, first world/third world, or the West and 'the Rest'?

I have discussed how the victim subject informs women's human rights discourse in the international context in ways that reinforce gender and cultural essentialism. I suggest that in order to partly avoid these traps, the engagement with human rights involves more than simply a claim to formal equal rights. We need to unpack how feminist arguments contribute to the very construction of the subject, reinforce the regulatory project, and reinforce normative understandings about the gendered subject, sexuality and culture. I have also examined some of the rather reactionary, and unanticipated, consequences of promoting the victim subject. Regardless of whether it is a product of the dominance feminism of the West or of the authenticity position of Indian feminism, this subject has become central to the women's human rights movement. The victim subject has become a decontextualised, ahistorical subject, disguised superficially as the dowry victim, as the victim of honour killings, or as the victim of trafficking and prostitution. The subject is no longer distinctly Indian or European, let alone Eastern or Western. Oddly enough, this subject has created the basis for an alliance in the human rights arena between Western feminists and Indian feminists, amongst others, in their pursuit for the recognition of women's human rights.

In the context of India, I have argued that the very thing that represents the authentic subject for Indian women – the non-Western subject – bears an uncanny resemblance to the basis of the alliance between Indian women and Western women in the international arena. West and non-West, in effect, become one in the victim – discrete, and yet not. There is a convergence of Indian women's realities with some

---

23 The event was the women's weightlifting event in the 69 kilogram category. *Times of India*, 2000; *The Indian Express*, 2000.
24 Slogan of the International Sex Workers Rights poster produced for the International Sex Workers Carnival, Calcutta, 3–6 March 2001.

notion of global sisterhood, but this has not provided them with an effective or distinct voice in the area of women's human rights.

Peripheral subjects, resistance and power eruptions

It is imperative to articulate a subject position in the domestic and international human rights arena that takes into account the subject's complex and contradictory locations in relation to different arenas of power. If a more progressive movement for women's rights is to develop within the arena of human rights, it is necessary to renegotiate and refashion new ways of legally and politically intervening and articulating women's concerns. This requires at least three major theoretical and practical shifts. First, it is important to recognise and centre women's multiple historical, cultural and socially determined subjectivities instead of falling back on universalised assumptions about women's realities and their subject position. Secondly, feminist legal politics needs to foreground the peripheral subject if any significant normative shifts or disruptions are to be brought about. Thirdly, in recognising and working with the peripheral subject, there is a need to understand resistance as more than simply a claim for rights, to ensure against producing a narrative that merely describes the multiple ways in which even women on the periphery are subjugated. It is this aspect which will provide the critical normative challenges which are essential in our engagements with human rights.

First, I endorse the suggestion of other scholars to focus on a more complex notion of the multi-dimensional subject as an important way to shift attention from an exclusive focus on the victim subject. This focus will assist in disrupting the linear narrative produced by the VAW campaigns and complicate the binary of the West and 'the Rest'. At a practical level, this strategy will complicate the narrative and guard against cultural and gender essentialism that characterises women's human rights campaigns and postcolonial feminist legal politics. For example, at the 1993 Vienna Tribunal on Violence Against Women, the personal testimonial of Perveen Martha, a woman from Pakistan, focused on the story of how she was set on fire when her husband doused her with kerosene in February 1984. The listener was left with the impression that the 'burning of brides' is a feature of 'Asian' culture. The framing of Perveen's life through the lens of violence and the mechanism of personal testimonial did not disrupt the gender and cultural assumptions present in the audience's imagination. What was marginalised in the telling of the story was the fact that Perveen was a Christian who had been married for several years and had several children who were no longer in her custody. Even in the transcript of her testimony, Perveen's broader story as a divorced Christian woman and parent is not in the foreground. The script focuses on the burning incident that took place in February 1984, even though she had been subjected to physical abuse prior to this incident. Constructing the story around the incident of burning is an exoticism move that plays into cultural essentialism and provides little insight into the reality of Perveen's life. Her husband had divorced her and she was struggling in court to secure maintenance and the custody of her children (whom she had not seen in five years). It is important to understand her multiple subject positions and location as a divorced Christian woman, at a time when the military dictatorship of General Zia-ul-Haq in Pakistan was clamping down on women's rights generally.

The burning episode is only part of the story. Highlighting the burning incident reinforces her victim status and a cultural stereotype. It excludes significant portions of her story as well as the broad array of human rights that are implicated. The fact that her rights to custody and maintenance were restricted because of her religious identity as a Christian, and not simply because of her gender identity, prompts a deeper understanding and a more sharply tuned response to her situation and her struggle. Her location as a divorced, Christian woman in a Muslim-dominated, non-democratic Pakistan, where strict laws against rape, adultery and fornication have been enacted, is critical to understanding her story.[25] These facts are also material to understanding the intersections between the politics of her struggle in court and the social context of her family and religious community, where she was both a marginalised and resistive subject, and not exclusively a victim of violence.[26]

However, the focus on multiple subjectivities is not in and of itself sufficient. My second point is that it is also necessary to focus on the subject situated at the periphery, as she has the power to bring about normative disruptions. For example, I have consciously highlighted the sex-worker in this essay. She is a 'speaking' and 'animated' subject who can and does make choices for economic empowerment, which includes migration. She is an unbounded subject who exists outside the supervision of the family. The sex-worker intensifies concerns about the threat to the family as well as to the purity of the nation. Her movement challenges the anti-trafficking regime being advocated as the new international regulatory mechanism for ostensibly protecting the human rights of women. She exposes how this new regime curtails mobility and economic opportunities for women and other migrants, and intensifies the moral surveillance of women's sexual conduct. It is a regime that does not necessarily restrict the number of women who are moving or migrating, but simply makes it more dangerous for women to cross borders. It is not directed towards protecting the rights of women who are in the sex industry or who migrate, albeit illegally, for purposes other than sex-work.

The sex-worker brings about several disruptions. Her claims to rights as a parent, entertainer, worker and sexual subject disrupt dominant sexual and familial norms. In postcolonial India, her repeated performances also challenge and alter dominant cultural norms. From her peripheral location, the sex-worker brings about a normative challenge by negotiating her disclaimed or marginalised identity within more stable and dominant discourses, that is, the way in which the intersection of the dominant sexual, familial and market ideologies structure her experience of the

---

25 Another speaker was Alpana Chandola, who was described as a 'survivor of dowry violence'. However, her testimony revealed that she was also a survivor of domestic violence, beaten and abused from the first day of her marriage. Focusing on the dowry demand deflected attention from other reasons for the violence that she experienced. Describing Chandola's experience of violence through the lens of dowry closed off a more complex socio-economic analysis of her experience and reinforced cultural stereotypes about how women in India experience domestic violence.

26 The theory of intersectionality was developed primarily by black feminist thinkers who explored the ways in which categories of race and gender intersect and suggested that black women's oppression was not simply racial oppression added to gender oppression: Crenshaw, 1991; Harris, 1990. Postcolonial feminists have also examined the extent to which gender intersects with colonial understandings of the 'native' subject: Spivak, 1988. For a more general discussion on the theory of multiple subjectives: see Powell, 1997.

world. By renegotiating and occupying dominant sexual, familial and cultural norms, she brings out the ambivalence of these norms. She simultaneously creates the potential for a more inclusive politics, opening up a space for subjects who have remained unaddressed in the women's human rights politics as it has emerged, such as single parents, other sexual minorities, and religious and cultural minorities.

The idea that the postcolonial sexual subaltern subject can consent to sex-work, and that she may consent to move or enter into a consensual arrangement with someone who arranges her transport from one port to another, free from coercion or violence, is also challenging at a normative level. Women from the third world can and do consent to commercial sex, and thus challenge sexual and cultural normativity, as well as the imperialist representations of women in the third world that have come to inform the international women's rights agenda as well as the policies of first world governments. Women from the third world move to the first world to engage in sex-work and other practices, such as domestic labour, thus challenging the dominant assumptions that inform both the contemporary international legal regime as well as feminist legal politics, which assumes that she is dragged, beaten, forced, kidnapped or abducted into this work. Women can and do choose to move and work in the sex industry, and even find clandestine means by which to enter into another country, searching for other economic opportunities if legal ones are not open to them. She is a market actor who understands the economic and other opportunities available to her in other parts of the world. As a market actor, she challenges the oversimplistic and patronising assumption that women in the third world enter the sex trade because of conditions of poverty, which belies the question why all poor women do not opt for sex-work. They can choose to cross borders in search of better economic opportunities, as do, for example, educated middle class graduates from the third world. As Jamie Chuang has argued, the focus on the normative question:

> ... of whether a woman should be able to consent to trafficking and prostitution overlooks the empirical fact that women actually do consent to these practices, and moreover, risks neglecting important descriptive facts regarding the quality of a woman's consent to these practices ... [I]n the case of a woman forced into prostitution who was deceived by a trafficker's lure of an attractive waitressing job abroad, or a woman who intended to engage in self-regulated prostitution and found herself in a debt-bondage situation, the source of exploitation might be misinformation or debt-bondage, respectively. Deeming consent irrelevant to the women's victimisation also risks portraying women as perennial victims of false consciousness, incapable of making autonomous choices regarding their means of migration and employment. (Chuang, 1998, pp 84–85)

The fact that women cross borders, and ought to be able to cross borders, has been conflated with the purpose of their journey, rather than with the conditions under which they cross borders. Recent literature in the area of international human rights continues to invoke the trope of poor, third world women's bodies, that is, the body of the third world subject exclusively as a victim, reinforcing arguments against sex-work *per se* as inherently exploitative, rather than supporting the rights of these women to move. Little attention is being given to the coercive and abusive practices that women may be subjected to in the course of movement, including a lack of interrogation of the racist, sexist and 'neo-colonial' anti-trafficking laws being advocated by first world governments (and reproduced in some feminist literature). These initiatives harm more women than they help and reinforce stereotypes of the third world as barbaric in the treatment of its women.

The beauty queens in the postcolonial world are also peripheral subjects who might be centred in our analysis. They have provoked serious opposition from state actors, religious conservatives and some feminists, and at the same time have opened up the space for Others to redefine the pageant space and understandings of beauty, culture, gender and the sexed body. As the example of the Miss World 1996 pageant illustrates, these subjects are implicated in human rights discourse because of the opposition – and indeed, the violations – they have encountered. The response of feminists and the religious right, who together threatened to disrupt the pageant and force the participants off the pageant stage in Bangalore, created a law and order problem in the city as well as a harassment threat to the participants. In the course of the disruption of the cultural spaces inhabited by the beauty contestants, they were denied recognition of their rights.

Another example would be the migrant woman – the travelling subject, whose very movement across borders, whether legal or illegal, challenges normative arrangements of gender, sex and culture. I elaborate on the implications of such cross-border movements in Chapter 5. Through her cross-border transgressions, she brings to the fore women's ability to choose to move, and belies cultural assumptions that imagine women, particularly third world women, as confined to the home in an oppressive familial and cultural space. Through the course of travel and the obstacles she encounters as she crosses borders, she exposes the shape-shifting of culture and the anti-migrant impact of recent anti-trafficking and immigrant legislation at the international, regional and domestic levels. She is a market actor, a traveller and a cultural importer, who brings an understanding about globalisation to the metropolis.

My third argument is that it is important to illuminate the moments of resistance of peripheral subjects. This involves more than simply viewing rights claims in and of themselves as acts of resistance. The claims of peripheral subjects incorporate a challenge to the normative assumptions about gender, sexuality and culture that inform human rights. For example, any claims to equality brought by a subject such as Malleswari, the female weightlifter, would challenge both gender and cultural essentialism. Malleswari's location as a working class, married woman, her body, and her commitment to weightlifting can provide a serious challenge to the emaciated, linear image of the third world woman that has colonised feminist imagination. Another example once again is the sex-worker in postcolonial India, who has been projected primarily in terms of her experience of victimisation and violence which ignore her struggle for, and claims to, rights in her multiple capacities. At the first and second International Sex Workers Carnival, the rights claimed by the sex-workers included the rights to: work; safe and non-discriminatory health care; mobility within as well as across national borders; keep their children; and the demand for recognition of their families as legitimate and entitled to state benefits. Identifying these claims as moments of resistance validates the sex-worker's agency, challenges normative assumptions about gender, culture and sexuality without invalidating the harms to which she may have been subjected. The claim for rights in these different guises amounts to more than a claim to equal treatment. The subject normatively challenges the legal and non-legal responses from state and non-state actors, including feminists and non-governmental organisations that treat her exclusively as a victim in need of rescue and rehabilitation or as a criminal to be incarcerated. Such responses ignore the fact that she is a woman, a worker and a parent with fewer legal rights than other women, workers and parents. She is left without any tools with which to fight violence, exploitation or discrimination.

A more complicated example of resistance by a peripheral subject involves the *hijra* or transsexual. Often referred to as eunuchs, when these subjects join regular models on the catwalk at the designer fashion show in Lucknow, a large metropolitan city in northern India, they rework the normative framework of femininity and immediately challenge any effort to cast culture in an essentialist mould or set it up in opposition to rights.[27] By participating in the fashion space as eunuchs, not as men or women, they denaturalise the normative framework of gender.[28] They also disrupt cultural norms that would deny this subject any visibility. A similar argument can also be applied to *hijras* from lower or working classes, who have mobilised to organise a celebration of their sexuality within, not in opposition, to their cultural context. The Hijra Habba (celebration of transsexuals) in Bangalore in early 2003 represented a spectacular array of sexualities that are rarely visible in the public arena. By exposing the diversity of the sexual sub-culture, the festival challenged the static and hermetically sealed representations of sexuality by the Hindu Right, some feminists and even human rights groups, and also challenged the confining and monolithic category of the 'global gay' that is

---

27 Manjul, 2000.

28 The disruption of the pageant space is not necessarily confined to the postcolonial world: see Butler's discussion of *Paris Is Burning*, and the practice of vogueing and theatrics among poor black and hispanic drag queens in Harlem and Brooklyn (Butler, 1993, pp 121–42); *Beautiful* (Destination Films, 2000), challenging the rule that mothers cannot be beauty queens; *Miss Congeniality* (Castle Rock Entertainment, 2000), where the main protagonist, an undercover FBI agent, is sent to secure the pageant space from a terrorist threat, but proves incapable of conforming to the cast-iron gender mould and performance required by the pageant. All of these representations move beyond the Barbie doll images of the beauty queen and are equally challenging of cultural and gender essentialism.

emerging in the international human rights arena (Phillips, 2000). These performances are not transformative, but placing the eunuch on the catwalk, or as a participant in a beauty contest in the Hijra Habba, represents an appropriation of a cultural space.[29] It also brings to the fore the material realities and differences within these different sexual subgroups. While the peripheral location of these subjects exposes at least one basis on which legal and economic entitlements and distributions operate, class advantage can have a distinct impact on the level of vulnerability to human rights violations of these sexual subjects (People's Union for Civil Liberties, 2003). At a normative level, in each location, dominant meanings are challenged as the subject blurs the line 'between that hegemonic call to normatising gender and its critical appropriation' (Butler, 1993, p 127). And at the international level, these spaces and subjects challenge cultural and gender stereotypes that have come to inform the politics of the women's human rights movement.

Foregrounding the resistance of the peripheral subject scatters hegemonic understandings of culture and gender that are reproduced at the international and domestic levels. The reproductions are invariably essentialist and invite imperialist, conservative or protective interventions. However, the claims made by the peripheral subject may not necessarily be successful or even heard. In fact, the more marginalised and subversive her politics, the more reluctant the state will be to cede her any ground. In particular, it will be reluctant to grant her human rights. Carol Smart has argued that the more conformist feminists are in their legal argument (by resorting to the language of individual rights, motherhood or sexual morality), the more likely they are to succeed. Thus, she says, the strength of radical or cultural feminists is that they deploy common sense notions, such as sexual and gender difference, in ways that seek to rearrange them rather than to challenge how we think about these categories (Smart, 1995, p 110). The success or failure of the peripheral subject is contingent on the interplay of dominant familial, cultural and sexual ideologies and the particular claims she puts forward. She may fail because of social, economic or historical constraints and oppositions. Her claims will not redefine gender or even culture instantaneously. Feminist efforts to destabilise dominant meanings have also encountered real oppositions firmly inscribed in dominant institutions and structures. Such oppositions cannot be countered through a single engagement. Feminist engagements with human rights require a constant and careful consideration of the way in which feminist claims may be

---

29 At the level of popular culture, such challenges have been posed by the representation of drag queens in the opening sequences of the 1995 film *To Wong Foo, Thanks For Everything, Julie Newmar* (Amblin Entertainment, 1995), where Patrick Swayze and Wesley Snipes prepare themselves to participate in the annual transgendered beauty pageant by applying makeup and wearing flamboyant outfits. Their performance inscribes the pageant space with notions of beauty, gender and sexuality that challenge the traditional pageant space. The performance is still limited, however, and does not necessarily lead to liberation from hegemonic constraints. See Judith Butler's discussion of the challenges posed by Venus Xtravaganza, who is represented in *Paris is Burning* as a transgendered woman who has an added 'desire to become a whole woman, to find a man and have a house in the suburbs with a washing machine' (Butler, 1993, pp 223–42). She does not appear to rework the heterosexual framework, indicating that the question of denaturalisation of gender and sexuality may not lead to a complete reworking of heteronormativity.

transformed through the powerful and complex interplay between dominant social relations and competing discourses. However, centring the peripheral subject and her moments of resistance is a disruptive move, destabilising universalised and naturalised claims made about women, poor women, third world women, or the culture from which these women emerge. The production and subjugation of identities are processes that go on simultaneously through legal engagement. The victim subject counters the atomised, ahistorical subject of liberal rights discourse, but it is not sufficiently disruptive of naturalised and universalised assumptions about gender and culture. The challenge is to disrupt and dispute the naturalness and originality of the victim subject.

Conclusion

The victim subject has highlighted that women suffer violence in the home and that such violence constitutes a human rights violation that is the responsibility of states to prevent or remedy. This is a very significant victory. Nonetheless, the creation and reinforcement of a victim subject has not necessarily proved to be empowering for women. In fact, there are hidden normative and regulatory traps that might result in a setback to the broader recognition of women's human rights. Nor is it sufficient to argue that rights claims by victim subjects constitute acts of resistance and are informed by a 'woman's point of view'. The rights claims by victims of sexual violence, though important, have in part constructed the terms on which women can claim and enjoy human rights: through reinforcing gender and cultural essentialism and without disrupting the normative assumptions about gender, sexuality and culture that inform these claims. The VAW campaign and the focus on the victim subject have led to a proliferation of rights for women, but it has not resolved the problem of gender subordination. Indeed MacKinnon was correct to point out in her early work that rights claims would serve to reinscribe the terms of male dominance in the law, mitigating the harms to which women are subjected without transforming the very terms under which they continued to be subjugated. Yet resorting to a 'women's point of view', whether by VAW campaigners who have lobbied for the recognition of violence in the private domain as a human rights issue, or as the grounds from which to build a feminist law or jurisprudence, has not brought about the political transformation that initially inspired the women's human rights campaign. This discussion reveals the consequences of a victim centred approach and the focus on VAW discourse for women's human rights claims. Such claims cannot be detached from the normative and discursive frameworks in which they are made and deployed.

In this chapter, I reveal the downside of VAW discourse and a victim subject politics for women. The focus on the authentic subject as a victim in Indian feminist discourse has not produced a liberated subject, but rather one that is based on a questionable authenticity and set up in opposition to the Western subject. This subject risks denying women the agency that they in fact demonstrate throughout their lives, whether by leaving an abusive relationship, soliciting for the purpose of sex-work, participating in a beauty pageant, or performing as a weightlifter.

In the international arena, the victim subject and the primary focus on violence against women, creates an exclusionary category built on racist perceptions and stereotypes of third world women. This category is disempowering and does not translate into an emancipatory politics. It produces the fiction of a universal sisterhood, bonded in its experience of victimisation and violence. There is no space in this construction for difference or for the articulation of a subject that is either empowered or provides a normative challenge to the gender, sexual and cultural assumptions that underlie the campaigns for women's rights or human rights discourse. Indeed, the victim subject collapses easily into Victorian/colonial assumptions of women as weak, vulnerable and helpless. It also feeds into conservative, right-wing agendas for women, which are protectionist rather than liberating (Buss, 1998; Herman, 2001). Additionally, it encourages states to resort to the criminal law to address women's rights issues, an arena of law in which nation-states enjoy powers of moral surveillance and regulation.

In challenging the universalising and disempowering implications of foregrounding the victim subject in feminist legal politics, I do not seek to revert to the fragmenting politics of identity. Instead, I argue in favour of recognising different subjectivities and peripheral subjects, primarily to counter the fictitious homogeneity and sisterhood created through the victim subject. The challenge for feminists has been to think of ways in which to express their politics without subjugating other subjectivities through claims to the idea of a 'true self' or a singular truth about all women. The re-envisioning of the subject of women's rights discourse leads to a reformulation of the notions of agency and choice. It is an agency that is neither situated exclusively in the individual nor denied because of some overarching oppression. It is situated in the structures of social relationships, the location of the subject, and the shape-shifting of culture. My arguments emanate from a postcolonial context. Although there have been some critiques of liberalism and rights discourse by feminist legal scholars in the West, it has rarely been amplified to address the ways in which the colonial encounter problematised rights discourse from its very introduction into the former colonies. Rights have not been received unequivocally as a liberating and emancipating project. Nor has 'inclusion' been regarded as the antidote for the subordination and exclusion that have constituted and sustained the boundaries of human rights and law projects. A postcolonial feminist position on human rights advocated in this essay accepts the value of rights without celebrating the colonial processes that justified imperialist intervention, and that continue to justify similar interventions in the postcolonial world. Also, it is engaged at the outset with bringing normative challenges to the regulatory edifice that entrenches assumptions about gender, sexuality and culture in law and continues to justify exclusions and subordination. Women cannot be incorporated into the human rights project through intervention strategies that replicate imperial interventions and the victimisation of women by the cultural Other, nor can they be recuperated through a project that seeks to distance itself from the West through the construction of an authentic subject, which is also thoroughly victimised and impoverished. There is a need to interrogate the normative assumptions about gender, sexuality and culture that remain in place and are partly reinforced in and through the VAW campaign and its focus on violence against women. This campaign continues to fall back on an uncomplicated position on rights, despite the critique of rights, and offers mitigation rather than transformation as a solution. The challenge lies in exposing the normative aspects of human rights discourse as it applies to gender, culture and sexuality, rather than merely consolidating the regulatory effect of these rights. This requires a revisiting of the women's rights strategies and claims, and bringing a normative challenge to human rights discourse. The recognition that the postcolonial subject can return the gaze and force an unpacking of the regulatory norms that underlie women's human rights claims and practices can perhaps provide that alternative and possibly transformative cosmology we are seeking to move towards.

Chapter 5
The Other Side of Universality: Cross-Border Movements and the Transnational Migrant Subject

> Before professors in business schools were talking about global economics, illegals knew all about it ... The illegal immigrant is the bravest among us. The most modern among us. The prophet ... The peasant knows the reality of our world decades before the Californian suburbanite will ever get the point. (Kumar, 2000, p xiv)

The current moment of globalisation is witnessing an extraordinary movement of people, legitimate and illegitimate, across national and international borders. These movements are exposing the porosity of borders, the transnational reality of subaltern existence, and the contingent foundations of international law. I examine how encounters with these constitutive Others, quite specifically the transnational migrant subject, disrupts and disturbs the universalist premise of international law. At the same time, these cross-border movements are countered, curtailed, restricted and even resisted, by a modernist narrative of international law, the legitimacy of which is constructed along the axis of progress, relations between sovereign nation-states, and the sovereign subject.

The contours of legitimacy in international law are re-shaped, altered and conferred according to the view one takes about the modernist narrative of human progress and development. One view is that international law constitutes a narrative of progress, the coming together of nations and the recognition of the need for a globalised legal order. It is a narrative sustained along legitimate borders of nation-states that participate in the global project through consensus. It is driven by a persistent belief that history has a purpose and direction coupled with an assumption that the world has emerged from a backward, more uncivilised era. International law reflects the metamorphosis of civilisation from the primitive into a modern and evolved form, and this progress has emanated from the heart of Europe.

This position has been challenged by those who do not regard international law as such an uncomplicated and linear project (Anghie, 1996; Engle, 1993; Kennedy, 2000; Koskenniemi, 2002; Marks, 1997). As I discuss in Chapter 2, some view modernity's thesis of 'history as progressive' as a fiction and exclusive, and law as the mechanism for sustaining unequal structures of power, whether in the form of slavery or Empire and a subordinating or 'civilising' tool of the superior power. Indeed, when Europe was in the midst of a struggle for liberty, equality and freedom, Europe's Others continued to be subjugated under the weight of colonialism and slavery. Even within Europe, gender apartheid established a hierarchy of what and who constituted the liberal subject: the white propertied male. These critiques expose what Wendy Brown describes as 'so much history and so many histories' of the world (Brown, 2001, p 5).

Another view is that international law is a corrosive tool that has eroded the legitimacy conferred or exercised through sovereignty, national and social cohesion, and the normative family. According to this view, the era of historical progress, coherence and totality has ceased, and we have entered the age of uncertainty and instability. It is a view that harks back to the past as a golden era, appeals to family values as a relic to be retrieved from a bygone age, and regards history as progress as meeting its final end. Today the immorality of sex, single parent families, and working mothers has in part brought about the demise of history and an end to progress. Gazing back to better times and a greater polity reflects the disillusionment, uncertainty and instability that characterises the contemporary moment. Legitimacy resides in the glories of the past and its certainties, which must be retrieved and the encroachments of international law on sovereignty arrested.

The challenge to foundational truth claims has resulted in an uncertainty, a questioning and indeterminacy. This challenge has exposed the fallacy of security and stability claimed by the modernist narrative of international law. Yet, as Wendy Brown argues, this challenge has not resulted in the abandonment of the modernist narrative and its truth claims. Current politics is informed by a 'Yes, I know. But ...' position that fears the consequences of abandoning such 'truth claims' (Brown, 2001, p 4). Nevertheless, the ambiguity and insecurity resulting from the erosion of the traditional building blocks of modernity, produces an uncertainty over how to formulate a grounded politics in the midst of such disorientation. In this chapter, I examine some of the implications of these challenges to the sovereign subject and the sovereign nation-state in relation to borders and the legal regulation of the border-crossings of the transnational migrant subject. The challenge that these border-crossings pose to the very foundations of liberal understandings of the state and the subject exposes the impact of the contemporary manifestations of globalisation, the ubiquitous quality of capitalism and labour, and the ascendance of new international non-state actors. And these disruptions create the possibility of new imaginations and legitimacies that move beyond merely grasping at the remnants of old and tattered foundations.

My intention in this chapter is not to provide a comprehensive global analysis of laws that regulate borders and border-crossings. My intention is to highlight how the transnational migrant subject is addressed through a spectrum of legal rules and criteria designed to question their legitimacy at the point of crossing borders. In the current moment, international and domestic laws intersect to resist and at times indict the legitimacy of the transnational migrant. I discuss three situations that demonstrate some of my concerns. I briefly examine: the legal regulation of women who migrate for work, including sex-work, focusing on both the international response to this issue as well as the recently enacted US anti-trafficking legislation; the response to global flows of migrants by countries such as Britain, which has adopted new criteria to determine eligibility for citizenship and immigration; and the global response to terrorism in and through the non-legal 'War on Terror', illustrating how this has impacted on Australia's legal response to refugees or asylum-seekers, fleeing from situations of persecution and conflict. In each instance, I discuss the impact of the legal interventions on the rights of the transnational migrant, and the underlying assumptions about women and the Other on which such interventions are based.

Colonial subjects and the meaning of 'universality'

Throughout this chapter I use the term 'transnational migrant subject', which refers quite specifically to the subject who crosses borders and occupies a subaltern position. In using the term 'subaltern', I borrow from the insights of postcolonial theory and the subaltern studies project that I discuss in Chapter 2, which have highlighted the fact that certain voices have been excluded from the dominant narratives and telling of history. The subaltern studies project regards hegemonic history as part of modernity's power/knowledge complex, which in the context of colonialism was deeply implicated in the 'general epistemic violence of imperialism' (Otto, 1996; Spivak, 1985, p 251). It focuses on 'listening to the small voice of history', including peasants, women and even religious, sexual and racial minorities (Guha, 1996, pp 1–12). In the context of law, the subaltern project challenges the assumptions about universality, neutrality and objectivity on which legal concepts are based, exposing such concepts to be products of the ruptures produced in and through the colonial encounter.

Subaltern studies and postcolonial scholarship have established how the identity of the West and the European has been constructed in opposition to an Other. And this opposition exposes an incommensurable tension and contradiction between the West's claims to universality and inclusion, while simultaneously justifying the exclusion of the Other from the project of universality (Fitzpatrick and Darian-Smith, 1999, pp 1–2). This tension is exposed in the context of the colonial relationship with the 'native subject' and the universal claim that all people are entitled to life, liberty and equality. The colonial relationship reveals how the meaning of these concepts is neither static nor uniformly assumed. The meaning and experience of each is mediated, amongst other things, by gender, sexual status, race, ethnicity and religion. Each of these concepts has been and continues to be a zone of contest, which at times exposes the paradox of liberalism and its potential for exclusion and arbitrariness.

Modernity posits a set of universal truth claims about equality, citizenship, and representation in law. In the context of Empire, colonialism was coterminous with modernity, but it also brought into sharp relief how exclusions were built into these supposedly universal concepts. While Europe was developing ideas of political freedom, particularly in France, Britain and Holland, it simultaneously pursued and held vast Empires where such freedoms were either absent or severely attenuated for the majority of native inhabitants (Mehta, 1999, pp 46–54). There were two primary ways in which it was possible to legitimise this relationship and reconcile the liberal notions of freedom with notions of Empire. This reconciliation involved first linking the capacity to reason with adherence to some notion of a universal natural law, applicable to all (Mahmud and Kapur, 2000, pp 1012–24; Williams, 1990). These norms were premised on European practices, to which the colonial subjects had to conform if they were to avoid sanctions and achieve full membership.

A second way in which to reconcile domination with freedom and equality was through the discourse of difference, whereby the eligibility and capacity for freedom and progress was biologically determined, and colonial subjugation legitimised as the natural subordination of lesser races to higher ones. The purportedly universal rights of man could be denied to those not considered to be men or human. Liberal discourses of rights, inclusion and equality could be reconciled with the colonial policies of exclusion and discrimination only by presuming differences between different types of individuals. A similar logic justified the continued subordination of women, where women were understood as different from men, more specifically as weaker, subordinate and in need of protection. In the colonial relationship, gender difference was also conflated with cultural backwardness, where the treatment of women was used in part as a justification for colonial intervention and the civilising mission (Sarkar, 2001; Sinha, 2000).[1] The Empire was able to position itself as the defender of women's rights in the colonial context, without, however, fundamentally affecting its position on gender difference and the representation of women as essentially weak and subordinate, that is to say, to continue to take the existence of gender difference as natural and inevitable. And difference was partly constructed through the capacity to consent and the capacity to reason. The Other was deemed unfathomable, inscrutable, distant and removed, demonstrating that this subject was civilisationally backward and savage or infantile (Fabian, 1983; Young, 1990).[2] Colonial subjugation became one means by which to rectify past deficiencies, and the civilising mission of Empire was justified in societies that were stagnant and mired in the stranglehold of custom.

Law became one site on which to deal with difference and legitimise the pursuit of the civilising mission (Anghie, 1996, pp 4–5). The 'universal' principles of liberty, equality and freedom were contingent on the native's ability to conform or be trained into civilisation. The native was entitled to certain rights and benefits, to the extent that he could reinvent himself as an Englishman, otherwise 'backwardness' and lack of 'civilisational maturity' was regarded as a limitation. It was a deficiency to be tolerated, even if it could not be altered, or to be eliminated if it was too threatening (Fein, 1977; Narain, 1998). These values meet with some of the same difficulties today, in their encounters with difference and unfamiliarity in a postcolonial and increasingly transmigratory, transnational world (Mahmud, 1997, p 634). Universality is always accompanied by what Denise Ferreira Da Silva evocatively describes as 'the other side of universality' (Da Silva, 2001, p 421). This 'moral and legal *no man's land*, where universality finds its *spatial* limit', is built upon the foundation of difference (Da Silva, 2001, p 422).

---

1 Sarkar discusses how Hindu ideas and traditions were in part products of the colonial encounter, which influenced the development of ideas and traditions that have shaped hegemonic and dominant conceptions of Indian womanhood, domesticity, wifeliness, mothering and the construction of India as a Hindu nation. The Hindu nationalists embraced the very aspects of the tradition that the colonial power argued were symbols of India's backwardness and a justification for the continued colonial rule.

2 Fabian discusses how the anthropologist engages with her subject as existing at a different time from herself, in some mythical and hence primitive past; Young also discusses how the notion of the Other as savage and primitive is partly contingent on the way in which history is recited. Young critiques various Marxist accounts of a single world history, which have represented the third world as unassimilable, and a surplus to the narrative of the West. Decolonising history is a part of the project of deconstructing the West and understanding how the 'truth' about the Other comes to be produced.

The Other in the contemporary moment

These responses to the Other remain present in the contemporary moment in the context of the legal treatment of the transnational migrant subject. I examine three responses, and unpack the assumptions about the Other and difference on which they are based. Difference in this context is at times cast as either an inherent or cultural defect, and at times as capable of being altered and assimilated. The response to cross-border movements has been addressed in international law as an issue of trafficking, smuggling or terrorism. At the domestic level, it has been addressed as a problem of immigration, ethnicity and more recently, national security. Both of these responses expose the failure to recognise the global movement of people through clandestine avenues as a part of the globalisation process, and resort to frameworks and legal tools that fail to engage with this transnational, transmigratory reality.

I examine the anti-trafficking initiatives and how these have failed to distinguish between consensual migration, albeit illegal, and coerced movement. The result is that trafficking initiatives have had a particularly adverse impact on women and their families. Such initiatives treat the movement of women as coerced, reinforcing assumptions about third world women as victims, infantile and incapable of decision making, an issue I discussed in Chapter 4. At the same time, their families are implicated in the trafficking chain and cast as criminals. As a result, these women and their families are excluded from access to legal recognition, rights and benefits, and rendered even more vulnerable and insecure. I specifically discuss the recently enacted US Anti-Trafficking Act 2000, which builds on similar assumptions about women and further collapses the distinction between trafficking and sex-work, adding a moralising dimension to the way in which issues of trafficking and women's cross-border movements are addressed.[3] I then examine how the global migration of people has been addressed by states such as Britain through recent immigration proposals and the targeting of the transnational migrant through new cultural, emotional and citizenship criteria. I examine these assimilationist moves against the backdrop of fear about the breakdown of the nation's cultural identity and social cohesion. This fear has been triggered in part by the race riots in Bradford, Oldham and Burnley in the summer of 2001 as well as the post-September 11 concern with securing the nation's borders from the threat posed by the dangerous Other. In my third example, I discuss how international law's response to terrorism and the global 'War on Terror' has produced an explicit demonisation and policy of incarceration of asylum-seekers in Australia. This policy illustrates how the transnational migrant is transformed from a victim into a manipulative, dangerous and contaminating force from which the normative family and the state need to be protected.

My discussion is episodic, drawing attention to the tensions that continue to inform law's encounters with difference at border-crossings. In the examples I discuss, the diverse responses to the transnational migrant are not necessarily clear cut and well defined, and they are frequently overlapping. These subjects are at times represented as victims and at times as also capable of the most terrifying

---

3   Victims of Trafficking and Violence Protection Act 2000, Pub L No 106–386, 114 Stat 1464.

violence. These examples also reveal a complex relationship between assumptions about gender and its relationship to the Other, which are either based on essentialist assumptions about women as weak, vulnerable and victims of a backward cultural Other, or as completely aligned with the identity of the Other as terrifying and dangerous. The common element in the examples I discuss is the attempt to examine and respond to border-crossings by transnational migrants along the rigid binaries of us and them, domination and subordination, which fail to address the complex, fragmented and blurred realities of our transnational world. These responses reflect the divide between Europe and its Others which continue to inform contemporary scholarship on colonial discourses and the direction, shape and relevance of international law in this area (Suleri, 1992).

Keeping the 'native' at home

On 3 March 2003, sex-workers, transgendered males and females, their families and support communities, crossed international borders to converge on the city of Trivandrum to celebrate the International Sex Workers Rights Day (as discussed in Chapter 4). At the epicentre of their debates and protests was a challenge to the anti-trafficking initiatives being promoted by Western and South Asian countries, feminists, human rights groups, and even religious groups (Bumiller, 2002). They argued that such measures targeted migration from the South, promoted a highly conservative moral agenda, and denied sexual and other subalterns the right to work, to family and to mobility. I discuss some of the international legal initiatives combined with some domestic responses, such as the US anti-trafficking legislation, in the arena of trafficking that impact on the right to migrate and the rights of migrants and their families. I discuss how these initiatives are based on the assumptions about trafficked persons, especially women, as 'victims' incapable of choosing to cross borders, as well as a failure to address the push factors that compel such 'unsafe' movements. These responses focus on border controls and the prosecution of 'traffickers', who range from transport agents to the so called victims' families who consent to the movement. I discuss how discouraging women's mobility and stigmatising their third world families conveys a simple message: to keep the 'native' at home.

(a) Conflations and confusions

The distinctions between the issue of trafficking and migration, and trafficking and sex-work, have been constantly blurred, resulting in the formulation of confused legal strategies that are both anti-migrant and anti-sex-work, and anti-the families of both. They fail to recognise why people move, and the consequences of trying to stop movement through border controls and displacing the problem onto individuals and their families. The legal responses construct women's movement as primarily forced and for the purpose of sex-work or prostitution. These responses are infused with assumptions about women's appropriate roles and conservative sexual morality. This narrow focus on women's migration excludes the complex social, economic, cultural and political factors that affect women's movement, and further stigmatises the women and their families.

In the context of trafficking, statistics on the number of persons who are moved are unavailable, primarily because of the clandestine nature of the activity. Nevertheless, cross-border movements have triggered a flurry of activity on behalf of Western governments, South Asian governments, and many human rights groups. Statistics are continuously cited about the ever growing spectre of trafficking and the urgent need to eliminate this activity. The source of these statistics remains unclear and frequently unreliable. The Global Alliance Against the Trafficking in Women undertook a study on behalf of the UN Special Rapporteur on Violence Against Women, and stated that it was extremely difficult to find reliable statistics on the extent of trafficking that was taking place (Wijers and Lap-Chew, 1997, p 15). There has been no systematic research on this subject, nor was it at the time possible to determine the accuracy of such statistics because of the imprecise nature of the definition of the term 'trafficking in women', and because so much of this activity had been pushed underground as a result of the illegal or criminal nature of sex-work and trafficking. Statistics are sometimes arbitrarily cited without any backup research to substantiate these findings. For example, the Coalition Against Trafficking in Women, Asia Pacific, sets out the numbers of women trafficked in a number of countries, without citing any research or the source of their statistics. According to the UN Special Rapporteur's *Report on Violence Against Women* in 2000, the UN has claimed that four million women are trafficked every year. Similarly, the US Central Intelligence Agency has estimated that nearly 40,000 to 50,000 women and children are trafficked annually to the US (Richard, 1999). These statements are not backed up by any verified data.[4] Similarly, the 1995 *Human Rights Report on Trafficking Between Nepal and India* states that 'At least hundreds of thousands, and probably more than a million women and children are employed in Indian brothels' (Human Rights Watch, 1995). This same group's report on trafficking between Burma and Thailand states that there are an estimated 800,000 to two million prostitutes currently working in Thailand (Thomas and Jones, 1993). In none of these reports are any sources for the statistics provided. Kempadoo questions the veracity of such figures, arguing that such discrepancies in figures would be grounds for questioning the reliability of the research. However, in the trafficking context (and its constant conflation with sex-work) these standards are compromised and the figures are often cited without any question (Kempadoo, 1998, p 15).

These questionable statistics have been combined with other confusions between trafficking, migration and sex-work. In contemporary discourse, human trafficking has come to be variously and yet integrally interwoven with migration, mainly illegal clandestine border-crossing, and smuggling of humans. On a parallel plane, trafficking in women and girls is resoundingly conflated with their sale and forced consignment to brothels in the sex industry. The conflation of trafficking in persons with various manifestations of migration and mobility on the one hand, and with prostitution and sex-work on the other, lies at the very core of the confusion that underpins the contemporary discourse on trafficking of women and girls globally, regionally and nationally.

---

4   Coalition Against Trafficking in Women – Asia Pacific, www.catw-ap.org; *Report of the Special Rapporteur on Violence Against Women, Its Causes and Consequences*, UN Doc E/CN 4/2000/68, para 72.

(b) Equating migration with trafficking

Recently, the UN adopted an international definition of trafficking, which is set out in the UN Protocol to Prevent, Suppress and Punish Trafficking in Persons, Especially Women and Children (2000), which supplements the UN Convention on Transnational Organised Crime. The Protocol defines trafficking as follows:

> Trafficking in persons shall mean the recruitment, transportation, transfer, harbouring or receipt of persons, by means of the threat or use of force or other forms of coercion, of abduction, of fraud, of deception, of the abuse of power or of a position of vulnerability, or of the giving or receiving of payments or benefits to achieve consent of a person having control over another person, for the purpose of exploitation. Exploitation shall include, at a minimum, the exploitation of the prostitution of others or other forms of sexual exploitation, forced labour or services, slavery or practices similar to slavery, servitude or the removal of organs.[5]

The definition reflects an important development and shift towards newer, relatively more widely acceptable and inclusive definitions of trafficking. As of March 2004, 117 countries had signed the Protocol. Since the definition is very recent, its impact will only be realised once it begins to be applied and tested. A striking feature of the definition is that the international community has only recently recognised the need to expand the definition of trafficking to include purposes other than prostitution, such as forced labour, forced marriage and slavery-like practices. There is also some acknowledgment that trafficking is a problem of human rights and not a law and order or public morality issue related to prostitution. But the problems of lack of coherency and the conflation of trafficking with migration, and trafficking with sex-work, have not been eradicated. Women move and are moved with or without their consent for a variety of reasons (Indra, 1999; Sassen, 1996). They frequently find their way into the job market as domestic helpers, or into the sex industry, partly because these are the largest enclaves in the job market of the receiving country (Wijers, 2000; Wijers and Lap-Chew, 1997; Zlotnik, 2003).

As discussed in Chapter 4, the definition of trafficking in the Protocol fails to distinguish between trafficking and voluntary consensual migration, and thus conflates the relationship between female migration and trafficking. A number of member countries have also interpreted the Protocol, both consciously and inadvertently, as foregrounding sex-work as the main site of trafficking, and consider the consent of the 'victim' irrelevant.[6] And finally, the Protocol does not impose any mandatory obligations on state parties to provide any redress measures or services to trafficked persons or their families. In all these ways, the trafficking definition delegitimises the woman's cross-border movement.

---

5 Article 3(a) of the Protocol to Prevent, Suppress and Punish Trafficking in Persons, Especially Women and Children, supplementing the UN Convention Against Transnational Organised Crime (discussed in Chapter 4).

6 *Ibid*, Art 3(b). Eg, the Council of Europe, in its parliamentary assembly recommendation 1545 in 2002, stated that 'In European societies, trafficking is a very complex subject which is closely linked to prostitution and hidden forms of exploitation, such as domestic slavery, catalogue marriages and sex tourism. Some 78% of women victims of trafficking are, in one way or another, exploited sexually'. No sources are provided for this statistic and it stands in contrast to another field report on the current situation and responses to trafficking in 10 south east European countries: Limanoska, 2002.

The Protocol reflects the tensions that characterise anti-trafficking initiatives. Equating trafficking with migration has led to simplistic and unrealistic solutions – in order to prevent trafficking there is a conscious or inadvertent move to stop those who are deemed vulnerable from migrating. Even when curbing migration is not a stated programmatic focus, an inadvertent impetus is to dissuade women and girls in particular from moving, in order to protect them from harm. Anti-trafficking measures are frequently applicable to 'women and girls', thereby failing to accord the woman an identity as an adult and confer rights that flow from that status, including the right to choose to move and have control over her life and body (Global Alliance, 1999, p 2). It also emphasises women's roles primarily as caretakers for children and fails to consider that women's roles have altered. Women's identity as the sole supporter of dependent family members and economic migrants in search of work are completely erased by these legal initiatives. Conflating trafficking with migration results in reinforcing the assumption that women and girls need constant male, state or trans-state protection, are incapable of decision making or consent, and therefore must not be allowed to exercise their right to movement or right to earn a living in the manner they choose. The construction of women who move as victims of a web of criminal networks sits in tension with the counter-narrative that regards the movement of labour as part of the globalisation process. The emergence of human trafficking and smuggling networks is part of the migration phenomenon that first world nation-states refuse to address other than as an issue of immigration or criminality.

This approach delegitimises women's movement, while the problem of trafficking, the ostensible purpose of these measures, never gets resolved. Curbing migration does not stop trafficking, it merely drives the activity further underground, and makes it more invisible. Borders cannot be impermeable, and stricter immigration measures result in pushing the victims further into situations of violence and abuse. As a result, women who migrate are pushed into further dependency on an informal and illegal network of agents, and rendered even more vulnerable to economic and physical abuse, exploitation and harm.

International law has constructed a response to 'trafficking' that fails to draw clear conceptual distinctions between migration and trafficking. As a result, migration becomes equated with trafficking, which also means that the number of victims of trafficking becomes equal to the number of those who have migrated voluntarily. This logic operates particularly in the case of adolescent girls and women migrants, rather than men. This practice has resulted in an extremely flawed methodology for conducting surveys on trafficking in 'risk-prone' and 'affected districts', for example in different South Asian countries. Absence of women or girls is routinely considered tantamount to 'missing persons', and therefore, trafficked. It is a logic that has resulted in the viewing of all consensual migrant females as trafficked and thus rendering women's cross-border movement as illegitimate.

Women's cross-border movements are also conflated with sex-work by anti-trafficking players, which produces at least two contradictory responses. By collapsing the process with the purpose, the abuse and violence that a woman may experience in the course of transport is equated with the purpose of her journey, and so many anti-trafficking measures are invariably anti-sex-work measures. Sex-work *per se* as the exclusive purpose of trafficking is an untenable definition, as not all victims are sex-workers nor have all sex-workers been trafficked. At the same time, if women are deemed to have participated in the process of trafficking, they are immediately recast as immoral or criminals, and undeserving of legal protection. The tension between the fact that women from the developing world who cross borders are predominantly victims of traffickers in need of protection, and that they are also sexually transgressive is never resolved through trafficking legislation or international initiatives.

Women who cross borders are not afforded the protection or legitimacy accorded to women who practise sex in the privacy of the family or who are victims of sexual violence. Familial ideology operates with dominant sexual ideology to contain women's sexuality and sexual conduct. Those who participate in the transgression of these norms are rendered exterior and no longer entitled to legal protection. Violence against women who are trafficked is taken up in ways that do not displace dominant constructions of women's sexuality and gender roles. And her identity as migrant and decision maker is never acknowledged, a construction that is only addressed in the context of sex-work; in which case she is regarded as a criminal and her breaching of borders regarded as a threat to the nation's security and moral integrity.

These responses not only reinforce assumptions about women and their families, especially if they are moving from the global South, they also fail to address the primary impetus behind trafficking. There is a dramatic decrease in the opportunities available for lawful migration at a time when the global movement of people is increasing sharply. The disjuncture between the number of people who wish to migrate and the legal opportunities for them to move has given rise to a growing market for irregular migration services which is being filled by traffickers and migrant smugglers (Gallagher, 2002; Ghosh, 1998, p 60).[7] It is the increasing anxiety on the part of states to control their borders that has led to an extraordinary level of international co-operation on the issues of trafficking and migrant smuggling. The issue of migration is addressed as a dilemma, a law and order problem and a question of transnational organised crime rather than a question of human rights. The emphasis therefore is on increasing border controls and strengthening law enforcement. The negotiations on the Trafficking Protocol did not take place under a human rights umbrella, but rather under the auspices of the UN Commission on Crime Prevention and Criminal Justice. Trafficking is an outcome of this need for people to migrate on the one hand and the growth of services in the migration market on the other, including exploitative and rights-violating practices.

---

7   The issue of people smuggling has been recently addressed in the Protocol Against the Smuggling of Migrants by Land, Sea and Air, supplementing the UN Convention Against Transnational Crime (GA Res 55/25, Annexe III, 55th Sess, 55 UN GAOR Supp No 49, at 65, UN Doc A/45/49 (2001), Vol 1), which came into force on 28 January 2004. The Protocol on the smuggling of migrants represents an important shift, as it is the first time that smuggling has been treated as distinct from trafficking. Smuggling of migrants addresses a very specific conduct that involves the transportation of women and men, through the provision of money or other material benefit, in order to acquire illegal entry into a country: Art 3.

The legal initiatives fail to recognise and respect the rights of transnational migrants, including women's agency and the rights of their families in the course of their movement. These initiatives continue to address women as victims and as incapable of choosing to move, either illegally or for work other than sex-work or prostitution.

These initiatives cast women who move exclusively as victims, failing to recognise that women move in part to seek better economic opportunities to support their families. By casting her as a victim, whose consent to move is irrelevant, she is rendered incapable of decision making. I do not mean to suggest that her choice to move is purely voluntary. It is conditioned by social and economic conditions as well as the discursive positioning of the subject as I discuss in Chapter 4. At the same time, the issue of trafficking is addressed under the Convention Against Transnational Organised Crime, that is, within the framework of criminal law, and this in turn treats any actors, including family members, who facilitate women's movement as alleged criminals. A further consequence is that by associating trafficking invariably with sexual exploitation, women who move are implicitly suspected of crossing borders for the purposes of sex, and in the process their movement is stigmatised. Thus the woman and the movement of women are viewed through the lens of criminality and stigma, and the woman herself is rendered both a victim as well as an immoral subject.

The association of women's victim status with protection reproduces assumptions about women, especially women from developing countries, as incapable of decision making, as passive and vulnerable. This approach conforms to an earlier approach in equality discourse that views women as in need of protection, naturally weak and incapable of exercising agency. This approach is based on the assumption that the category of gender is immutable and that women are just different. The assumption of women, especially from the global South, as in need of protection and rescue, also frames the response to trafficking in the US Victims of Trafficking and Violence Protection Act 2000. Although a number of countries have enacted anti-trafficking legislation, I specifically address the US Act because of its extra-territorial implications and the government's efforts to establish its anti-trafficking legal framework as the global standard. The various provisions of the Act tend both to reinforce the infantilisation of women and to render cross-border movements, especially by poor or working class women, suspect. It also imposes a series of punitive measures on states that fail to comply with the US anti-trafficking criteria.

The term 'trafficking' is not defined in the Act. The only definitions that appear in the Act relate to 'sex trafficking' (s 103(9)) and 'severe forms of trafficking in persons' (s 103(8)(A) and (B)).[8] Most of the provisions deal with combating severe

---

8 Sex trafficking is defined as recruitment, harbouring, transportation, provision or obtaining of a person for the purpose of a commercial sex act. Severe forms of trafficking in persons are defined as follows: (A) sex trafficking in which a commercial sex act is induced by force, fraud or coercion, or in which the person induced to perform such act has not attained 18 years of age; or (B) the recruitment, harbouring, transportation, provision or obtaining of a person for labour or services, through the use of force, fraud or coercion for the purpose of subjection to involuntary servitude, peonage, debt bondage or slavery.

forms of trafficking in persons, especially into the sex trade, slavery and slavery-like conditions. The Act incorporates the language of 'luring' victims and 'false promises' ostensibly made by traffickers to innocent victims for a better, more prosperous life elsewhere (s 102(4)). This language reinforces the division between those who deliberately transgress borders, including sexual norms, and those who are 'duped' into it. As Jo Doezema argues, such a dichotomy obscures the reactionary and often moralistic assumptions that underlie these concerns, and results in 'advocating a rigid sexual morality under the guise of protecting women' (Doezema, 1998, p 45).

The Act further establishes a task force, which includes among others, the Secretary of State, the Administrator of the US Agency for International Development and the Director of the Central Intelligence Agency (s 105(b)). The Act authorises the task force to develop measures to combat the 'sex tourism' industry, facilitate strengthening of the local and regional capacities to prevent trafficking, prosecute traffickers, and assist trafficking victims partly by reintegrating them into their place of origin (s 105(d)). It also provides benefits to victims of 'severe' trafficking who have not attained the age of 18, or who are willing to provide assistance in every reasonable way in the investigation and prosecution of severe forms of trafficking in persons (s 107(b)).[9]

Victims are entitled to a temporary visa or 'T' visa, but there is an annual cap of 5,000 such visas, even though the Act itself states that over 50,000 women and children are trafficked into the US each year (s 102(b)(1)). The 'T' visas are granted only if the victim can credibly establish 'victim' credentials. Such proof includes the person being a victim of a severe form of trafficking, not having attained the age of 15, or being induced to participate in the sex trade or slavery-like practices by force, coercion, fraud or deception (s 107(e)(1)). No evidence should exist of voluntary agreement to any arrangement, including participation in the sex trade, and the victim should agree to provide reasonable assistance in the investigation or prosecution of trafficking acts. In addition, the victim must prove that she has a well founded fear of retribution involving the infliction of 'severe' harm, or that she will suffer extreme hardship in connection with the trafficking, if she is removed from the US. The Attorney General is authorised to convert the 'T' visa into permanent resident status provided the victim has resided in the US for three years, has been a person of good moral character during that period, has continued to assist in the investigation or prosecution of trafficking acts, and would be harmed if she were to be sent home. Presumably, the 'good moral character' requirement would disqualify a woman who has engaged in sex-work.

The overriding assumption of these provisions is that the victim must be able to demonstrate that she is not responsible for her condition. If she participates in any way in the facilitation of her illegal movement, she is implicated in the trafficking chain and subject to criminal sanctions. If a woman pays for her transport, she is

---

9   Such benefits include the provision of shelter, medical care, food, legal and other assistance, including protection if the victim is at risk of harm or danger from the trafficker.

regarded as having participated in her trafficking. She is also stigmatised by the fact that the underlying assumption of this legislation is that women are trafficked primarily for sexual purposes. If she is regarded as having participated in her movement, she is also exposed to the assumption that she is sexually promiscuous and no longer entitled to the protection of the criminal law but rather subject to it. Although the Act ostensibly prioritises concern for the victim, women who cross borders to work in the sex industry and are harmed or experience violence during their travels, or are exploited in the course of this work are not a concern. Access to benefits thus becomes partly conditional on a woman's chastity, purity and innocence.

The Act also supports punitive measures towards states that do not comply with the anti-trafficking criteria in the Act. Countries must demonstrate that they have fulfilled certain minimum standards for eliminating trafficking, which include enacting laws that deal seriously with trafficking and provide harsh punishment for such crimes (s 108(a)(1–3), (b)(1) and (b)(7)). The US is to provide assistance to foreign countries to meet the minimum criteria, such as drafting legislation to prohibit and punish acts of trafficking, investigating and prosecuting traffickers, and creating facilities, programmes and activities for the protection of victims. Specific criteria for determining if a country has tried to eliminate trafficking are also laid down in the Act, including official monitoring of emigration and immigration patterns for evidence of severe forms of trafficking (s 108(b)(6)).

If a government does not comply with the minimum standards for eliminating trafficking, it will be subjected to punitive sanctions, such as the withholding or denial of non-humanitarian assistance (s 110(d)(1)(A)(i)). If the country accused of failing to comply with the dictates of the new legislation does not receive non-humanitarian assistance from the US, the US can deny funding for educational and cultural exchanges between the two countries (s 110(d)(1)(A)(ii)). The President of the US will also instruct the directors of multilateral banks and the International Monetary Fund (IMF) to vote against any loan or other funds to the erring government until it complies with the minimum standards (s 110(d)(1)(B)).

The Act leaves little space for addressing the issue of trafficking from the perspective of human rights. The entire effort is primarily directed towards restricting the movement of people across US borders. Trafficking becomes a guise for not only keeping people out, but also casting suspicion on those who go to the US to work as nannies, domestic labourers, dancers, factory workers or restaurant workers. The Act places an onus on countries of origin to undertake effective measures to deal with the problem of trafficking, that is, to contain people within their own borders. The extra-territorial reach of this legislation, through the threat of sanctions, is directed primarily at countries that receive economic assistance and other forms of non-humanitarian aid from the US. The Act is primarily concerned with the considerable increase in the traffic across borders, especially from developing countries into the US, that needs to be stopped. The paranoid approach to this 'problem' is demonstrated by the extreme measures to be imposed on those countries that fail to curtail the stream of migration and exit from their countries. Little distinction is being drawn between migration and trafficking. And the fact that every border-crossing can be rendered suspect, given the broad assumption that a whole host of actors are characterised as being victims of trafficking, will render the crossing of borders more difficult.[10]

Anti-trafficking initiatives are infantilising of women, especially women from the global South, who are regarded as lacking the capacity to reason or choose. Women who cross borders are regarded exclusively as victims, 'lured' or 'duped' by the 'false promises' ostensibly made by traffickers for a better, more prosperous life elsewhere. Such initiatives also tend to criminalise women and their families, regarding such families as part of the trafficking chain, and do not recognise that women move and are moved partly to seek out economic opportunities. The conflation has had a particularly adverse affect on women who migrate. It creates a schizophrenic response to the transnational migrant subject – one that views him or her as a victim in need of rescue and rehabilitation, which underscores the anti-trafficking initiatives. And another response that reinforces the fear of the Other as a potential threat to the nation's social cohesion or the nation's security, intensifying the regulation of borders and the scrutiny of the Other.

Assimilating the Other

These trans-border and in-country movements and migrations are occurring for a plethora of reasons: the reconfiguration of the global economy; displacement and dispossession of marginalised populations; the awareness through consciousness raising that there are better options elsewhere; armed conflict; and of course the basic human aspiration to explore the world (Hollifield, 1998; Weiner, 1995). The global patterns of economics and trade have increased the demand for low wage labour, as well as the demand of poor countries for remittances from immigrants in the global North that will assist in social welfare that the state is neither able nor willing to perform (Brodie, 1995; Puri and Ritzema, 1999; Rittich, 2000). The World Bank's *Report on Global Development Finance 2003* estimates that migrant remittances to developing countries reached almost $80 billion in 2002, and that these remittances exceeded the net foreign direct investment for the first time (IMF, 2002; Ratha, 2003; Russell, 1992). Poorer countries thus have little interest in controlling outward movement, legal or illegal (Buch, Kucklenz and Le Manchec, 2002; International Organisation on Migration, 2003).

Accurate statistics on migration flows are not readily available. This lack is due in part to the absence of a universal methodology for collecting such statistics. In addition, there is a lack of commitment on the part of governments to collect these

---

10 Even the Special Rapporteur on Violence Against Women in her very recent report has been critical of the way in which most governments have responded to the issues of trafficking in women. She states that while governments have sought ways and means to combat trafficking, they (particularly governments of northern countries) simultaneously have fortified their external borders against the perceived threat of unfettered immigration. *Report of the Special Rapporteur on Violence Against Women, Its Causes and Consequences*, UN Commission on Human Rights, UN Doc E/CN 4/2000/68 (2000).

statistics, a common definition amongst countries in respect of determining who is an international migrant, and the difficulty in collecting data given the clandestine nature of some forms of migration. However, some official UN estimates provide information about the numbers involved in cross-border movements. The UN's *International Migration Report 2002* estimated there were 175 million migrants – defined as persons outside their country of birth or citizenship for 12 months or more.[11]

There are several human rights documents and provisions that address some of the harms and abuses to which migrants may be exposed, such as slavery, forced labour and debt bondage, in existing international and human rights law.[12] And the recently ratified International Convention on the Protection of the Rights of All Migrant Workers and Members of Their Families 1990 (MWC) is the first international convention to address the issue of irregular migration from a rights perspective. It affords some recognition and substantial rights to migrants and undocumented workers.[13] The primary purpose of the Convention is to protect the human rights of legal and illegal migrants and their families, and ensure there is no arbitrary interference with their families, and their rights to liberty and security.[14] The MWC provides rights to equality and due process to migrant workers and their families, regardless of whether they are documented or undocumented.[15] It also imposes positive obligations on the state to provide housing and other benefits to such persons.[16] Despite the rights provided under the MWC, it does not address the obstacles posed by immigration laws and restrictions, nor has it been ratified by a single industrial country.

New legal regimes have been erected to negotiate the relationship between national sovereignty and transnational corporate actors and capital. There is a recognition that the free flow of capital requires that the market remain unencumbered if it is to flourish. However, a similar determination has not been made in respect of labour and migration. Partly in response to the global movement

---

11 Department of Economic and Social Affairs, *Recommendations on Statistics of International Migration*, Revision 1, UN Statistics Division 12–15 ST/ESA/STAT/SER M/58/Rev 1 (1998), pp 12–15. About 60% of migrants were in 'developed countries', including 56 million in Europe, 50 million in Asia, and 41 million in North America. During the 1990s, the number of migrants in developed countries rose by 23 million or 28%, and immigration accounted for almost two-thirds of the population growth in industrial countries. Between 1995 and 2000, the more developed countries received nearly 12 million migrants from the less developed countries, about 2.3 million migrants a year, including 1.4 million a year in North America and 800,000 a year in Europe. In 2001, the UN Commission for Refugees estimated that of the 21.8 million people the Commission was responsible for, 12 million were refugees (Populations Data Unit, 2001). Several million people are missing from these estimates because they are illegal and do not appear in the official census (Sassen, 2000).

12 Some of these include the Supplementary Convention on the Elaboration of Slavery, the Slave Trade and Institutions and Practices Similar to Slavery 1956; International Covenant on Civil and Political Rights, Art 8; International Covenant on Economic Social and Cultural Rights, Art 6; Universal Declaration of Human Rights, Arts 4 and 23; ILO Convention No 129 (1930); ILO Convention No 105 (1957). See also Bassiouni, 1991.

13 International Convention on the Protection of the Rights of All Migrant Workers and Members of Their Families, UN GA Res 45/158, Annexe 45, UN GAOR Supp No 49A, at 262, UN Doc A/45/49 (1990), entered into force 1 July 2003.

14 *Ibid*, Preamble, Parts II and III.

15 *Ibid*, Part IV.

16 *Ibid*, Art 43.

of people, states throughout Europe are enacting new citizenship and nationality laws to enable transnational migrants to be part of the universal project of rights and acquire legitimacy through the process of assimilation. However, these initiatives are also being promoted alongside tighter immigration laws and procedures, and increased border controls that target those who refuse to assimilate. The transnationalisation of labour and migration cannot be addressed within the framework of immigration, which is based on notions of loyalty to and identification with the nation. Such movements are challenging nation-states, and their borders, and reconfiguring the map of national, political and cultural identity. The lack of willingness to countenance such a challenge operates from the need to secure the sovereign nation-state and the sovereign subject. It also perpetuates continued (neo-colonial) anxieties about the Other.

It is in the context of such anxieties that we need to understand the UK government's new policy on immigration and citizenship. The policy set out in *Secure Borders, Safe Haven*, is part of the government's response to the racial tensions that gripped the country in the summer of 2001 and the need to restore social and cultural cohesion as well as address the country's security concerns.[17] The policy targets the transnational migrant through new cultural, emotional and citizenship criteria. Most of these criteria have found their way into the UK Nationality, Immigration and Asylum Act 2002. The White Paper is based on two primary objectives. The first is to build social cohesion and a sense of British identity in 'an increasingly diverse world'.[18] The second is to meet the economic challenge, partly by ensuring that people who want to work in the UK can do so without entering into the country through illegal routes. These two challenges are to be confronted under a policy of 'managing migration'.[19] Managing migration is designed to set up a system of entry into the country that is orderly and organised. It is also directed towards assisting in the integration of migrants into the British economy and society in ways where they will be welcomed by the existing population. These migrants are to be managed in the crossing of borders as well as in terms of their identity construction once they have crossed borders.

The flows of migration are partly stimulated by global economic processes. As a result, a large number of people are crossing borders and their arrival is disrupting social cohesion and harmony within the UK. It is therefore crucial for the government to introduce measures that will ensure that local residents are secure in their own community, and that those who want to settle in the UK 'develop a sense of belonging, an identity and shared mutual understanding which can be passed from one generation to another'.[20] One answer is to re-shape the migrant into a

---

17 UK Home Office, White Paper, *Secure Borders, Safe Haven: Integration with Diversity in Modern Britain*, 10 February 2002, p 10, stating that: 'The reports into last summer's disturbances in Bradford, Oldham and Burnley painted a vivid picture of fractured and divided communities, lacking a sense of common values or shared civic identity to unite around. The reports signalled the need for us to foster and renew the social fabric of our communities, and rebuild a sense of common citizenship which embraces the different and diverse experiences of today's Britain.' See also, Cantle, 2003; and Oldham Independent Review, 2001, for a general discussion and analysis of race riots and community relations in Britain.

18 *Secure Borders, Safe Haven*, p 11.

19 *Ibid*, p 22.

20 *Ibid*, p 27.

British mould through a new nationality, citizenship and integration policy. They must be trained to 'uphold common values and understand how they can play their part in our society while upholding our status as subjects of HM The Queen'.[21] In pursuit of this goal, the government proposes that people who want to become UK citizens take a compulsory English language test and an exam on the ways of British life, British society and British institutions.[22] The sole previous requirement was just a passport. They will also be required to take a citizenship pledge.[23] These measures are justified by the Home Secretary in the following terms: 'Our future social cohesion, economic prosperity and integrity depends on how well we rise to the global challenge of mass migration, communication and flight from persecution.'[24]

The White Paper targets what are described as 'bogus marriages'.[25] The recommendations on these marriages have yet to be explicitly enacted into law. They nevertheless serve as a telling illustration about some of the cultural, sexual and gendered assumptions that the government holds with respect to foreigners; assumptions that will no doubt inform the discretion of those who evaluate immigration applications. The assimilationist aspect of the policy that I examine is the focus on legitimate marriages. The White Paper sets out that only marriages that conform to recognised norms will be acceptable. This normative arrangement is constructed as heterosexual, monogamous, genuine and long-term. This normative arrangement also forms the backdrop to targeting what are described as 'sham marriages'. In the White Paper the Home Secretary states:

> There has been a tradition of families originating from the Indian subcontinent wanting to bring spouses from arranged marriages to live with them in the UK ... We ... believe there is discussion to be had within those communities that continue the practice of arranged marriages as to whether more of these could be undertaken within the settled community here. Our changes will not penalise those in authentic relationships, but provide a longer period to test the genuineness of the marriage and increase the chance of exposing any marriages that are a sham.[26]

He suggests that there has been a steady increase in the number of people seeking leave to remain in the country on the basis of marriages which are not genuine.[27] He is particularly concerned with the 'innocent' local resident who is 'duped' into a marital arrangement by the manipulative outsider, who has every intention of leaving that person as soon as they have obtained settlement status.[28] The Home Secretary is also concerned with the number of suspicious marriage cases that have been brought to the attention of the Immigration Services.[29] The criteria for

---

21 *Ibid*, p 29.

22 *Ibid*, pp 32–33.

23 *Ibid*, pp 34–35, 111. See Nationality, Immigration and Asylum Act 2002, s 1, which pertains to knowledge of language and society for naturalisation; and s 3, which brings into effect Sched 1 to the Act, pertaining to the citizenship ceremony, oath and pledge. See also Tempest, 2002 and Cantle, 2003.

24 *Secure Borders, Safe Haven*, p 3.

25 *Ibid*, pp 99–102.

26 *Ibid*, p 18.

27 *Ibid*, p 99.

28 *Ibid*, pp 99–100.

29 *Ibid*, p 100.

determining if a marriage may be deemed suspicious are not explicitly stated, though there is an implicit assumption that it would be evaluated against normative understandings of marriage.

The Home Secretary seeks to introduce a 'probationary period' of two years for new marriages before allowing the couple to apply for settlement.[30] Under the current law, couples are subjected to a one year probationary period before settlement is granted, regardless of whether they are newly married or have been married for several years and living abroad. The new rule for granting leave to remain is to be based on proof that the relationship is genuine and intended to be permanent.[31] During those two years:

> ... the couple will need to prove that ... they have been able to maintain and accommodate themselves without recourse to public funds. While this will not greatly inconvenience or penalise those in genuine relationships, it will provide a longer period to test the genuineness of the marriage and increase the chance of exposing sham marriages.[32]

The subjection of the relationship to some form of economic hardship and proximity over the course of two years would, according to the Home Secretary's view, be unsustainable in the context of sham marriages: 'It would be harder to sustain a relationship for this longer period with a duped partner and more likely that, when questioned or interviewed, the lack of genuine and subsisting relationship will become apparent.'[33]

The proposal to introduce separate standards into the relationships of new immigrant populations to prove the 'authenticity' of their marriages is based on two assumptions – one is instrumental and the other is emotional. The instrumental element requires that the strength and genuineness of the marital arrangement be contingent upon the length of time a couple remains together. The longer they are together the more legitimate the arrangement. The other is the emotional requirement – quite specifically proof of love. The proposals assume that arranged marriages are illegitimate because they are not based on love, are coercive, not durable, and have a limited survival rate. These are not real relationships. The duration requirement sets up a hierarchy of legitimate social and marital arrangements. It is a new element that is being imposed on ethnic groups or outside groups. As for the love criteria: when the law starts regulating emotional and intimate aspects of people's lives, it exposes its preference for certain normative arrangements and its impetus to universalise and naturalise those arrangements.[34]

A further proposal to check 'sham marriages' is the introduction of a 'no switching provision'. As of April 2003, this provision has entered into force and requires that those persons who are given leave to enter the country for six months or less, lose their status if they get married in the UK during that time.[35] They

---

30 *Ibid*.

31 *Ibid*, p 101.

32 *Ibid*, p 18.

33 *Ibid*, p 100.

34 There have been some angry responses to these statements. See, eg, Blackstock, 2002, p 1, where the National Assembly Against Racism argued that 'Telling established British communities whom they should or should not marry is quite abhorrent to these communities'.

35 Statement of Changes of Immigration Rules, HC 538, 31 March 2003.

cannot switch or apply in the UK for leave to remain as the spouse of a British citizen, and must leave the UK and submit their application from abroad. This proposal is intended to prevent persons from applying for leave to remain on the grounds of marriage after they have entered into the UK in a different category. The White Paper states that 76% of those who were granted leave to remain in the UK on the basis of marriage in 1999 had originally been admitted under a different category.[36] In addition, 50% of this group switched into the marriage category within six months of their entry.[37] The White Paper concludes:

> As it seems unlikely that such a large percentage of this number would develop permanent relationships within such a short period of time, the indication is that many of these persons had intended to marry all along but had not obtained leave to enter on this basis and had therefore lied about their intentions to the entry clearance officer. Alternatively they may have entered into a bogus marriage to obtain leave to remain after arrival.[38]

This proposal introduces another extraordinary requirement into the subaltern relationship, namely that legitimacy and genuineness of the relationship is contingent on how quickly a relationship is forged and materialises in marriage. This requirement would render even 'love marriages' between migrants suspect if they took place at least within six months of arrival. The requirement further serves to infantilise the subaltern as incapable of taking a mature and informed decision about adult relationships. At the same time, the subaltern is cast as manipulative and scheming, one who can 'dupe' the unsuspecting, passive, local resident into an intimate relationship for self-serving utilitarian goals. The local resident is represented as devoid of agency or decision making. These relationships are rendered suspect if they happen too quickly, even if they are based on love. They are also rendered suspect if they do not survive the longevity requirement of at least two years. And even if they are sustained over a long period of time, they must conform to the normative criteria for marriage in the UK.

In the effort to curtail illegal migration, the White Paper targets a legal arrangement. Marriage provides institutional access to a spectacular array of state benefits, and the right to settle is simply one of them. The proposals in the White Paper are based on monolithic, linear and essentialist understandings of marriage and culture in Britain and postcolonial India. That individuals marry for a variety of reasons is as true in the postcolonial world as it is in the metropolis. People 'here' and 'there' marry for love, for economic status, for title and privilege, for procreative purposes, as well as the fact that the marital arrangement is the only arrangement that is accorded the maximum legitimacy by the state and receives the greatest share of state benefits, rights and privileges. Arranged marriages also encompass all or some of these motives and cannot be explained exclusively in cultural terms.

---

36 *Secure Borders, Safe Haven*, p 101, fn 17.
37 *Ibid*.
38 *Ibid*.

The complex understandings of the marital arrangement in the Indian subcontinent are explored in Mira Nair's recent production, *Monsoon Wedding* (see Kapur, 2002a). The complexities of the 'Indian marriage' and wedding space are examined through the lens of the postcolonial present. While the main narrative takes place in the overarching framework of an arranged marriage, a secondary romantic plot also gathers momentum and culminates in what is popularly described as a 'love marriage'. Even the central relationship is scripted through a narrative of emotional detours. In the finale, the spectator catches glimpses of new relationships in the making through the weft and warp of the marriage ceremony. Yet these complexities are belied in the UK White Paper. The tensions, ambiguities and contradictions of marriages in India cannot be explained through a monochromatic static representation of the woman as largely coerced and obedient, the family as greedy and exploitative, and the culture which permits such an arrangement as barbaric and backward.

In the White Paper, arranged marriages are discussed in a reductionist way. Arranged marriages are not defined in the White Paper, but there is an assumption that they are loveless and hence the motivations for the marriage must be subject to greater scrutiny. These marriages have either been arranged in complicity with the family members, the primary objective being to obtain the right to settle in the UK through a 'cultural' guise; or they are arranged without the consent of the women and are therefore coerced. At its most extreme, this second assumption views families in the postcolonial world as encouraging the abuse, rape and kidnapping of their girl children through the coercive practice of arranged marriage.[39] The Other is cast as either conniving, or a victim of a barbaric cultural practice who must be protected and rescued by the more enlightened and civilised norms of British society. Arranged marriages are simply rendered suspect, and cast as a cultural practice of a majority of Indians, which are largely coercive and do not conform to dominant marital norms in Britain. The White Paper thus subjects arranged marriages to a double illegitimacy. Either the marriage is not genuine because it is used for immigration purposes and is a sham, that is, it is not a *real* arranged marriage; or it is a real marriage, but then the whole practice of arranged marriages is rendered suspect.

Women in these communities are further cast as victims of their culture, which is regarded as backward and uncivilised. The Other is regarded as a violator of rights and the 'British' cultural standard as the civilised measure against which the cultural Other must be assessed. Championing women's rights in the subaltern community and family also becomes a way of delegitimising the community and its familial structures. Arranged marriages become a cultural peg for constructing the Other as subordinating in its treatment of women, denying women their rights to autonomy and consent.

These views are also based on cultural essentialism; the idea that the arranged marriage is a universal practice amongst Indians and is part of a long, ancient, cultural practice, at times even equated with the Hindu religion or Asian culture.

---

39 The fact that the legal age of marriage under the law in India is 18 for women and 21 for men is not addressed. Marriages between minors are illegal and cannot be overridden by custom or local practice.

Even those who have critiqued the proposal have done so on the assumption that arranged marriages constitute a part of 'Asian culture'.[40] Not only is this an inaccurate assumption, it erases any understanding of culture in the postcolonial context as heterogeneous, fluid and malleable. For example, arranged marriages constituted a part of the political and cultural authenticity move against the British colonial power during the period of Empire. As Tanikar Sarkar has set out in her meticulous account of the cultural consequences of the colonial encounter for women, the non-consensual, indissoluble, infant marriage was projected as a higher form of love that countered the 'utilitarian, materialist and narrowly contractual western arrangements' (Sarkar, 2001, pp 40–41). It was an arrangement that was also cast as a more loving and spiritual union than those practised in the West. The Hindu wife remained chaste and pure, and her purity derived in part from the fact that she was not contaminated by exposure to the colonial education system, urbanisation and an office routine. As I have discussed in Chapter 2, conjugality was a site of pure Hindu culture, and marked out as sacred and beyond the reach of colonial intervention. It was the primary site of power for the Hindu male who was otherwise thoroughly subjugated in the public arena by the colonial regime. Culture was constructed initially by the cultural revivalists and subsequently by the political nationalists in opposition to the West and Empire. The practice of the few was universalised to represent the culture of the whole community. Arranged marriages have become a symbol of cultural distinction amongst diasporic communities in Britain and elsewhere. However, it cannot be universalised and projected as a deeply embedded religious and cultural practice of all Indians or Asians.

The proposals put forth in the White Paper are also framed against the unstated normative understandings of marriage and culture in Britain. The Home Secretary expresses the need for future generations of these immigrants to grow up 'feeling British'.[41] Yet this 'feeling' is assumed but never examined. It encapsulates a return to a crude and simple mythology of a 'mono-racial, culturally uniform British identity in which non-white people's presence is tolerated – and even then only conditionally'.[42] The 'British' identity is neither defined nor explained, but it does involve integration by adopting British 'norms of acceptability', studying British history and culture, and the embracing of 'our laws, our values, our institutions'.[43] The deputy mayor of Oldham, one borough where race riots erupted in the summer of 2001, stated that he could 'visualise the BNP putting up election literature at the next local elections, quoting these words from the home secretary'.[44] Part of being British includes more than simply not tolerating practices unacceptable in the UK, such as arranged marriages. It involves a more aggressive assimilation move, which seeks in part to reshape the Other to conform to sexual, marital and cultural norms. Being British to some is understood as historical subordination of the 'native', through the vessel of Empire, to the one who occupies the unstated norm. For the

40 Burrell, 2002.
41 BBC, 'Immigrants should try to feel British', BBC News, 9 December 2001, http://news.bbc.co.uk/hi/English/uk_politics/newsid_1699000/1699847.stm (last visited 7 May 2002).
42 Younge, 2002.
43 Hodge, 2002a and 2002b.
44 Hodge, 2002a.

Home Secretary, being British involves assimilation into a society that is assumed to be advanced, civilised and homogenous. To ensure that their practices do not infiltrate or compromise on 'British values', the White Paper lays down the criteria for encouraging assimilation with the norm and excludes all those subaltern arrangements that do not conform to or resemble the norm. The norm against which one is to assimilate is clearly white, Christian and middle class. Blunkett explicitly challenges what he views as 'political correctness', stating that if you are 'white and middle class you can't say or do anything that might upset someone who's black or Asian'.[45] The proposal does not address the fact that more than half of the non-white people who live in the UK were born in the country and are part of a second or third generation of immigrants. Their presence has had an impact on what constitutes British values, culture and history and the meaning of these concepts is neither static nor agreed. They are subject to constant change, especially in the current context of devolution, European integration, globalisation and the decline of the monarchy.

The White Paper recognises that the Other always has the opportunity of being embraced by the universal project, through his or her willingness to assimilate. It provides the possibility for the Other to metamorphose into someone who is familiar and recognisable, and access to rights and benefits is contingent on the ability of the native to reinvent himself as an 'Englishman', a regular 'good chappy'. And one way in which to achieve this goal is to 'legislate for love', by encouraging marriage along the new lines proposed by the government, which introduce a love and duration criteria. Those relationships that fail to conform to the new criteria are rendered suspect and may be denied family or spousal reunion benefits. The goal to control who should and should not live in Britain is being partly secured through the proposal to regulate who a section of society should and should not marry. And this is reinforced through a cultural move, whereby arranged marriages, which are consensual, are subtly conflated with forced marriages and cast as an unacceptable cultural practice of the Other, and that such practices are wrong and also un-British. The White Paper represents a return to a strongly centred and highly exclusivist form of cultural and national identity. It is reminiscent of a time when English identity felt it could command, 'within their own discourses, the discourses of almost everybody else; not quite everybody, but almost everyone else at a certain moment in history' (Hall, 1997, p 20). The underlying message of the policy is to try to be like everyone else, and thereby entitled to be treated the same as everyone else. The 'everyone else' is the universal standard, the point of viewlessness that is positioned on a point of view, what Martha Minow describes as the starting point from which differences are described (Minow, 1987). It is the unstated norm from which 'being British' emerges.

Demonising the Other

The treatment of the Other has remained ambiguous and contested, based at times on simply a lack of knowledge or desire to know the Other, or at times on a fear that the Other was arriving in hordes to disrupt the social cohesion of the (Caucasian, Christian) global North or to take away jobs. At the same time, demographic deficits

45 Blunkett, 2002.

and labour demands for nannies, maids and domestic workers amongst others, have pressed nations into adopting policies that negotiate between a nation's cultural purity, economic priorities and national cohesion. The tensions generated by these negotiations could not be addressed within the exclusive confines of administrative and ministerial decisions. There was an explosion of actors involved in the debates on immigration, including non-governmental networks or organisations representing the rights of migrants, ethnic lobbies and anti-immigrant parties. The issue has been the centrepiece of elections and at the heart of cultural debates and cultural wars. Underlying this approach to difference is the premise that the Other is an ambiguous category – one who can in some ways be neutralised, though despised, or made into a friend, and even assimilated.

However, post-September 11 and the new 'War on Terror', we are witnessing a heightened anxiety about the Other, who is increasingly perceived as a threat or someone who is dangerous to the security of the nation. The boundary line of difference is being redrawn along very stark divides – between friend and enemy, those who are good and those who are evil (Porras, 1994). After September 11 the Other is transformed into a fanatic and potential enemy, although there are several grades of distinction.[46] The failure to define either the purpose or limits of the War on Terror has resulted in a serious casualty – targeting groups and communities we simply do not like.[47] In addition, the failure of any international legal definition on terrorism, precisely because of the disagreement over who is a terrorist and what

---

46 There is the distinct enemy, Al Qaeda and the Taliban. There are the rogue states, referred to in Bush's State of the Union Address on 29 January 2002, where he declared that Iran, Iraq and North Korea collectively constituted the axis of evil. And then there is a category that is less distinct, but nevertheless an enemy – the plethora of 'terrorists'. There are the suspected terrorists, the ones who are subject to racial profiling because of their affiliations with a 'hostile' or 'rogue state'. And there are those who walk the fine line between hostile enemy and friend, who can in an instant be cast as foe in the rhetoric of good and evil or us and them. These may include allies, as well as outspoken critics. Finally there are those who consort with, support, or even talk about giving the enemy rights – they are also the enemy. The enemy is to be annihilated through war pursued in the exercise of the right of self-defence and/or disenfranchised through the denial of rights. Thus denying rights to Guantanamo Bay prisoners, to which they are entitled under the Geneva Conventions, or denying due process or arbitrarily incarcerating 'the enemy' who resides within its borders, are all justified in the case of those who are not human or simply evil. See The New York Times, 2002; Shenon, 2002.

47 Human Rights Watch has reported that the broad scope and breadth of legislation that has been enacted by some states in pursuit of the War on Terror attests to the fact that they are using the legislation for purposes other than merely targeting terrorism (Human Rights Watch, 2002b). The report criticises legislation enacted immediately after the September 11 attacks as being over-inclusive and compromising on civil liberties. Eg, it states that the emergency legislation rushed through the US Congress, the US Patriot Act, 'permits the indefinite detention of non-deportable non-citizens once the Attorney General "certifies" that he has "reasonable grounds to believe" that the individual is engaged in terrorist activities or endangers national security' (Human Rights Watch, 2002b, p xxiv). These broad and vague criteria could allow the Attorney General to certify and detain any alien in the US who had any connection, however tenuous or distant in time, with a group that had once unlawfully used a weapon to endanger a person. The report is critical of several other measures by governments in different parts of the world which feed an anti-immigrant agenda rather than an anti-terrorist concern.

constitutes terrorism, has also made possible the unbounded, unrestrained use of the non-legal War on Terror.

The casting of the Other as a dangerous and negative force to be contained and confined finds its most explicit expression in Australia. The plight and desperation of asylum-seekers has been recast as a method by which to blackmail the Australian government. In response, the Australian government has adopted a policy which regards asylum-seekers with fear and loathing and, post-September 11, as a danger and threat to the nation. This policy has built on assertions of national sovereignty and a history of a white or discriminatory immigration policy that have been at the core of the Australia's treatment of its 'Others' (McMaster, 2000; McMaster, 2002, pp 3–9).

Australia is party to the 1951 Convention Relating to the Status of Refugees. Australian law defines refugees as people who are outside their country of nationality or usual country of residence, and are unable or unwilling to return to or seek the protection of that country because of a well-founded fear of being persecuted for reasons of race, religion, nationality, membership of a particular social group or political opinion.[48] The state has declared its commitment to provide protection to refugees under the terms of the Convention and ensure that asylum-seekers within Australia are treated in accordance with internationally recognised human rights standards, including the standards laid down in the International Covenant on Civil and Political Rights.[49] These commitments include an undertaking not to send back or refoule people to a country where they would be exposed to human rights violations. Some of these risks are defined in Art 33 of the Refugee Convention, and Arts 1 and 3 of the Convention Against Torture and Other Cruel, Inhuman or Degrading Treatment or Punishment.[50] In January 1993, the

---

48 The definition of 'refugee' is incorporated into the Migration Act 1958 (Cth) by s 36(2), which deals with the granting of protection visas and provides that a criterion for a protection visa is that the applicant is a non-citizen 'to whom ... Australia has protection obligations under the Refugees Convention as amended by the Refugees Protocol'. In September 2001, the Australian Parliament passed the Migration Legislation Amendment Act (No 6) 2001 (Cth). The amendments to the Migration Act 1958 (Cth) included definitions of key Convention definition terms: persecution; particular social group; non-political crime; and serious crime. The definitions are contained in Pt 2, Div 3, Sub-Div AI of the Migration Act 1958 (Cth). Persecution is defined in s 91R(1) as: '(a) the Convention grounds (or "reasons") must be the "essential and significant" reason/s for persecution; (b) the persecution must involve serious harm; (c) the persecution must involve "systematic and discriminatory conduct"'. Section 91R(2) lists some examples of 'serious harm', eg threat to life or liberty or 'significant economic hardship that threatens the person's capacity to subsist'. The definition of membership of a particular social group is refined in s 91S by stating that when the particular social group is a family, then the administrative decision maker should disregard any persecution experienced by other members of the family.

49 See also Human Rights and Equal Opportunity Commission, *Those Who've Come Across the Seas: Detention of Unauthorised Arrivals*, 11 May 1998.

50 Article 33.1 of the Refugee Convention prohibits '[the expulsion] or return [of] a refugee in any manner whatsoever to the frontiers of territories where his life or freedom would be threatened on account of his race, nationality, membership of a particular social group or political opinion'. And Art 3.1 of the Torture Convention prohibits the return of people to another country where they might face torture or ill-treatment: 'No state party shall expel, return ("refouler") or extradite a person to another state where there are substantial grounds for believing that he would be in danger of being subjected to torture.' The Torture Convention permits a wide interpretation to the term torture, but includes acts of cruel, inhuman or degrading treatment and punishment. Convention Against Torture and Other Cruel, Inhuman or Degrading Treatment or Punishment, 26 June 1987, Arts 1.2, 16, 1465 UNTS 85.

Australian government also recognised the right of people in the country to submit complaints under Art 22 of the Refugee Convention to the UN Committee Against Torture.

These international commitments have not been directly incorporated into domestic law, largely because Parliament considers that the domestic law is already in compliance with international standards. It is also reflective of a deeper tension between refugee law, which is governed by international law, and asylum law, which is considered to be part of a state's preserve, and governed by domestic law (Kennedy, 2004, pp 199–233). Under the domestic law, asylum-seekers are categorised into two groups: those who enter legally and those who enter unlawfully.[51] There is a legitimate means of entry through Australia's 'Humanitarian Program', where a quota has been set for the numbers who will be allowed entry from different parts of the world.[52] They are referred to as refugees and entitled to permanent residency on arrival and health checks. If a candidate arrives in an authorised manner, either through a visitor's visa or student's visa, they are allowed to remain in the community while their applications are processed. Others who arrive in Australia outside of this scheme may be provided with 'temporary safe haven'. The country provided safe haven for over 4,000 ethnic Albanians in 1999 when they were flown in from Kosovo.

Those who enter the country illegally and without proper travel documents are treated as 'unlawful non-citizens' and confined to a detention centre until their cases are reviewed and they are either granted a visa to remain in Australia, or ordered to leave the country voluntarily, or deported. Since October 1999, asylum-seekers who arrive without authority are released from detention if their application is successful, but they are only entitled to receive a temporary protection visa (TPV) for a period of three years.[53] If they leave the country for any reason, they cannot re-enter.[54] Every three years they must reapply for their visa and their cases are re-evaluated to determine whether or not they still face persecution. The temporary visa affords asylum-seekers limited access to healthcare, but relatively few other services.[55] A critical feature of this category of visa is that family members are not allowed to join those who hold a TPV. Those persons who arrive in an unauthorised manner are refused family reunification rights for a minimum of 30 months after they receive refugee status and are not provided with travel documents. Women and children can be detained even though they may have a male family member in Australia who is on a TPV. The reasoning of the government is that they do not want to reward people who disrespect the laws by paying someone to smuggle them into the country by then sending an invitation to their families to join them.

---

51 Department of Immigration and Multicultural and Indigenous Affairs, *Fact Sheet 61: Seeking Asylum in Australia*, www.immi.gov.au/facts/61asylum.htm (visited 2 November 2003).

52 Department of Immigration and Multicultural and Indigenous Affairs, *Fact Sheet 60: Australia's Refugee and Humanitarian Program*, www.immi.gov.au/facts/60refugee.htm (visited 2 November 2003).

53 Migration Amendment Regulations 1999 (No 12) to Migration Regulations 1994 (Cth).

54 Regulation 785.511, Migration Regulations 1994 (Cth).

55 For a comparison of the entitlements of holders of TPVs and holders of protection visas, see Human Rights and Equal Opportunity Commission, *Temporary Protection Visas: Operation and Impacts*, www.hreoc.gov.au/racial_discrimination/Erace/tpvs/tpvs.html.

Philip Ruddock, the former Minister for Immigration and Multiculturalism, justified the policy stating that these are suspect cases: 'If somebody comes to Australia without authorisation and is allowed to remain in Australia in order to ensure that they are not refouled, doesn't give them a family reunion entitlement. Their families are in situations of safety and security. Otherwise they wouldn't have left them, I am sure.'[56] He has implicitly accused TPV holders of blackmail by 'using our good feelings ... to get money to send out of Australia ... and using the money that is provided for food to buy mobile telephones and then go to charities to try to top up their income'.[57] The policy has had two inadvertent implications. Women and children are increasingly accompanying husbands and fathers on boats for fear of otherwise being permanently separated. Secondly, if it is not possible to raise enough funds for the entire family to travel, those individuals who are on a TPV are encouraged to maintain contact with criminal networks as their only hope of being reunited with their family members.[58]

Australia's mandatory detention policy was adopted in 1994 when nine detention centres were set up to deal with the increasing number of persons fleeing to Australia through smuggling routes via Indonesia. One of the effects of this policy has been to incarcerate illegal immigrants and their families arbitrarily in detention centres, the conditions of which have been regarded as bordering on inhuman.[59] Under international standards, the policy of detention should be temporary and must be exceptional and not used as a form of punishment.[60] Some people, including children, are locked up in medium security prisons, often in

---

56 Ruddock, P, 'Interview: Philip Ruddock: regarding asylum-seekers, unlawful arrivals, refugee conventions and detention', 'Hard Talk', BBC TV, 14 December 2001.

57 ABC Radio, *The World Today*, 9 August 2000; National Nine Television Network, Sunday, 13 August 2000.

58 Since August 2003, there have been further changes made to the migration regulations. Prior to September 2001, lawful entrants who had been granted a TPV were entitled to apply for a permanent protection visa after 30 months. This option has now been withdrawn. TPV holders who did not apply for a permanent protection visa prior to 21 September 2001 are ineligible to do so after that date. All TPV holders, even those who entered Australia lawfully on genuine documents, are covered by the changes. A TPV holder can apply for another TPV if he or she can demonstrate that he or she is in continuing need of protection: see Migration Amendment Regulations 2003 (No 9) to Migration Regulations 1994 (Cth).

59 The detention policy has been criticised by a number of the human rights groups, including Amnesty International (*Amnesty International Australia* (Newsletter Aug–Sept: Mandatory Detention), www.amnesty.org.au/airesources/index-92as2001.html) and the Human Rights Committee, as violating Art 7 of the International Covenant on Civil and Political Rights, adopted 16 December 1966, 999 UNTS 171.

60 See Conclusion No 44 (XXXVII), *Detention of Refugees and Asylum Seekers*, Executive Committee of UN High Commissioner for Refugees, para (b) (1986), which states 'in view of the hardship which it involves, detention should normally be avoided', although the Conclusion does recognise the right of a state to detain an asylum-seeker temporarily in exceptional cases where detention is necessary in order to:

- verify his or her identity;
- determine the elements on which the claim to protection is based;
- deal with cases where refugees or asylum-seekers have destroyed their travel and/or identification documents in order to mislead the authorities of the state in which they intend to claim asylum; or
- to protect national security and public order.

See also Convention Relating to the Status of Refugees, 28 July 1951, Art 31, 189 UNTS 150, which provides that state parties 'shall not impose penalties, on account of their illegal entry or presence, on refugees who, coming directly from a territory where their life or freedom were threatened ... enter or are present in their territory without authorisation, provided they present themselves without delay to the authorities and show good cause for their illegal entry or presence'.

remote and inhospitable locations. Some inmates have spent years behind razor wire fencing while their applications are processed (Flood, 2001). In March 2001, Ron McLeod, Commonwealth Ombudsman with the Department of Immigration and Multicultural Affairs, stated in his report on the conditions prevailing at immigration detention centres (IDC) that refugees had fewer rights than convicted criminals in Australia, and that as of 30 June 2001 he was concerned that there were almost 800 women and children in detention (McLeod, 2001, p 19). He condemned the conditions of the IDCs, holding that he found evidence:

> ... at every IDC of self-harm, damage to property, fights and assaults, which suggested that there were systemic deficiencies in the management of detainees ...The evidence available to me suggests that what was provided in late 1999 to mid 2000 was not adequate at that time, especially at Woomera where large numbers of detainees were held. (McLeod, 2001, pp 2–3)

Amnesty International has expressed serious concerns regarding the lack of access to due process of asylum-seekers. Its report states that the government 'regularly refuses requests by lawyers and other organisations to visit the detention centres to meet new arrivals and advise them of their rights under Australian and international law' (Amnesty International, 1998, p 15). In July 2000, the Human Rights Committee also stated, in its concluding observations on the third and fourth periodic report submitted by Australia, that the government should reassess its policy and legislation on mandatory detentions.[61]

After September 11, the government also enacted several pieces of legislation prioritising border controls and ensuring that the illegitimate and illegal 'migrants' were restricted or confined, partly in the interests of the security of the nation. In September 2001, Parliament amended the Migration Act 1958, introducing certain populist measures designed to discourage non-citizens from seeking to enter Australia unlawfully, and provide clear legislative authority for the government to take action to stop unlawful entry into Australia (Maley, 2003). The Migration Amendment (Excision from Migration Zone) Act 2001 permits certain Australian territories and excised offshore places to be removed from the migration zone for the purposes of limiting the ability of 'unlawful non-citizens' to make a valid visa application.[62] The Migration Amendment (Excision from Migration Zone) (Consequential Provisions) Act 2001 introduces a new regime for people who arrive unlawfully at an offshore excised place. It includes powers to move the person to another country where claims for Australia's protection can be considered.[63] The

---

61 Office of the High Commissioner for Human Rights, *Concluding Observations of the Human Rights Committee, Australia*: 24 July 2000, paras 498–528, A/55/40 (2000). The Committee specifically stated the mandatory detention under the Migration Act of 'unlawful non-citizens', including asylum seekers, raised questions about compliance with Art 9.1 of the International Covenant on Civil and Political Rights. This Article provides that no person shall be subjected to arbitrary detention. The Committee also questioned the policy of not informing detainees of their right to seek legal advice and not allowing access to non-governmental human rights organisations.

62 This Act amends the definition of 'excised offshore place' in the Migration Act 1958 (Cth), s 5. The note accompanying the definition is: 'The effect of this definition is to excise the listed places and installations from the migration zone for the purposes of limiting the ability of offshore entry persons to make valid visa applications.'

63 The 2001 Act inserts s 198(A) into the Migration Act 1958 (Cth).

legislation also prevents any legal proceeding from being initiated against the government in respect of the entry, status, detention and transfer of any unlawful non-citizen entering Australia at an excise offshore place.[64] These Acts were enacted in part to respond to several efforts by asylum-seekers to arrive in Australia by landing at offshore places that constitute parts of Australian territories. The specific targets of this legislation are boat people. By removing any infrastructure or facilities to process claims, the intention was to discourage boats from landing at the nearest land destination or to undertake the journey in the first place. The amendments applied to the boat people taken to Nauru and Papua New Guinea after being rescued, by *the Tampa*, a Norwegian cargo ship, from their sinking ship. Australia refused the ship access to its waters, adamant to 'keep these people out' as part of its broader 'Pacific solution' (MacCallum, 2002, pp 38–46).

The policy in Australia has treated the families of asylum-seekers as responsible for their condition, criminal and dangerous. And this policy is reinforced through the representations of these families as uncaring, even brutal and barbaric. In October, the Australian navy fired at an Indonesian ship carrying over 300 asylum-seekers, in an attempt to force it to leave Australian waters. The government announced that the refugees were throwing their children overboard to force the navy to rescue them, and in an attempt to blackmail the government.[65] The government stated that they had photographs of these outrages, proving that the actions of the refugees were premeditated.[66] The result was to fuel the image of the uncaring and uncivilised Other, at a time when the issue of asylum-seekers was a hot election issue.[67] Prime Minister Howard stated, 'There is something to me incompatible between somebody who claims to be a refugee and somebody who would throw their own child into the sea ... It offends the natural instinct of protection and delivering security and safety to your children'.[68] In February, well after the Howard government was safely ensconced back in power, the Prime Minister confessed that the photographs were not genuine, and that he had knowledge of this fact just three days prior to the election but chose not to divulge the information.[69]

During 2002, refugees in detention centres across the country began to protest against the government's repressive policy and the appalling conditions of the centres. In February 2002, detainees at Woomera began a hunger strike, protesting against the conditions in the centres, especially the situation of children and young adults. Refugees flee from their countries of origin often in search of a better life for their children. To find themselves incarcerated with their families is tantamount to

---

64 This Act inserts s 494AA into the Migration Act 1958 (Cth). However, this amendment does not exclude the original jurisdiction of the High Court of Australia under s 75 of the Australian Constitution.

65 Douez and Forbes, 2001.

66 Cock and Ludlow, 2001.

67 Barkham, 2001.

68 Newsfeed, 2001.

69 Clennell, 2002; Walker, 2002.

the ultimate humiliation. Several of the detainees, including children, began the horrifying method of protest by drinking detergent and shampoo and sewing their lips together in a symbolic gesture of protest against the oppression and imposed silence that they experienced in the detention centres. The government once again cast the refugees as uncivilised, and as child abusers for stitching together the lips of their children. Howard stating that children who are in the proper, positive care of their parents do not sew their lips together.[70] One columnist supporting the government's tough policies towards illegal immigrants deplored the acts of lip stitching, stated, 'The test is simple: who wants as neighbours the people who have stitched shut the mouths of their children?'[71] The actions of the families were characterised as a form of blackmail of the government, rather than an act of desperation.[72] The chairman of the Council for Multicultural Australia challenged these assertions, stating that: 'Every time a humanitarian issue is raised in relation to asylum-seekers, their deviousness and criminal intent is proclaimed.'[73] Although the method of resistance was a particularly disturbing one, it was characterised by the Australian Human Rights and Equal Opportunities Commission as a response to the 'atmosphere of despair in which they live' (Tay and Ozdowski, 2002).

There was also a demonstration by Australian activists outside Woomera, where several activists helped detainees break out and escape from the centre. Howard reiterated that these demonstrations would only serve to strengthen the resolve of the government in relation to its policy on illegal immigration. He reasserted the commitment of the government to pursue the policy of mandatory detention as a method for sending a signal to the world that no one can come to Australia illegally, despite the fact that punitive detentions contravene the Refugee Convention. Several letters to the editor of the *Daily Telegraph*, a national daily newspaper, echoed the position of the government towards the outsider and the image of the Other as barbaric. One such letter stated:

> Some of these refugees come from countries where life is cheap and national pride is unheard of. They are so busy killing each other and supporting violence that they reduce their countries to rubble, only caring about the outside world when they want something such as aid or, in this case, refuge … The asylum seekers should be grateful that they are alive at all, despite their conditions, and realise that the demonstrators outside Woomera share the same destructive, unethical and selfish traits as those governments or individuals the asylum seekers were originally escaping.[74]

In April 2003, the Woomera detention centre was shut down. However, the government remains steadfast in the pursuit of its policy. In response to the protests, it proposed that the children be placed in care with foster parents to meet the needs in detention centres without allowing their parents into the country. The proposal is

---

70 Mackay, 2002.
71 Tyler, 2002.
72 Steketee and Henderson, 2002.
73 Marks, 2002.
74 *Daily Telegraph*, 2002.

reminiscent of the notorious policy to place Australia's aboriginal children in the care of Christian, white families who would teach them how to be real Australians. It is simultaneously an assimilationist move as well as a civilising strategy that relegates the parents of subaltern families into the category of savage and criminal (Human Rights and Equal Opportunities Commission, 1997; Manne, 2001).

The Australian policy towards asylum-seekers has historically been problematic (Maley, 2001). A trickle of people, especially those who are non-white and non-Christian, triggers a fear of an imminent flood. This fear, in the contemporary moment, has been most explicitly expressed against the Muslim. The breakdown of numbers of refugees worldwide, published in 2001, indicates that the largest number of refugees in the world come from the Middle East and South Asia (57%) (Solomon, 2001). However, in Australia, a European refugee (6%) has a 14.7 times greater chance of being granted asylum in Australia than someone from the Middle East.[75] At the same time, a disproportionate number of individuals from Islamic and third world countries are placed in detention.[76] And these 'boat people' have been subjected to a new form of hate-speech and Islamaphobia, which expresses itself in terms of a fear of a 'Muslim invasion'.

The fear of hordes of immigrants flooding into the country is not substantiated by statistics.[77] In part this fear has been constructed in and through the rhetoric of the far right, especially the 'One Nation' party which was a significant force in 1998. Since then the party's fortunes have declined, but their rhetoric has succeeded in influencing public discourse on asylum-seekers. Since September 11, the Howard government has been able to capitalise on the fear and the rhetoric through recourse to the 'War on Terror', which casts the Other as quite simply evil and dangerous. This dehumanising move serves to justify the denial of rights to those who cross Australia's borders illegally, regardless of the reasons or context. Howard was able to fight a successful election campaign by casting the cross-border movements by immigrants, refugees and asylum-seekers into Australia as a potential terrorist threat. Ruddock stated on several occasions that 'these people' had to be detained to determine if they posed 'a security risk to our country ... and assess whether or not they have criminal backgrounds ... or ... a contagious disease'.[78] In the build up to

75 Department of Immigration, Multicultural and Indigenous Affairs, *Population Flows: Immigration Aspects*, Part 4, 2000, pp 24–27.

76 By November 2001 there were some 3,400 people detained in immigration detention facilities in Australia. The five main nationalities of detainees in 2001–02 were Iranian, Afghan, Chinese, Indonesian and Sri Lankan. In 2000–01, the five main nationalities were Afghan, Iraqi, Iranian, Palestinian and Chinese: Department of Immigration and Multicultural and Indigenous Affairs, *Fact Sheet 82: Seeking Asylum in Australia*, www.immi.gov.au/facts/82detention.htm (visited 2 November 2003).

77 In a recent report by the UN High Commissioner for Refugees, the total number of boat people arriving in Australia between 1999–2000 was only 4,174, in sharp contrast to the number of asylum applications received in the UK, which was 97,660 in 2000. The number of applications received in other liberal democracies also far outnumbers the ones received by Australia. In 2000, Germany received 78,760; the Netherlands 43,890; Belgium 42,690; and France 38,590: Registration and Statistics Unit, Division of Operational Support, United Nations High Commissioner for Refugees, *Asylum Applications Submitted in Europe*, 2000, 25 January 2001.

78 Loane, 2002. See also Anthony Burke who discusses how the security discourse and Australia's general security concern may have affected the country's refugee policies (Burke, 2001).

the national elections in 2001, the two main national parties resorted to the powerful rhetoric of the threat of terrorism and evil. Howard declared, 'You don't know who's coming, and you don't know whether they do have terrorist links or not'.[79] Howard's hardline position that these asylum-seekers were unwelcome, would not be allowed into Australia and would be incarcerated, won the day.

In the Australian context, the transnational migrant is undermined through two delegitimising moves. These subjects are cast as blackmailers, using their situations of hardship to extract sympathy and material benefits from the Australian government. They are also cast as primitive and barbaric, as demonstrated in the representation of these families in the media and government statements in *the Tampa* case, the 'children overboard' fiction, as well as the Woomera protests. And the (Christian) 'Western family' is cast as autonomous, egalitarian and freedom loving, in contrast to the family of the transnational migrant subject, which is represented as oppressive and dictatorial, and where the overarching identity is a religious one (invariably Muslim).[80] Both of these responses are based on a fear of the Other that has characterised Australian policy in an increasingly borderless world, as well as assumptions that the 'subaltern family' is not a 'real' family and has no claims to be treated as a 'real family'.

Through these various delegitimising moves, the transnational migrant subject is dehumanised and thus regarded as not deserving rights and freedoms. They are invading hordes of 'natives' who deserve to drown should their vessels capsize, or be incarcerated should they make it to shore. The nearly xenophobic features of this policy demonstrate the ideological success of the conservative right and the legacy of its One Nation agenda (despite its electoral defeats), which have been reinforced by the recent War on Terror. The transnational migrant subject must be held at bay, as someone who is not only barbaric in his or her treatment towards children, but also a subject who is crossing borders to undermine 'Australian values' and the Australian way of life. Women are regarded as complicit with their male counterparts, regarded as equally backward or dangerous, and not deserving of any different treatment, as is highlighted in the housing of all inmates in crowded non-private arrangements in the detention centres. They are all treated as either criminal or contaminating and a force to be feared, regardless of gender. The complex factors that push people to migrate are overshadowed by the construction of this savage Other. The human security that is central to the debate on refugee and asylum

---

79 Mydans, 2001.

80 Even those subjects who propose to come to Australia through legitimate means, especially from the Middle East, are discouraged through a complete Othering of their habits, lifestyles and relationships as distinct and incompatible with Western (civilised) norms and values. A kit prepared for Phillip Ruddock for a tour in the Middle East contained a document entitled, Department of Immigration Multicultural and Indigenous Affairs, 'Questions and Answers Provided by the Australian Minister for Immigration and Multicultural Affairs, Philip Ruddock', 2001. In response to a query, 'Wouldn't my family have a better life?', the response suggested stated as follows: 'No. Even if you can bring your family to join you, your children will abandon your traditional way of life in favour of modern "western" ways. You will lose control of your children, who will rebel and question your authority and your religious beliefs.' The relationships of the Muslim or Middle Easterner are constructed as repressive and undemocratic, and Australia as a land only suitable to 'Westerners' and a family structure that comprehends 'Western values' and autonomy (Maley, 2001, p 12).

policy is displaced by one that prioritises the security of the nation-state and its citizens and families (Rundle, 2001). The measures put in place serve to push those who seek to flee from their circumstances further into the network of human smugglers and traffickers.

The new War on Terror is not bounded by any international definition on terrorism, and has created space for a more strident and alarming response to the global movements of people, reducing it at times to nothing more than an evil threat. It is a non-legal War being pursued at times in and through international institutions such as the UN Security Council, and/or through the fear of the Other by Western liberal democracies and nation-states. The unrestrained possibilities of this polemical device can target a host of activities that blur any distinctions between terrorism, trafficking, smuggling, migration and illegal movement. If terrorism is defined as a transnational crime, then by merely committing the crime of seeking illegal movement and illegal entry these people could be defined as terrorists. Because the smugglers offer travel services to illegal migrants, they would easily fall within the category of transnational organised crime, criminals and potential terrorists. At the very worst they are terrorists and the very best they are criminals who have sought to cross the border illegally. These simple equations again led to a disjuncture between the reality of the illegal migrant and the issue of terrorism. The conflation of the migrant with the terrorist is not new, but it has received greater attention since September 11. It has afforded more space for the representation of the Other as a fanatic, dangerous and opposed to freedom.

All three responses fail to engage with the transnational, transmigratory processes that have been triggered by new global processes. Cross-border movements have become a feature of the contemporary moment and an integral aspect of globalisation. Although a new legal order has emerged to deal with and facilitate the cross-border movement of capital, there has not been a simultaneous response to deal with the concomitant cross-border movement of people and labour through legal processes that accommodate this new reality. Instead, states have sought refuge in traditional notions of nation-state identity and sovereignty to resist cross-border traffic (Beneria and Bisnath, 2004, p 2). And this assertion of national identity is being deployed through assimilationist moves as well as through the production of fear of the Other as a threat to the nation's security. Prior to September 11, there was some recognition that cross-border movements needed to be addressed in more transnational terms. These conversations have become muted ever since the September 11 attacks took place.

The space for the transnational migrant is being eroded through the discourse of trafficking and through the discourse of terrorism and threats to the security of the nation. These initiatives operate to keep 'the Rest' away from the West. This shift is troubling given that movement and migration is partly a phenomenon of the current phase of globalisation and hence it is and will continue to be a feature of our transnational world. Criminalising or victimising the transnational migrant, forces this subject to continue to move through illicit channels, and remain vulnerable, stigmatised and illegitimate. It seems unlikely that the security of what is left of the nation-state can be achieved at the cost of the security of the transnational migrant.

Indeed it will only serve to encourage the construction of a paradox, where the security of the transnational migrant is perhaps less threatened by people smugglers and traffickers than by the current international system of protection offered to people who move as migrants, refugees or asylum-seekers.

The spectre of the Other and the *Death of the West*

Across Europe and North America, the conservative voice is building on the fear of the Other crossing borders, the threat they pose to the nation-state and the values of 'western civilisation'. Pat Buchanan voices this fear when he predicts the death of the West from immigrant hordes, amongst others, in his recent book *Death of the West* (Buchanan, 2002).[81] He argues that the very survival of the West is under threat, as a result of depopulation, surrender of nationhood, and the flood of third world immigration:

> Now that all the western Empires are gone, Western Man, relieved of his duty to civilise and Christianise mankind, revelling in luxury in our age of self-indulgence, seems to have lost his will to live and reconciled himself to his impending death. Are we in the twilight of the West? Is the Death of the West irreversible? (Buchanan, 2002, p 1)

And these fears have been accentuated post-September 11. Buchanan argues that the events of September 11 exposed a new divide, 'Suddenly we awoke to the realisation that among our millions of foreign-born, a third are here illegally, tens of thousands are loyal to regimes with which we could be at war, and some are trained terrorists sent here to murder Americans' (Buchanan, 2002, p 2). And there are some specific races or ethnic groups that are particularly averse to changing, or assimilating. Unlike the Europeans who were willing to change, melting and reforming, 'the largest population transfer in history is coming from all the races of Asia, Africa and Latin America, and they are not melting and reforming' (Buchanan, 2002, p 3). There is a fear of some fanatical, uncontrolled migration from places that have nothing in common with America's history (all two hundred years of it), heroes, language or culture. And that Other is mostly 'Arab looking' and Muslim. Their cultures are often essentialised and pitted against universal norms and values such as freedom or liberty.[82] For example, the religious right leader Pat Robertson described Islam as a violent religion that seeks 'to dominate and then if need be

---

81 Pat Buchanan's position is not representative of the entire conservative right. Nevertheless, I present the views of Buchanan partly because he has been a senior advisor to three American presidents. From 1966 to 1974 he was confidant and assistant to Richard Nixon. In 1974, he served as assistant to Gerald Ford. From 1985 to 1987 he was White House Communications Director for Ronald Reagan. In December 1991, Mr Buchanan challenged President George Bush for the 1992 Republican presidential nomination and received 3 million Republican primary votes.

82 'The clash between Islamic religious and political authority is more widespread and in some places more threatening now than it was then ... This is the dark side of Islam, which shows its face in violence and terrorism intended to overthrow modernising, more secular regimes and harm the western nations that support them. Its influence far outweighs its numbers ... these disparate cells of angry young men seem to boil up from the broad opposition growing in the largely undemocratic countries of the region, in a self-proclaimed war to force pure, undiluted Islamic law on the societies that have failed them' (Nelan, 1993).

destroy'.[83] In contrast, the culture of the West is represented as freedom loving and committed to liberty. In his address to the nation on September 11, President Bush concluded that the US had been attacked by 'evil' because 'we're the brightest beacon for freedom and opportunity in the world'.[84] The Italian Prime Minister, Silvio Berlusconi, 'praised Western civilisation ... as superior to that of the Islamic world and urged Europe to reconstitute itself on the basis of its Christian roots'.[85] And Dick Cheney argued that the civilised world was under threat:

> I think the world increasingly will understand that what we have here are a group of barbarians ... So it's an attack not just upon the US but upon, you know, civilised society. ... We also have to work, through, sort of the dark side, if you will ... That's the world these folks operate in, and so it's going to be vital for us to use any means at our disposal, basically to achieve our objective. And I think we have to recognise we are the strongest, most powerful nation on Earth.[86]

The conservatives and religious right have been able to deploy this rhetoric to simultaneously further their domestic agenda. Jerry Falwell is reported as stating that 'liberal civil liberties groups, feminists, homosexuals and abortion rights supporters bear partial responsibility for Tuesday's terrorist attacks because their actions have turned God's anger against America'.[87]

The threat from those who have nothing in common with the West is also able to take advantage of the declining birth rate. For Buchanan this is the Achilles heel of the West, which will ultimately lead to its demise. His biggest concern is over the decline in the birth rate of European-Americans and the simultaneous increase in immigration from non-white countries. Buchanan argues that those who are celebrating diversity 'will spend their golden years in a Third World America' (Buchanan, 2002, p 5). His solution to this decline is to reclaim the white, Christian origins of the West and the traditional family. Although the extreme bigotry of Buchanan is not likely to appeal to a majority, he expresses explicitly the fears that remain unstated amongst moderates. The regulation of immigration, appeals to security, national cohesion, and keeping the 'alien' at bay have popular appeal in many countries in the developed north. Prior to September 11, in countries such as the Netherlands, France, Germany, Austria, Italy, Australia, Britain and the US, conservative and right-wing parties raised the spectre of the native Other as a creature who is depriving their nations and citizens of jobs, a discrete identity and its national moorings.

The conservative right's agenda plays out differently in different political and cultural contexts. However, their commonality lies in their resort to imagined notions of a homogenous community and a homogenous culture, and how these have now come under threat. In Denmark, refugees have been exempt, since January 1999, from the requirement to show that they have the means to support

---

83 Robertson, 2002.
84 *The New York Times*, 2001.
85 Erlanger, 2001.
86 Russert, 2001.
87 Harris, 2001.

family members who wish to join them, except for parents over 60 years old.[88] However, some municipalities which accepted refugees under the new dispersal scheme have criticised the family reunification rules as over-liberal and socially inflammatory. In response, the government has drafted an amendment to the 'Aliens Law', which will limit access to family reunion. The European Commission against Racism and Intolerance (ECRI) has criticised Denmark's 'recent growth in hostility' to refugees and immigration, especially in areas of housing and employment.[89] Denmark's refugees number only about 4.5% in a population of 5.5 million. There has been an increase in the spread of Nazi propaganda, and despite relatively small levels of poverty and the fairest distribution of wealth in the European Union, Danes have propelled a far-right nationalist party, the Danish People's Party, led by Pia Kjaersgaard, to respectability in the polls.[90] The Commission has expressed specific concern over the treatment of those perceived to be Muslims, especially from Somalia, who are vulnerable to problems of xenophobia and discrimination.[91] The ECRI has also been concerned over the increasing use of racist and xenophobic propaganda in politics, especially by the Austrian Freedom Party, which has enjoyed unexpected electoral successes in the past few years.[92] The main targets of these attacks are non-EU citizens, including immigrants, asylum-seekers, and refugees:

> Typically these categories of people are held to be responsible for unemployment, street crime, social security abuse and increased expenditure in border control and internal security budgets. The presence of people of non-Austrian origin in Austria, presented as excessive, is portrayed as a threat to the preservation of Austrian national identity and of a secure environment.[93]

Although the Austrian Freedom Party fared badly in the last set of national elections, the success of the right wing does not lie as much in its electoral success as in its ability to shift the discourse to the right, forcing other parties to embrace their policies and promote their agenda. For example, the Austrian Freedom Party was able to force the government to enact new alien laws in 1998. In 1999, the Social Democratic Interior Minister announced that there would be *de facto* no more immigration. In Holland, polls taken in late 2001, revealed that 46% of the 18–30 age group polled in favour of zero Muslim immigration.[94] The anti-Islamic sentiment was given legitimacy by the maverick Dutch politician, Pim Fortuyn, who authored *Against the Islamisation of Our Culture*. In an interview with *The Guardian* newspaper, prior to his assassination in May 2002, he stated that Islam was a backward culture, and when asked about immigration, he stated, 'This country is full'.[95] In Germany,

---

88 European Council on Refugees and Exiles, *Country Report*, 1999, www.ecre.org/publications/3legaldevel.shtml.
89 European Commission Against Racism and Intolerance, *Second Report on Denmark*. Adopted 16 June 2000.
90 *Ibid*, p 4.
91 *Ibid*.
92 European Commission Against Racism and Intolerance, *Second Report on Austria*. Adopted 16 June 2000, p 3.
93 *Ibid*, p 5.
94 Osborn, 2002.
95 *Ibid*, p 19.

the ex-Chancellor Helmut Schmidt, declared that there were too many foreigners in the country and that they could not be assimilated simply because Germans were 'racist deep down'.[96] The extraordinary victory of French neo-fascist Jean-Marie Le Pen, in the first round of the French presidential election in April 2002, on an anti-crime and anti-immigration platform, exposed an anxiety about the loss of identity. This anxiety was not analysed in the broader context of Europeanisation and globalisation, but targeted against the most visible manifestation of change and loss of cultural moorings – the arrival of immigrants.

The targeting of the Other as the source of the woes of the local resident found a strident voice after the attacks on the World Trade Centre. After September 11, the urgency of the situation has been underscored by the War on Terror and imminent threats to national security. The conservative right has been able to build on the fear of the Other and the xenophobia pre-dating September 11, and turn it into a hostile antagonistic fear of the Other who is threatening the security of the nation. Although these concerns are most explicitly voiced by the extreme right or religious right, less noticed is the more uniformly pervasive emergence of similar forms of conservatism within mainstream discourses. The mainstreaming of the right wing's discourse is combined with the current hostility to cultural difference, and the reassertion of family values. This shift is underscored by an approach that seeks to retrieve a golden era that has been ruptured as a result of the cross-border infiltrations, and the challenges this poses to the legitimacy of the nation-state, national cohesion and the family. This shift justifies legal reforms that further alienate those who have been cast as the 'new enemy' and also justifies the resort to punitive measures on the grounds that these people are evil or dangerous and not entitled to due process or rights. The recourse to border controls, ethnic purity, cultural values and nationalism is constructed along the anxieties of dealing with difference and serves to stigmatise, penalise and criminalise the transnational migrant. These responses push us further away from addressing the complexity of cross-border movements and the equally complex legal and political responses required to address the issues raised by such movements.

And this brings me to the normative consequences of the current response to the transnational migrant subject. The autonomous sovereign subject, which is bounded by the nation-state, is afforded the maximum protection, even at the cost of the liberty or freedom of the transnational migrant subject. My three examples reveal that the transnational migrant has fewer rights, and at times is subjected to criteria or a punitive regime that is in part designed to ensure the security and legitimacy of the autonomous sovereign subject. States remain reluctant either to confer rights or benefits on this subject in international law or to force it to assimilate and conform to an 'everyone else' standard. It is also regarded as an entity to be kept at arm's length, incarcerated or kept out lest it corrupt and contaminate and ultimately destroy the security and freedom of the sovereign subject and the culture of the West.

The assertion of normative values and truth claims has enabled conservative and right-wing forces, buttressed by the War on Terror, to pursue a political and legal agenda that is diametrically opposed to women's rights and others who cross

---

96 Hooper, 2002.

borders in their capacities as migrants, refugees or asylum-seekers. International and domestic legal responses illustrate how law is being contained within cultural, familial and sexual normativity. The War on Terror has enabled bright lines to be drawn along artificial divides of civility and barbarity. The construction of the transnational migrant subject as a savage, enables liberal democracies to treat the Other as undeserving and incapable of participating in the universal rights project. It is an approach that produces a paradox – though the project of law is based on the Enlightenment's foundations of universality and inclusivity, the transnational migrant, a subaltern subject, ends up challenging these claims of completeness and finality. Fitzpatrick and Darian-Smith discuss the incommensurability of the law with the perspective of postcolonialism, stating:

> ... we can say that postcolonialism holds apart what the discourse of universal human rights would oppressively unite ... the problem postcolonialism has with human rights is not they are universal ideals or that they have a particular practical purchase, or even that they contain both these qualities. The problem lies in these two things being made to correspond to each other. (Fitzpatrick and Darian-Smith, 1999, p 10)

The legal interventions in the lives of transnational migrants have been articulated primarily from the perspective of the host country. The subaltern voices are omitted from these conversations and yet these are the voices that can assist in untangling the conflations and confusions that are taking place between trafficking, migration and terrorism in the international and domestic legal arenas. The voice of the transnational migrant must be foregrounded – not as a terrorist, nor as a victim, but as a complex subject who is affected by global processes and seeking safe passage across borders.

Contingent legitimacies

In all three situations, I have discussed how the legitimacy of the transnational migrant is challenged at the point of crossing borders, whether through lawful or unlawful means. The focus of the regulatory effort by industrialised states is on borders. These efforts are based on the assumption that the movement of the transnational migrant is a consequence of either organised criminal networks and 'evildoers' or their manipulative and devious manoeuvres. The consequence of this assumption is that the receiving country is not regarded as in any way implicated in these movements. It is the passive recipient. This assumption is not universally the case, but the initiatives I have discussed in this chapter suggest that the larger part of the responsibility lies with those who move. As a result, the transnational migrant becomes the site for accountability and enforcement.

The dichotomous and simplistic responses to cross-border movements have several important implications. First, they do not respond to the global reality. As Sassen argues, the increased control over immigration, as well as over resident immigrants, after September 11, will reduce civil liberties but will not in turn 'help us learn how to accommodate more immigration to respond to the future demographic turn' (Sassen, 2003). The War on Terror has taken us further in a direction that is insular, prioritises the security of the nation and operates to reinforce the sovereign subject. It also provides the new discourse through which the Other comes to be viewed, and conflates the issues of trafficking, migration and refugees with terrorism. The fact that there is no internationally agreed definition of terrorism leaves open the possibility for states to go after anything they simply do not like.[97] Cross-border movements have been caught within the framework of a War fought along the simple binaries of good versus evil, civilisation versus barbarism. A response to border-crossing cannot be adequately addressed through such binaries. Indeed this myopic response will do little to discourage the illegal crossing of borders or the determination of those who want to move.

Secondly, the treatment of women's cross-border movements within the framework of trafficking perpetuates the assumption that she is a victim in need of rescue from the conniving, manipulative, culturally primitive subaltern family, or is herself equated with the demonised Other. Her complex subjectivity remains unaddressed in the legal and policy approaches being pursued at the national and international levels. Her legitimacy resides primarily in her status as a victim and/or in her role as a mother or wife, ascribed to her through the operation of dominant sexual and cultural norms. Women's choice or agency remains either non-existent, questionable or tainted. Her choice to move must be distinguished from other situations where her consent is absent or her movement is compelled by strife or conflict.

Thirdly, the transnational migrant poses a challenge to the nation-state and the fictional boundaries being buttressed in this current moment of globalisation. She challenges the notion of the autonomous sovereign subject, proposing a reconstitution of the subject, and she challenges assumptions about the world's Others who are moving, taking advantage of the opportunities afforded by globalisation, and revealing the vicissitudes of their own complex locations. Assimilative moves in Britain and elsewhere seek the surrender of subaltern spaces in exchange for being treated the same as everyone else. The politics of assimilation are based on the assumption that the state is a democratic institution that needs to simply rectify certain inequalities, rather than a space which institutionalises dominant social powers. The radical and subversive potential of the transnational migrant subject as posing a challenge to these power arrangements, and the norms that sustain the edifice of the sovereign state and the sovereign subject, is rendered benign through assimilation. The potential for a transformative political project is made impotent, and the scope of the radical challenge posed by the subaltern location narrowed if not altogether extinguished.

Finally, it is important to recognise that the erection of borders through immigration policies, anti-terrorist legislation and anti-trafficking laws, or simply incarceration, will not succeed in stopping cross-border movements, meeting a

---

97 In the US, the lack of a definition has also encouraged an attack on difference especially on the Arab-American community or those who are Arab-looking. Neighbours and colleagues are willing to provide information to the FBI and intelligence sources about anyone they deem 'suspicious'. 'Most of the detainees are Arabs or Muslims, and many have spent more than 100 days in jail waiting to leave the country with no end to detention in sight. Nearly all were jailed after being picked up on visa violations at traffic stops or because of neighbours' suspicions' (Drew and Miller, 2002).

nation's security needs or protecting the sovereign subject. People will continue to move, illegally if legal means are not available. This process cannot be arrested through stricter border controls or immigration policy. Further, as Sassen has pointed out, there has been a significant reconfiguration of the nation-state in two directions. The first is the relocation of certain attributes of the state onto a supranational regime of authority, such as the World Trade Organisation, the European Union or certain human rights codes and institutions (Sassen, 1999, p 5). Secondly, there is an increased significance of transnational private actors that are produced through the emergence of a transnational legal and illegal regime for cross-border transactions that include labour mobility and exit options for refugees (Sassen, 1999, p 5).

Law has served as an important site for the regulation of cross-border movements. It is a site of contest over the extent of legitimate encroachment on state sovereignty, over the legitimacy of border-crossings, over the legitimacy of the players and participants, be they non-state actors such as transnational corporations, trafficking, terrorist or smuggling networks. International law is combining with domestic legal responses to the crossing of borders primarily from two perspectives – protection and security. Protection has implications specifically for women, resonating with an earlier moment in history when protectionist responses were based on certain gender stereotypes. And security emanates from the desire to return to secure borders, a cohesive society, and a defence against the threat posed by these global Others. The examples discussed in this essay bring out how these contests are being fought out. In the international arena, the view that women's consensual movement should also be included within the definition of trafficking has won over the struggle to articulate women's consensual movement within a migration and human rights framework. In the UK, the institution of marriage and its cultural underpinnings are sites of contest, where the legal regime is being implicated to outlaw culturally unfamiliar or suspicious arrangements in favour of those which are familiar and dominant. In the context of Australia, there is a struggle over who is or is not a threat to the security of the nation and the white, Christian normative family. The government is invoking the non-legal War on Terror, to expand the scope of its anti-immigration policies to include those who are also victims of persecution, terror, and displacement, and recast them as dangerous, threatening and subject to incarceration.

In order to address the issue of cross-border movements, we cannot simply remain confined to the domestic arena, where regulatory enforcement is focused on the individual and the border. Nor can this process be addressed in the international legal arena purely in terms of criminality or trafficking. These responses fail to understand the global context in which such movements are occurring. In order to understand and respond to the relationship between the transnational migrant subject and the law, it is necessary to revisit this issue as one that is not cast in terms of binaries – the security and cohesion of the state versus the invasion of hordes of Others. It must be addressed against this broader canvas of transnationalism. Transnational movements require a transnational response and analysis – they cannot be caught within older frameworks.

The challenges posed by transnational migrant subjects reveal the fact that legal responses to cross-border movements, internationally and domestically, need to be reorganised. The sovereign state and the sovereign subject are being bared through these challenges posed by the world's constitutive Others. The liberal state and the liberal subject are based on the idea of fixed borders, with clearly identifiable interests and identities. They are imbued with the power to decide, choose and act autonomously. Yet the challenge of globalisation, which brings the challenge of migration and non-state actors to the legitimacy of the borders of the sovereign state and the autonomous subject, indicates otherwise. The complexity of new global formations and the dynamic character of the individual who crosses borders exposes any notion that the state and individual are hermetically sealed or capable of exercising control through self-contained power. The inability to distinguish those who constitute national subjects from those who are alien or foreign is blurred, reflecting the uneasy location of a distinct national entity with distinct borders and a distinct national subject with borders. The legitimising tools of cohesion, unity and especially sovereignty become blunt in the face of a more complex and integrated world and global economy (Knopp, 1993).

Taking the international and transnational interventions in the legitimacy of border-crossings as the focal point, I have argued that the legal regulation of cross-border movements is premised on assumptions about difference, the subject, and gender. In the contemporary moment, the legitimacy of these movements has been defined in and through the War on Terror and the UN Security Council resolutions that followed the September 11 attacks. Security of the sovereign state and its citizens become the overarching frame through which to determine the legitimacy of interventions at the border and the response to border-crossings. This frame opposes the primitive Other who seeks to destroy all that is 'good' and 'civilised', and also amplifies the voice of those whose reference point is a golden age, a return to family values, faith based practices, and the social cohesion of the nation.

The idea that either or both of these positions are fictions that ignore the uneven development of history has found its expression in the questions provoked by the transnational migrants who are living the global reality. They are moving – across national, regional and international borders – and they are simultaneously drawing attention to the disparate arenas of power with which we must engage in order to understand the global movement of people and the normative and political significance of the transnational migrant subject.

Abrams, K, 'Sex wars redux: agency and coercion in feminist legal theory' (1995) 95 Columbia Law Review 304

Abu-Odeh, L, 'Comparatively speaking: the "honor" of the "East" and the "passion" of the "West"' (1997) 2 Utah Law Review 287

Agnes, F, 'Law, ideology and female sexuality: gender neutrality in rape law' (2 March 2002) 37(9) Economic and Political Weekly 844

Ahmad, A, 'Fascism and national culture: reading Gramsci in the days of Hindutva', in *Lineages of the Present: Ideological and Political Genealogies of Contemporary South Asia*, 2000, London and New York: Verso

AIDS Bhedbhav Virodhi Andolan, 'Homosexuality in India: culture and heritage', in Ratti, R (ed), *A Lotus of Another Colour: An Unfolding of the South Asian Gay and Lesbian Experience*, 1993, Boston: Alyson Publications Inc

Alexander, JM, 'Erotic autonomy as a politics of decolonization: an anatomy of state practice in the Bahamas tourist economy', in Alexander, JM and Mohanty, CT (eds), *Feminist Genealogies, Colonial Legacies, Democratic Futures*, 1st edn, 1996, London: Routledge, pp 63–100

Amin, S and Chakrabarty, D (eds), *Subaltern Studies IX: Writings on South Asian History and Society*, 1996, Delhi: OUP

Amnesty International, *Australia – A Continuing Shame: The Mandatory Detention of Asylum-Seekers*, June 1998, New York: Amnesty International

Anderson, B, *Imagined Communities: Reflections on the Origin and Spread of Nationalism*, revised edn, 1991, London and New York: Verso

Anghie, A, 'Finding the peripheries: sovereignty and colonialism in nineteenth century international law' (1990) 40 Harvard International Law Journal 1

Anghie, A, 'Franscisco de Vitoria and the colonial origins of international law' (1996) 5(3) Social and Legal Studies 321

Anzaldua, G, *Borderlands/La Frontera: The New Mestiza*, 2nd edn, 1999, London: Consortium Book Sales and Distributors

Appadurai, A, *Modernity at Large: Cultural Dimensions of Globalization*, 1996, Minneapolis: Minnesota UP

Appiah, A, *In My Father's House: Africa in the Philosophy of Culture*, 1992, London: Methuen

Arnold, D and Hardiman, D (eds), *Subaltern Studies VIII: Essays in Honour of Ranagit Guha*, 1994, Delhi: OUP

Asian Age, 'Deepa Mehta leads candlelit protest' (1998a) *Asian Age*, 8 December

Asian Age, 'Macauby's law haunts Calcutta's guys' (1998b) *Asian Age*, 5 August

Bachetta, P, 'When the (Hindu) Nation exiles its queers' (1999) 17(4) Social Text 141

Banerjee, S, *Dangerous Outcast: The Prostitute in Nineteenth Century Bengal*, 1998, Calcutta: Seagull Books

Barkham, P, 'Australia votes on how tightly to close the door' (2001) *The Guardian*, 10 November

Barry, K, *Female Sexual Slavery*, reprint, 1990, New York: New York UP

Bassiouni, MC, 'Enslavement as an international crime' (1991) 23 New York University Journal of International Law and Politics 445

Basu, A, 'Hindu women's activism in India and the questions it raises', in Jeffrey, P and Basu, A (ed), *Resisting the Sacred and the Secular: Women's Activism and Politicised Religion in South Asia*, 1998, London: Routledge, pp 167–84

Basu, T, Datta, P, Sarkar, S, Sarkar, T and Sen, S, *Khaki Shorts, Saffron Flags: A Critique of the Hindu Right*, 1993, Delhi: Orient Longman

Belak, B, *Gathering Strength: Women from Burma and Their Rights*, 2003, Thailand: Images Asia, pp 194–225

Beneria, L and Bisnath, S (eds), *Global Tensions: Challenges and Opportunities in the World Economy*, 2004, London: Routledge

Benhabib, S, 'On contemporary feminist theory' (1989) 36 Dissent 366

Berman, N, 'The Grotius lecture series' (1999) 14(6) American University International Law Review 1515

Beverley, J, *Subalternity and Representations: Arguments in Cultural Theory*, 1999, Durham, NC, London: Duke UP

Bhabha, H, '"Race", time and the revision of modernity' (1991) 9(12–13) The Oxford Literary Review 193

Bhabha, H, *The Location of Culture*, 1994, London: Routledge

Bhadra, G, Prakash, G and Tharu, S (eds), *Subaltern Studies X: Writings on South Asian History and Society*, 1999, Delhi: OUP

Bhaskaran, S, 'The politics of penetration: section 377 of the Indian Penal Code', in Vanita, R (ed), *Queering India: Same-Sex Love and Eroticism in Indian Culture and Society*, 2002, New York: Routledge, pp 17–29

BJP Mahila Morcha (BJP Women's Front), 'Women's decade: Mahila Morcha response', in *Dashak Ke Jharokhe Mein* (Reflections on a Decade), 1991, p 1

Blackstock, C, 'Blunkett in clash over marriages' (2002) *The Guardian*, 8 February

Blunkett, 'Love and legislation' (2002) *The Guardian*, 13 February

Bower, LC, 'Queer acts and the politics of "direct address": rethinking law, culture and community' (1994) 28 Law and Society Review 1009

Boyd, S, 'Challenging the public/private divide: an overview', in Boyd, S, *Challenging the Public/Private Divide: Feminism, Law and Public Policy*, 1997, Toronto: Toronto UP, pp 3–33

Boyd, S, 'Family, law and sexuality: feminist engagements' (1999) 8(3) Social and Legal Studies 369

Brodie, J, *Politics on the Margins: Restructuring and the Canadian Women's Movement*, 1995, Halifax: Fernwood

Brown, W, 'Feminist hesitations, postmodern exposures' (1991) 3(1) Differences 63

Brown, W, *States of Injury: Power and Freedom in Late Modernity*, 1995, Princeton: Princeton UP

Brown, W, *Politics Out of History*, 2001, Princeton and Oxford: Princeton UP

Brown, W, 'Suffering the paradoxes of rights', in Brown, W and Halley, J (eds), *Left Legalism/Left Critique*, 2002, Durham and London: Duke UP, pp 420–34

Brown, W and Halley, J, 'Introduction', in Brown, W and Halley, J (eds), *Left Legalism/Left Critique*, 2002, Durham and London: Duke UP, pp 1–37

Buch, CM, Kucklenz, A and Le Manchec, M, 'Worker remittances and capital flows', 2002, Kiel Institute for World Economics, Working Paper No 1130

Buchanan, P, *Death of the West: How Dying Populations and Immigrant Invasions Imperil Our Country and Civilization*, 2002, New York: St Martin's Press

Bulbeck, C, *Re-Orienting Western Feminism: Women's Diversity in a Post-Colonial World*, 1997, Cambridge: Cambridge UP

Bumiller, E, *May You Be the Mother of a Hundred Sons: A Journey Among the Women of India*, 1990, New York: Random House

Bumiller, E, 'Evangelicals sway White House on human rights issues abroad' (2002) *The New York Times*, 26 October

Bunch, C, 'Women's rights as human rights: toward a re-vision of human rights' (1990) 12 Human Rights Quarterly 486

Bunch, C, 'The intolerable status quo: violence against women and girls', in *The Progress of Nations*, 1997, New York: Unicef, pp 41–43

Bunting, A, 'Theorizing women's cultural diversity in feminist international human rights strategies', in Bottomley, A and Conaghan, J (eds), *Feminist Theory and Legal Strategy*, 1993, London: Blackwell, pp 6–18

Burke, A, *In Fear of Security: Australia's Invasion Anxiety*, 2001, Sydney: Pluto Australia

Burrell, I, 'Is Blunkett "attacking Asian culture" with criticism of arranged marriages?' (2002) *The Independent*, 8 February

Burton, A, *Burdens of History: British Feminists, Indian Women and Imperial Culture*, 1994, Chapel Hill: North Carolina UP

Buss, D, 'Robes, relics, and rights: the Vatican and the Beijing Conference on Women' (1998) 7(3) Social and Legal Studies International Law Journal 339

Butler, J, *Bodies that Matter*, 1993, New York: Routledge

Butler, J, 'Merely cultural' (1998) 227 New Left Review 33

Butler, J, *Gender Trouble: Feminism and the Subversion of Identity*, 1999, New York: Routledge

Cain, P, 'Feminist jurisprudence: grounding the theories' (1989–90) 4 Berkeley Women's Law Journal 191

Cantle, T, *Community Cohesion: A Report of the Independent Review Team*, 1 January 2003, London: Community Cohesion Unit, Home Office

Chakrabarty, D, 'Postcoloniality and the artifice of history: who speaks for "Indian" pasts?' (1992) 37 Representations 1

Chakrabarty, D, 'Radical histories and questions of Enlightenment Rationalism' (1995) 30(14) Economic and Political Weekly 751

Chakrabarty, D, *Provincializing Europe*, 2000, Ewing, New Jersey: Princeton UP

Chakrabarty, D and Bhabha, H, *Habitations in Modernity: Essays in the Wake of Subaltern Studies*, 2002, Chicago: Chicago UP

Chandra, B, *Communalism in Modern India*, 1984, Delhi: Stosius Inc/Advent Book Division

Chari, H, 'Colonial fantasies and postcolonial identities: elaboration of postcolonial masculinity and homoerotic desire', in Hawley, JC (ed), *Postcolonial Queer*, 2001, New York: New York UP, pp 277–304

Charlesworth, H, Chinkin, C and Wright, S, 'Feminist approaches to international law' (1991) 85(4) American Journal of International Law 613

Chatterjee, P, *Nationalist Thought and the Colonial World*, 1986, Delhi: OUP

Chatterjee, P, 'The Nationalist resolution of the women's question', in Sanghari, KK and Vaid, S (eds), *Recasting Women: Essays in Colonial History*, 1989, New Delhi: Kali for Women, pp 233–53

Chatterjee, P, 'A religion of urban domesticity: Sri Ramakrishna and the Calcutta middle class', in Chatterjee, P and Prasad, G (eds), *Subaltern Studies VII*, 1991, Delhi: OUP, pp 40–68

Chatterjee, P, *The Nation and Its Fragments: Colonial and Postcolonial Histories*, 1993, Ewing, New Jersey: Princeton UP

Chatterjee, P, 'The Cowgirl goddess' (1994) *The Economic Times*, 23 August

Chatterjee, P and Jeganathan, P (eds), *Subaltern Studies XI: Community, Gender, and Violence*, 2000, Delhi: Permanent Black

Chatterjee, P and Pandey, G (eds), *Subaltern Studies VII: Writings on South Asian History and Society*, 1992, Delhi: OUP

Chaudhuri, M, *Indian Women's Movement: Reform and Revival*, 1993, Delhi: Radiant Publishers

Chaudhuri, N and Strobel, M (eds), *Western Women and Imperialism: Complicity and Resistance*, 1992, Bloomington: Indiana UP

Choudhary, A, 'Canning the controversy: the saga of the *Bandit Queen*' (1996) 4 Voices: A Journal on Communication and Development 27

Chuang, J, 'Redirecting the debate over trafficking in women: directions, paradigms, and context' (1998) 11 Harvard Human Rights Journal 65

Chugtai, I, *The Quilt and Other Short Stories*, Naquvi, T and Hameed, S (trans), 1990, Delhi: Kali for Women

Clennell, A, 'Overboard photos: I knew they were doubtful, PM admits' (2002) *Sydney Morning Herald*, 20 February

Cock, A and Ludlow, M, 'Parents throw children off ship – navy intercepts asylum boat' (2001) *Daily Telegraph*, 8 October

Cohn, B, *Colonialism and Its Forms of Knowledge*, 1996, Princeton: Princeton UP

Collini, S, Geuss, R and Skinner, Q (eds), *JS Mill: 'On Liberty' and Other Writings*, 1989, Cambridge: CUP

Collins, P, *Black Feminist Thought: Knowledge, Consciousness, and the Politics of Empowerment*, 2nd edn, 2000, New York: Routledge

Cossman, B, 'Turning the gaze back on itself: comparative law, feminist legal studies, and the postcolonial project' (1997) 2 Utah Law Review 525

Crenshaw, K, 'Demarginalizing the intersections of race and sex: a black feminist critique of antidiscrimination doctrine, feminist theory, and antiracist politics' (1989) University of Chicago Legal Forum 139

Crenshaw, K, 'Mapping the margins: intersectionality, identity politics, and violence against women of color' (1991) 43 Stanford Law Review 1241

Daily Telegraph, 'Letters to the editor' (2002) *Daily Telegraph*, 1 April

Daly, M, *Gyn/Ecology: The Metaethics of Radical Feminism*, 1978, Boston, Mass: Beacon Press

Das, A and Das, Y, *AIDS aur Hum*, 1999, Almora: Sahyog

Da Silva, DF, 'Toward a critique of the socio-logos of justice: the analytics of raciality and the production of universality' (2001) 7(3) Social Identities 421

Delgado, R and Stefancic, J, 'Hateful speech, loving communities: why our notion of "a just balance" changes so slowly' (1994) 82 California Law Review 851

Department of Women and Child Development, *Report of the Committee on Prostitution, Child Prostitutes and Children of Prostitutes and Plan of Action to Combat Trafficking and Commercial Sexual Exploitation of Women and Children*, 1998, New Delhi: Department of Women and Child Development

Department of Women and Child Development, 'An overview', *Annual Report 2001–2002*, 2001a, Delhi: Government of India

Department of Women and Child Development, *National Policy for the Empowerment of Women*, 2001b, Delhi: Government of India

Diamond, I and Quinby, L (eds), *Feminism and Foucault: Reflections on Resistance*, 1988, Boston, Mass: Northeastern UP

Dirlik, A, 'The postcolonial aura: third world criticism in the age of global capitalism' (1994) 20 Critical Inquiry 328

Doezema, J, 'Forced to choose: beyond the voluntary v forced prostitution dichotomy', in Kempadoo, K and Doezema, J (eds), *Global Sex Workers' Rights*, 1998, New York: Routledge, pp 34–50

Douez, S and Forbes, M, 'Boat people threw children overboard' (2001) *The Age*, 8 October

Drew, C and Miller, J, 'Though not linked to terrorism many detainees cannot go home' (2002) *The New York Times*, 18 February

Dubin, L, 'The direct application of human rights standards to, and by, transnational corporations' (1999) 61 International Commission of Jurists: The Review 35

Dugger, C, 'Kerosene weapon of choice for attacks on wives in India' (2000) *The New York Times*, 26 December

Dworkin, A, *Woman Hating*, 1991, reissue edition, New York: Plume

Dworkin, A and MacKinnon, C, *Pornography and Civil Rights: A New Day for Women's Equality*, 1988, Minneapolis: Organizing Against Pornography

Engineer, AA, 'On Bombay' (1995) 30(26) Economic and Political Weekly 1556

Engle, K, 'After the collapse of the public/private distinction: strategizing women's rights', in Dallmeyer, D (ed), *Reconceiving Reality: Women and International Law*, 1993, Washington DC: American Society of International Law, pp 143–47

Erlanger, S, 'Italy's Premier calls West superior to Islamic world' (2001) *The New York Times*, 27 September

Everett, JM, *Women and Social Change in India*, 1979, New Delhi: Heritage

Fabian, J, *Time and Its Other: How Anthropology Makes Its Objects*, 1983, New York: Columbia UP

Fein, H, *Imperial Crime and Punishment: The Massacre at Jallianwala Bagh and British Judgment, 1919–1920*, 1977, Honolulu: Hawaii UP

Fineman, ML, 'Challenging law, establishing differences: the future of feminist legal scholarship' (1990) 42 Florida Law Review 25

Fitzpatrick, F and Darian-Smith, E, 'Laws of the postcolonial: an insistent introduction', in Darian-Smith, E and Fitzpatrick, P (eds), *Laws of the Postcolonial*, 1999, Ann Arbor: Michigan UP, pp 1–15

Fitzpatrick, P, 'The immanence of Empire', in Passavant, P and Dean, J (eds), *Empire's New Clothes: Reading Hardt and Negri*, 2004, London: Routledge, pp 31–56

Flood, P, *Report of Inquiry into Immigration Detention Procedures*, 23 February 2001, Canberra: Department of Immigration and Multicultural Affairs

Foucault, M, *The Archaeology of Knowledge*, Sheridan, AM (trans), 1972, London: Tavistock

Foucault, M, *The History of Sexuality, Volume 1: An Introduction*, 1978, New York: New York Vintage

Foucault, M, *Power/Knowledge: Selected Interviews and Other Writings 1972–1977*, Gordon, C (trans), 1980, New York: Pantheon

Foucault, M, 'Nietzsche, genealogy, history', in Rabinow, P (ed), *The Foucault Reader: An Introduction to Foucault's Thought*, 1984a, Harmondsworth: Penguin, pp 76–100

Foucault, M, 'What is enlightenment', in Rabinow, P (ed), *The Foucault Reader: An Introduction to Foucault's Thought*, 1984b, Harmondsworth: Penguin, pp 32–50

Franke, K, 'Theorizing yes: an essay on feminism, law and desire' (2001) 101 Columbia Law Review 181

Frazer, N, *Justice Interruptus: Critical Reflections on the 'Postsocialist' Condition*, 1997, New York: Routledge

Fukuyama, F, *The End of History and the Last Man*, 1992, New York: Avon Books

Fuss, D, *Essentially Speaking: Feminism, Nature, and Difference*, 1989, New York: Routledge

Gabriel, K, 'Designing desire: gender in mainstream Bombay cinema', in Bose, B (ed), *Translating Desire: The Politics of Gender and Culture in India*, 2002, Delhi: Katha, pp 48–81

Gallagher, A, 'Consideration of the issue of trafficking: background paper', prepared for the Asian Pacific Forum of National Human Rights Institutions, New Delhi, 11–12 April 2002

Gandhi, L, *Postcolonial Theory: A Critical Introduction*, 1998, New Delhi: OUP

Ghosh, B, *Huddled Masses and Uncertain Shores: Insights into Irregular Migration*, 1998, The Hague: IOM-Martinus Nijhoff

Ghosh, S, 'Unfair victory for Saamna' (1995) 2(8) Journal of Peace Studies 28–33

Ghosh, S, 'The troubled existence of sex and sexuality: feminist engagements with censorship', in Butcher, M and Brossius, C (eds), *Image Journeys*, 1999, London and New Delhi: Sage, pp 233–56

Global Alliance Against the Trafficking in Women, Foundation Against Trafficking in Women and the International Human Rights Law Group, *Human Rights Standards for the Treatment of Trafficked Persons*, 1999, Bangkok, Thailand: Global Alliance Against the Trafficking in Women

Government of India, Ministry of Home Affairs, *Report of the Committee on Reforms of Criminal Justice System*, Vol 1 (2003), available at http://mha.nic.in/criminal_ justice_system.pdf

Gowalkar, MS, *We or Our Nationhood Defined*, 1939, Delhi: Bharat Publications

Grewal, I, 'Autobiographic subjects and diasporic locations: meatless days and borderlands', in Grewal, I and Kaplan, C, *Scattered Hegemonies: Postmodernity and Transnational Feminist Practices*, 1994, Minneapolis: Minnesota UP, pp 231–54

Grewal, I and Kaplan, C, 'Introduction', in Grewal, I and Kaplan, C, *Scattered Hegemonies: Postmodernity and Transnational Feminist Practices*, 1994, Minneapolis: Minnesota UP, pp 1–33

Grosz, E, 'Sexual difference and the problem of essentialism', in Schor, N and Weed, E (eds), *The Essential Difference*, 1994, Bloomington: Indiana UP, pp 82–97

Guha, R (ed), *Subaltern Studies I: Writings on South Asian History and Society*, 1982, Delhi: OUP

Guha, R (ed), *Subaltern Studies II: Writings on South Asian History and Society*, 1983, Delhi: OUP

Guha, R (ed), *Subaltern Studies III: Writings on South Asian History and Society*, 1984, Delhi: OUP

Guha, R (ed), *Subaltern Studies IV: Writings on South Asian History and Society*, 1985, Delhi: OUP

Guha, R (ed), *Subaltern Studies V: Writings on South Asian History and Society*, 1987, New York: OUP

Guha, R (ed), *Subaltern Studies VI: Writings on South Asian History and Society*, 1989, Delhi: OUP

Guha, R, 'The small voice of history', in Amin, S and Chakrabarty, D (eds), *Subaltern Studies IX: Writings on South Asian History and Society*, 1996, Delhi: OUP

Gujjar, 'Debate on how vulgar is *Bandit Queen*' (1996) *The Pioneer*, 17 February

Gunning, I, 'Arrogant perception, world-travelling, and multicultural feminism: the case of female genital surgeries' (1992) 23 Columbia Human Rights Law Review 189

Hall, S, 'Culture, community, nation' (1993) 7 Cultural Studies 349

Hall, S, 'Cultural identity and cinematic representation', in Baker, H, Diawar, M and Lindeborg, R (eds), *Black British Cultural Studies: A Reader*, 1996a, Chicago: Chicago UP, pp 210–22

Hall, S, 'When was "the postcolonial"? Thinking at the limit', in Chambers, I and Curti, L (eds), *The Post-Colonial Question: Common Skies, Divided Horizons*, 1996b, London: Routledge, pp 242–60

Hall, S, 'The local and the global: globalization and ethnicity', in King, AD (ed), *Culture Globalization and the World System: Contemporary Conditions for the Representations of Identity*, 1997, Minneapolis: Minneapolis UP, pp 19–40

Halley, J, 'Sexuality harassment', in Brown, W and Halley, J (eds), *Left Legalism/Left Critique*, 2002, Durham and London: Duke UP, pp 80–104

Hansen, TB, *The Saffron Wave*, 1999, Princeton: Princeton UP

Hardt, M and Negri, A, *Empire*, 2000, Cambridge: Harvard UP

Harris, A, 'Race and essentialism in feminist legal theory' (1990) 42 Stanford Law Review 581

Harris, J, '"God gave US what we deserve" Falwell says' (2001) *Washington Post*, 14 September

Hawley, JC (ed), *Postcolonial Queer*, 2001, New York: New York UP

Heng, G, 'A great way to fly: nationalism, the state, and the varieties of third-world feminism', in Alexander, J and Mohanty, CT (eds), *Feminist Genealogies, Colonial Legacies, Democratic Futures*, 1996, London: Routledge

Hennessy, R and Ingraham, C (eds), *Materialist Feminism: A Reader in Class Difference and Women's Lives*, 1997, New York: Routledge

Herman, D, 'Globalism's "siren song": the United Nations and international law in Christian Right thought and prophecy' (2001) 49 Sociological Review 77

Higgins, T, 'Anti-essentialism, relativism and human rights' (1996) 19 Harvard Women's Law Journal 89

Hindustan Times, 'Stall move to legalise prostitution, say NGOs' (2001) *Hindustan Times*, 2 March, p 4

Hodge, W, 'Britain proposes changes in asylum process' (2002a) *The New York Times*, 9 February

Hodge, W, 'Britain's non-whites feel un-British, report says' (2002b) *The New York Times*, 4 April

Hollifield, J, 'Migration, trade and the nation-state: the myth of globalization' (1998) 3(2) UCLA Journal of International Law and Foreign Affairs 595

Home Office, *Secure Borders Safe Haven*, Home Office White Paper, February 2002, London: HMSO

hooks, b, *Feminist Theory: From Margin to Centre*, 2nd edn, 2000, Boston: South End Press

Hooper, J, 'Ex-Chancellor complains country has too many foreigners as a result of guilty feelings over the Nazis' (2002) *The Guardian*, 29 March

Human Rights and Equal Opportunities Commission, *Bringing Them Home: Report of the National Inquiry into the Separation of Aboriginal and Torres Strait Islander Children from Their Families*, 1997, Sydney: Human Rights and Equal Opportunities Commission

Human Rights Watch, *Rape for Profit: Trafficking of Nepali Girls and Women to India's Brothels*, 1995, New York: Human Rights Watch

Human Rights Watch, *World Report*, 2000, New York: Human Rights Watch

Human Rights Watch, *Epidemic of Abuse: Police Harassment of HIV/AIDS Outreach Workers in India*, 2002a, New York: Human Rights Watch

Human Rights Watch, *World Report*, 2002b, New York: Human Rights Watch

Human Rights Watch Women's Rights Project, 'Trafficking in women and girls', in Human Rights Watch, *Global Report on Women's Human Rights*, 1995, New York: Human Rights Watch

Iglesias, EM and Valdes, F, 'Religion, gender, sexuality, race, and class in coalitional theory: a critical and self-critical analysis of Latcrit social justice agendas' (1998) 19 Chicano Latino Law Review 503

The Indian Express, 'She lifts 240 kg and the hopes of a billion' (2000) *The Indian Express*, 9 September

The Indian Express, '2001 will be year of women's power' (2001) *The Indian Express*, 3 January

Indra, D, *Engendering Forced Migration: Theory and Practice*, 1999, London: Berghahn Books

International Monetary Fund (IMF), *Balance of Payments Statistics Yearbook*, 2002, Washington: IMF

International Organisation on Migration, 'Facts and figures on international migration' (2003) 2 Migration Policy Issues 1

Jaffrelot, C, *The Hindu Nationalist Movement in India*, 1998, New York: Columbia UP

Jain, M, 'Coming to their aid' (1994) *Sunday*, 31 March

Jain, M and Raval, S, 'Controversy: ire over fire' (1998) *India Today*, 21 December

Jameson, F, *Postmodernism or the Cultural Logic of Late Capitalism: Post-Contemporary Interventions*, 1991, Durham and London: Duke UP

Jayaprasad, K, *RSS and Hindu Nationalism*, 1991, Delhi: Deep and Deep Publications

Jayawardena, K, *Feminism and Nationalism in the Third World*, 1986, London: Zed Books

Jethmalani, R (ed), *Kali's Yug: Empowerment, Law and Dowry Deaths*, 1995, New Delhi: Har-Anands Publications

John, M and Nair, J, 'Introduction', in John, M and Nair, J (eds), *Questions of Silence: The Sexual Economies of Modern India*, 1998, Delhi: Kali for Women, pp 1–51

Jones, KB, 'The trouble with authority' (1991) 3 Differences: A Journal of Feminist Cultural Studies 105

Kakkar, S, *Intimate Relations: Exploiting Indian Sexuality*, 1989, Delhi: Penguin

Kannabiran, K and Kannabiran, V, *De-Eroticising Assault: Essays on Modesty, Honour and Power*, 2002, Calcutta: Stree

Kapur, R, 'The profanity of prudery: the moral face of obscenity law in India' (1997) 8 Women: A Cultural Review 293–302

Kapur, R, 'The fundamentalist face of secularism and its impact on women's rights in India' (1999a) 47 Cleveland State Law Review 323

Kapur, R, 'The two faces of secularism and women's rights in India', in Howland, C and Buerganthal, T (ed), *Religious Fundamentalisms and the Human Rights of Women*, 1999b, New York: Palgrave Macmillan

Kapur, R, 'Imperial parody' (2001) 2(1) Feminist Theory 79

Kapur, R, 'Monsoon in a teacup' (2002a) Legal Affairs, September/October 46

Kapur, R, 'The right to freedom of religion and secularism in the Indian Constitution', in Tushnet, M and Jackson, V (eds), *Defining the Field of Comparative Constitutional Law*, 2002b, Westport: Praeger Publishers, pp 199–213

Kapur, R and Cossman, B, *Subversive Sites: Feminist Engagements with Law in India*, 1996, London: Sage

Kapur, R and Cossman, B, *Secularism's Last Sigh? Hindutva and the (Mis)Rule of Law*, 2001, reprint, Delhi: OUP

Kapur, R and Ghosh, S, '*The Bandit Queen* comes out on top' (1995) The Bulletin: Rights of Women 10

Kapur, R and Ghosh, S, 'Beauty queens: what a drag?' (1996) 9(4) Forum News 11, Kuala Lumpur: Asia Pacific Forum on Women Law and Development

Kempadoo, K, 'Introduction: globalizing sex-workers' rights', in Kempadoo, K and Doezema, J (eds), *Global Sex Workers' Rights*, 1998, New York: Routledge, pp 1–33

Kempadoo, K, 'Women of color and the global sex trade: transnational feminist perspectives' (2001) Meridians: Feminism, Race, Transnationalism 28

Kennedy, D, 'When renewal repeats: thinking against the box' (2000) 32 International Law and Politics 335

Kennedy, D, *The Dark Side of Virtue: Reassessing International Humanitarianism*, 2004, Princeton: Princeton UP

Khanna, S, 'Gay rights' (1992) Lawyer's Collective, June

Kim, N, 'Toward a feminist theory of human rights: straddling the fence between Western imperialism and uncritical absolutism' (1993) 25 Columbia Human Rights Law Review 49

Kishwar, M, '*The Bandit Queen*: film review' (1994) 84 Manushi 34

Kline, M, 'Race, racism, and feminist legal theory' (1989) 12 Harvard Women's Law Journal 115

Knopp, K, 'Re/statements: feminism and state sovereignty in international law' (1993) 3 Transnational Law and Contemporary Problems 293

Kosambi, M (ed), *Pandita Ramabai Through Her Own Words: Selected Works*, 2000, Delhi, London and New York: OUP

Koskenniemi, M, 'Fragmentation of international law? Postmodern anxieties' (2002) 15(3) Leiden Journal of International Law 553

Koso-Thomas, O, *The Circumcision of Women: A Strategy for Eradication*, 1997, London: Zed Books

Kotiswaran, P, 'Preparing for civil disobedience: Indian sex-workers and the law' (2001) 21 Boston College Third World Law Journal 161

Kumar, A, *Passport Photos*, 2000, Berkeley and Los Angeles: California UP

Lacey, N, *Unspeakable Subjects*, 1998, Oxford: Hart Publishing

Lai, SY and Ralphy, RE, 'Female sexual autonomy and human rights' (1995) 8 Harvard Human Rights Journal 201

Lal, V, 'John Stuart Mill and India' (1998) 54 New Quest 54

Lal, V, *Empire and Knowledge: Culture and Plurality in the Global Economy*, 2002, Sterling, Virginia: Pluto

Lawyers' Collective Women's Rights Initiative, 'Campaign for a Civil Law on Domestic Violence 2002: Update and Briefing', 2002, Lawyers' Collective Women's Rights Initiative, pp 22–23

Lewis, H, 'Between Irua and "female genital mutilation": feminist human rights discourse and the cultural divide' (1995) 8 Harvard Human Rights Journal 1

Lewis, H and Gunning, I, 'Cleaning our own house: "exotic" and familiar human rights violations' (1998) 4 Buffalo Human Rights Law Review 123

Liddle, J and Rai, S, 'Feminism, imperialism, and orientalism: the challenge of the "Indian Woman"' (1998) 7(4) Women's History Review 495

Limanoska, B, *Trafficking in Human Beings in South Eastern Europe*, 2002, UNICEF, UNOCHR and OSCE-ODIHR

Loane, S, 'Interview: Philip Ruddock' (2002) ABC, 1 February. See also Anthony Burke who discusses how the security discourse and Australia's general security concern may have affected the country's refugee policies (Burke, 2001)

Longfellow, B, 'Rape and translation in *Bandit Queen*', in Bose, B (ed), *Translating Desire: The Politics of Gender and Culture in India*, 2002, Delhi: Katha, pp 238–54

Loomba, A, *Colonialism/Postcolonialism (The New Critical Idiom)*, 1998, London and New York: Routledge

Lourde, A, *Sister Outsider: Essays and Speeches by Audre Lourde*, 1984, Freedom, California: Crossing

Ludden, D (ed), *Reading Subaltern Studies: Critical History, Contested Meaning and the Globalization of South Asia*, 2002, London: Anthem Press

Lugones, M, 'Playfulness, world-travelling, and loving perception', in Anzaldua, G (ed), *Making Face, Making Soul/Haciendo Caras: Creative and Critical Perspectives by Women of Colour*, 1990, San Francisco: Aunt Lute Foundation Books, pp 390–400

MacCallum, M, 'Girt by sea: Australia, the refugees and the politics of fear' (2002) 5 Quarterly Essay 1

Mackay, H, 'Australians all let us be judged' (2002) *The Age*, 30 March.

MacKinnon, C, 'Feminism, Marxism, method and the state: an agenda for theory' (1982) 7 Signs 515

MacKinnon, C, 'Feminism, Marxism, method and the state: toward feminist jurisprudence' (1983) 8 Signs 635

MacKinnon, C, *Feminism Unmodified: Discourses on Life and Law*, 1987, Cambridge: Harvard UP

MacKinnon, C, *Toward a Feminist Theory of the State*, 1989, Cambridge: Harvard UP

MacKinnon, C, 'On torture: a feminist perspective on human rights', in Mahoney, K and Mahoney, P (eds), *Human Rights in the Twenty-First Century: A Global Challenge*, 1992, Amsterdam: Martinus Nijhoff

MacKinnon, C, 'Crimes of war, crimes of peace', in Shute, S and Hurley, S (eds), *On Human Rights: The Oxford Amnesty Lectures*, 1993a, New York: Basic Books/Harper Collins, pp 83–109

MacKinnon, C, 'Turning rape into pornography: postmodern genocide' (1993b) 4(1) *Ms Magazine*, pp 24–30

MacKinnon, C, 'Rape, genocide, and women's human rights', in Stiglmeyer, A (ed), *Mass Rape: The War Against Women in Bosnia-Herzegovina*, 1994, Lincoln, Nebraska: Nebraska UP, pp 183–96

McClintock, A, *Imperial Leather: Race, Gender and Sexuality in the Colonial Contest*, 1995, New York: Routledge

McLeod, R, *Report of an Own Motion Investigation into the Department of Immigration and Multicultural Affairs' Immigration Detention Centres* (2001), March, www.ombudsman.gov.au./publications_information/Special_Reports/IDCMarch1.pdf

McMaster, D, 'Asylum-seekers and the insecurity of a nation' (2000) 56(2) Australian Journal of International Affairs 279

McMaster, D, 'Refugees: where to now?: White Australia to Tampa: the politics of fear' (2002) 21(1) The Academy of the Social Sciences in Australia Dialogue 3

McNay, L, Foucault and Feminism: Power, Gender and the Self, 1992, London: Polity

Mahmud, T, 'Migration, identity and the colonial encounter' (1997) 76(3) Oregon Law Review 633

Mahmud, T and Kapur, R, 'Hegemony, coercion, and their teeth-gritting harmony: a commentary on power, culture and sexuality in Franco's Spain' (2000) 33(3) University of Michigan Journal of Law Reform 995

Majeed, J, Ungoverned Imaginings: James Mill's The History of British India and Orientalism, 1992, reprinted 2001, Oxford: Clarendon

Maley, W, 'Security, people-smuggling and Australia's new Afghan refugees', Working Paper No 63, 2001, Australian Defence Studies Centre

Maley, W, 'Asylum-seekers in Australia's international relations' (2003) 57(1) Australian Journal of International Affairs 187

Mani, L, 'Multiple mediations: feminist scholarship in the age of multinational reception' (1990) 35 Feminist Review 24–41

Mani, L, 'Cultural theory, colonial texts: reading eyewitness accounts of widow burning', in Grossberg, L, Nelson, C and Treichler, P (eds), Cultural Studies, 1991, London: Routledge, pp 392–404

Mani, L, Contentious Traditions: The Debate on Sati in Colonial India, 1998, Berkley and Los Angeles: California UP

Manjul, T, 'Models don't find eunuchs a drag' (2000) Hindustan Times, 17 November

Mankekar, P, Screening Culture, Viewing Politics: Television, Womanhood and Nation in Modern India, 1999, New Delhi: OUP

Manne, R, 'In denial: the stolen generations and the right' (2001) 1 The Australian Quarterly Essay 1

Marks, K, 'Far from Guantanamo Bay, desperate Afghans try to grab the world's attention' (2002) The Independent, 24 January

Marks, S, 'The end of history? Reflections on some international legal theses' (1997) 3 European Journal of International Law 449

Marks, S, 'Empire's law' (2003) 10(1) Indiana Journal of Global Legal Studies 449

Matsuda, M, Lawrence, C and Delgado, R, 'Public response to racist speech: considering the victim's story' (1989) 8 Michigan Law Review 2320

Matsuda, M, Lawrence, C and Delgado, R, Words that Wound: Critical Race Theory, Assaultive Speech and the First Amendment (New Perspectives on Law, Culture and Society), 1993, Boulder, Colorado: Westview

Mehta, US, *Liberalism and Empire: A Study in Nineteenth Century British Liberal Thought*, 1999, Chicago: Chicago UP

Memmi, A, *Dominated Man: Toward a Portrait*, 1968, London: Orion

Mendoza, B, 'Transnational feminisms in question' (2002) 3 Feminist Theory 295

Menon, N, 'Embodying the self: feminism, sexual violence and the law', in Chatterjee, P and Jeganathan, P (eds), *Subaltern Studies Volume XI: Community and Gender Violence*, 2000, Delhi: OUP, pp 67–104

Mernissi, F, *Dreams of Trespass: Tales of a Harem Girlhood*, 1994, Boulder, Colorado: Perseus Books

Mignolo, W, *Local Histories/Global Designs*, 2000, Princeton: Princeton UP

Mill, JS, *The Subjection of Women*, 1997, Mineola, New York: Dover Publications

Mill, JS, 'Civilization', in *Dissertations and Discussions*, 2002, Honolulu: Pacific UP, pp 130–67

Minow, M, 'Justice engendered' (1987) 101 Harvard Law Review 10

Minow, M, 'Surviving victim talk' (1993) 40 UCLA Law Review 1411

Mishra, S, *Chameli*, 2004, Mumbai: Pritish Nandi Communications Ltd

Mohanty, CT, 'Under western eyes: feminist scholarship and colonial discourses', in Mohanty, CT, Russo, A and Torres, L (eds), *Third World Women and the Politics of Feminism*, 1991, Indianapolis: Indiana UP, pp 51–80

Mohanty, CT, '"Under western eyes" revisited: feminist solidarity through anti-capitalist struggles' (2003) 28(2) Signs: Journal of Women in Culture and Society 499

Mukherjee, K, 'Unique sex-worker fair rekindles legitimisation debate' (2001) *Asian Age*, 5 March

Mydans, S, 'Which Australian candidate has the harder heart' (2001) *The New York Times*, 9 November

Nair, J, 'Nationalist patriarchy and the regulation of sexuality', in *Women and Law in Colonial India: A Social History*, 1996a, New Delhi: Kali for Women

Nair, J, 'The Devadasi, Dharma and the State', in Kapur, R (ed), *Feminist Terrains and Legal Domains: Interdisciplinary Essays on Women and Law*, 1996b, New Delhi: Kali for Women, pp 243–66

Narain, S, *The Historiography of the Jallianwalla Bagh Massacre, 1919*, 1998, New Delhi: Lancer Publishers and Distributors

Narayan, U, *Dislocating Cultures: Identities, Traditions, and Third World Feminism*, 1997, London: Routledge

Narayan, U, 'Essence of culture and a sense of history: a feminist critique of cultural essentialism' (1998) 13 Hypatia 86

National Commission of Women, *Report on Societal Violence on Women and Children in Prostitution, 1995–96*, 1996, New Delhi: National Commission of Women

Nelan, B, 'The dark side of Islam' (1993) *Time*, 4 October

Nessiah, V, 'The ground beneath her feet: TWAIL feminisms', in Anghie, A, Chimni, B and Mickelson, O (eds), *The Third World International Order: Law, Politics and Globalizations*, 2003, London: Kluwer, pp 133–43

Newsfeed, 'PM accuses boat people of moral blackmail' (2001) *AAP Newsfeed*, 8 October

The New York Times, 'A day of terror: Bush's remarks to the nation on the terrorist attacks' (2001) *The New York Times*, 12 September

The New York Times, 'US fighting suit for names of New Jersey September 11 inmates' (2002) *The New York Times*, 19 February

Nussbaum, MC, *Sex and Social Justice*, 1999, New York, Oxford: OUP

Nussbaum, MC, *Women and Human Development: The Capabilities Approach*, 2000, Delhi: Kali for Women

Okin, SM, *Justice, Gender and the Family*, 1989, New York: Basic Books

Okin, SM, 'Feminism, women's human rights, and cultural differences' (1998) 13(2) Hypatia 32

Oldenburg, VT, 'Lifestyle as resistance: the case of the courtesans of Lucknow, India' (1990) 16 Feminist Studies 259

Oldenburg, VT, *Dowry Murder: The Imperial Origins of a Cultural Crime*, 2002, New York: OUP

Oldham Independent Review, *Panel Report*, 2001, Oldham: Oldham Metropolitan Borough Council and Greater Manchester Police

Ong, A, 'Strategic sisterhood or sisters in solidarity? Questions of communitarianism and citizenship in Asia' (1996) 4 Indiana Journal of Global Legal Studies 107

Osborn, A, 'Dutch youth back far-right immigration policy' (2002) *The Guardian*, 23 February

Otto, D, 'Challenging the "New World Order": international law, global democracy and the possibilities for women' (1993) 3 Transnational Law and Contemporary Problems 371

Otto, D, 'Subalternity and international law: the problems of global community and the incommensurability of difference' (1996) 5(3) Social and Legal Studies 337

Pandey, G, *The Construction of Communalism in Colonial North India*, 1990, Delhi: OUP

Parekh, B, 'Superior people: the narrowness of liberalism from Mill to Rawls' (1994) *The Times Literary Supplement*, 25 February

Parekh, B, 'Liberalism and colonialism: a critique of Locke and Mill', in Pieterse, JN, Parekh, B and Nederveen, J (eds), *The Decolonization of Imagination: Culture, Knowledge and Power*, 1995, London: Zed Books, pp 81–98

Parry, B, 'Problems in current theories of colonial discourse' (1997) 9 Oxford Literary Review 27

Passavant, P, 'A moral geography of liberty', in Darian-Smith, E and Fitzpatrick, P (eds), *Laws of the Postcolonial*, 1999, Ann Arbor: Michigan UP, pp 61–85

People's Union for Civil Liberties, Karnataka, *Human Rights Violations Against the Transgender Community: A Study of Kothi and Hijra Sex Workers in Bangalore, India*, 2003 Bangalore: PUCL-K

Phillips, O, 'Constituting the global gay: individual subjectivity and sexuality in southern Africa', in Herman, D and Stychin, C (eds), *Sexuality in the Legal Arena*, 2000, London: Athlone, pp 17–34

Populations Data Unit, Population and Geographical Data Section, UN High Commissioner for Refugees, *A Statistical Overview of Refugee Populations, New Arrivals, Durable Solutions and Refugee Status, Determination Procedures in Some 90 Countries*, Global Refugee Trends: January–September, 2001, 14 December 2001, Geneva: UNHCR

Porras, I, 'On terrorism: reflections on violence and the outlaw', in Danielson, D and Engles, K, *After Identity: A Reader in Law and Culture*, 1994, New York: Routledge

Powell, A, 'Conference on bride-burning in India' (1998) *Harvard University Gazette*, 3 December, www.news.harvard.edu/gazette/1998/12.03/bride/html

Powell, J, 'The multiple self: exploring between and beyond modernity and postmodernity' (1997) 81 Minnesota Law Review 1481

Pradhan, S, 'Beauty pageants trying to promote cosmetics market: Rajnath' (2000), 15 December, news.indianinfo.com/2000/12//12/15beauty.html

Prakash, A, 'Law, prejudice block condom supply to Tihar inmates' (1994) *The Pioneer*, 24 February

Prakash, G (ed), *After Colonialisms: Imperial Histories and Postcolonial Displacements*, 1995, Princeton: Princeton UP

Prasad, P, 'Besides Manusmriti Kapur should have quoted Kama Sutra' (1994) *The Sunday Observer*, 24 August

Probyn, E, 'Travels in the postmodern: making sense of the local', in Nicholson, L (ed), *Feminism/Postmodernism*, 1990, New York: Routledge, pp 176–89

Puri, P, *Women, Body, Desire in Post-Colonial India: Narratives of Gender and Sexuality*, 1999, New York: Routledge

Puri, S and Ritzema, T, 'Migrant worker remittances, micro-finance, and the informal economy: prospects and issues', 1999, International Labour Organization, Enterprise and Co-operative Development Department, Social Finance Unit, Working Paper No 21

Radhakrishnan, R, 'Nationalism, gender, and the narrative of identity', in Parker, A, Russo, M, Sommer, D and Yaeger, P, *Nationalisms and Sexualities*, 1992, London: Routledge, pp 77–95

Raghavan, RK, 'The crime scene' (2003) 20(23) Frontline 129

Rai, 'Condoms for prisoners opposed' (1994) *The Pioneer*, 23 February

Rajalakshmi, K, 'Targeting NGOs' (1–14 September 2001) 18(18) Frontline 113–14

Ratha, D, 'Workers' remittances: an important and stable source of external development finance', in *Global Development Finance*, 2003, Washington, DC: World Bank, p 157

Ray, S, *En-gendering: Women and Nation in Colonial and Post-Colonial Narratives*, 2000, Durham: Duke UP

Richard, AO, *International Trafficking in Women to the United States: Contemporary Manifestation of Slavery and Organized Crime*, November 1999, Washington: Center for the Study of Intelligence, p iii

Rittich, K, 'Transformed pursuits: the quest for equality in globalized markets' (2000) 13 Harvard Human Rights Journal 231

Robertson, 'Islam is violent in nature' (2002) *The New York Times*, 23 February

Romany, C, 'Women as aliens: a feminist critique of the public/private distinction in international human rights law' (1993) 6 Harvard Human Rights Journal 87

Roy, KK, 'Unravelling the Kamasutra', in John, M and Nair, J (eds), *A Question of Silence? The Sexual Economies of Modern India*, 1998, Delhi: Kali for Women, pp 52–76

Rubin, G, 'Thinking sex: notes for a radical theory of the politics of sexuality', in Vance, C (ed), *Pleasure and Danger: Exploring Female Sexuality*, reprint, 1989, Boston: Routledge, pp 267–319

Rundle, G, *The Opportunist: John Howard and the Triumph of Reaction*, 2001, Melbourne: Black Inc

Russell, S, 'Migrant remittances and development' (1992) 30(3/4) International Migration Quarterly 267

Russert, T, 'Interview: meet the press, with Vice President Cheney', 17 September 2001, www.whitehouse.gov/vicepresident/news-speeches/speeches/vp20010916.html

Said, E, 'Foreword', in Guha, R and Spivak, G (eds), *Selected Subaltern Studies*, 1988, London, New Delhi: OUP, pp i–x

Said, E, 'Representing the colonized: anthropology's interlocutors' (1989) 15(2) Critical Inquiry 205

Said, E, *Culture and Imperialism*, 1993, London: Chatto & Windus

Said, E, *Orientalism*, reprint, 1995, Harmondsworth: Penguin

Sangari, K and Vaid, S, 'Institutions, beliefs and ideologies: widow immolation in contemporary Rajasthan', in Menon, N (ed), *Gender and Politics in India*, 2001, New Delhi: OUP

Sanghera, J and Kapur, R, *Report on Trafficking in Nepal: Policy Analysis – An Assessment of Laws and Policies for the Prevention and Control of Trafficking in Nepal*, 2001, New Delhi: Population Council

Sangram, *A Statement of Women in Prostitution*, 1997, p 2

Sarkar, S, *A Critique of Colonial India*, 1985, Calcutta: Papyrus

Sarkar, S, 'The decline of the subaltern in subaltern studies', in Sarkar, S, *Writing Social History*, 1997, Delhi: OUP, pp 82–108

Sarkar, T, 'Rhetoric against the age of consent: resisting colonial reason and death of the child-wife' (1993) 28(36) Economic and Political Weekly 1869

Sarkar, T, 'Colonial lawmaking and lives/deaths of Indian women: different readings of law and community', in Kapur, R (ed), *Feminist Terrains in Legal Domains: Interdisciplinary Essays on Woman and Law*, 1996, New Delhi: Kali for Women, pp 210–38

Sarkar, T, *Hindu Wife and Hindu Nation*, 2001, New Delhi: Permanent Black

Sarvarkar, VD, *Hindutva: Who is Hindu?*, 4th edn, 1949, Delhi: SP Gokhale

Sassen, S, 'Toward a feminist analysis of the global economy' (1996) 4 Indiana Journal of Global Legal Studies 7

Sassen, S, *Globalization and Its Discontents: Essays on the New Mobility of People and Money*, 1999, New York: The New Press

Sassen, S, 'The state and economic globalization: any implications for international law?' (2000) 1 Chicago Journal of International Law 109

Sassen, S, 'A universal harm: making criminals of migrants' (2003) *Open Democracy*, 28 August, www.opendemocracy.net/debates/article-10-96-1444.jsp

Schneider, E, 'The violence of privacy', in Fineman, MA and Mykitiuk, R (eds), *The Public Nature of Private Violence: The Discovery of Domestic Abuse*, 1991, New York: Routledge, pp 36–58

Schultz, V, 'Reconceputalizing sexual harassment' (1998) 107 Yale Law Review 1685

Scott, J, *Gender and the Politics of History*, 1999, New York: Columbia UP

Sen, A, *Development as Freedom*, 1999, New York: Random House

Sen, S, 'Citizen and the law: a case for decriminalization' (1994) *The Statesman*, 1 March

Shenon, P, 'Suit to be filed on behalf of three detainees in Cuba' (2002) *The New York Times*, 19 February

Shifman, P, 'Trafficking and women's human rights in a globalised world', in *Gender and Development: Women Reinventing Globalisation*, 2003, Oxford: Oxfam, pp 125–32

Singha, R, *A Despotism of Law: Crime and Justice in Early Colonial India*, 2000, New Delhi: OUP

Sinha, M, *Colonial Masculinity: The 'Manly Englishman' and the 'Effeminate Bengali' in the Late Nineteenth Century*, 1995, Manchester: Manchester UP

Sinha, M (ed), *Mother India: Selections from the Controversial 1927 Text by Katherine Mayo*, 2000, Ann Arbor: Michigan UP

Skinner, E, Melkote, S and Muppidi, S, 'International satellite broadcasting in India and other areas: a critical summary', in Melkote, S, Shields, P and Agrawal, B (eds), *International Satellite Broadcasting in South Asia: Political, Economic and Cultural Implications*, 1998, Maryland: University Press of America

Smart, C, *Feminism and the Power of Law*, 1989, London: Routledge

Smart, C, *Law, Crime and Sexuality: Essays in Feminism*, 1995, London: Routledge

Smith, B (ed), *Home Girls: A Black Feminist Anthology*, 1983, New York: Kitchen Table, Women of Colour Press

Solanki, G and Gangoli, G, 'The official discourse around PITA' (1996) 31 Economic and Political Weekly 3298

Solomon, A, 'Fallacy: Australia's offshore program is a fair and equitable way of helping the world's refugees', 2001, www.illywhatcker/net/asylum/page2.php

Spelman, E, *The Inessential Woman: Problems of Exclusion in Feminist Thought*, 1998, Boston, Mass: Beacon Press

Spivak, G, 'Three women's texts and a critique of imperialism' (1985) 12 Critical Inquiry 242

Spivak, G, 'Can the subaltern speak?', in Nelson, N and Grossberg, L (eds), *Marxism and the Interpretation of Culture*, 1988, Chicago: Illinois UP

Spivak, G, 'Questions of multi-culturalism', in Harasym, S (ed), *The Post-Colonial Critic: Interviews, Strategies, Dialogues*, 1990, New York: Routledge

Spivak, G, 'Neocolonialism and the secret agent of knowledge' (1991) 13(1–2) Oxford Literary Review 220

Spivak, G, *Outside in the Teaching Machine*, 1993, New York: Routledge, pp 45–46

Spivak, G and Rooney, E, 'In a word: interview', in Schor, N and Weed, E (eds), *The Essential Difference*, 1994, Bloomington: Indiana UP

Stetketee, M and Henderson, I, 'PM labels lip sewing blackmail' (2001) *Australian*, 26 January

Stoler, A, *Carnal Knowledge and Imperial Power: Race and the Intimate in Colonial Rule*, 2002, Berkley, Los Angeles, London: California UP

Subramanyam, C, 'War over lesbianism: is it un-Indian?' (1998) *Asian Age*, 10 December

Suleri, S, *The Rhetoric of English India*, 1992, Chicago: Chicago UP

Sullivan, E, 'Liberalism and imperialism: John Stuart Mill's defence of the British Empire' (1983) 44(4) Journal of the History of Ideas 599

Sunder Rajan, R, *Real or Imagined Women: Postcolonialism, Gender and Culture*, 1995, London and New York: Routledge

Sunder Rajan, R, 'The Third World academic in other places; or, the postcolonial intellectual revisited' (1997) 23 Critical Inquiry 598

Swaraj, S, 'AIDS campaign must advocate sex only with life partner, not just safe sex' (2001) *The Week*, 11 April

Symposium, 'Feminism and globalization: the impact of the global economy on women and feminist theory' (1996) 4 Indiana Journal of Global Legal Studies 7

Tandani, G, *Sakhiyani: Lesbian Desire in Ancient and Modern India*, 1996, London: Cassell

Tay, A and Ozdowski, S, *Human Rights Commissioner OAM, Media Statement: Woomera Immigrations Detention Centre Report of Visit by HREOC Officers*, 6 February 2002, www.hreoc.gov.au/media_releases/2002/05_02.html

Tempest, M, 'Immigrants to face language and citizenship tests', 7 February 2002, politics.guardian.co.uk/hjomaffairs/story/0,11026,646478,00.html; see also Cantle, 2003

Thackeray, B, 'Kick them out – no compromise with Muslims: the rhetoric of hatred from Shiv Sena's Bal Thackeray' (1993) *Time*, 25 January, p 43

Thackeray, B,'The AIDS scare: whose interest does it serve?' (2000) *The Organizer*, 20 August, pp 49–50

Thackeray, B, 'Shiv Sena suicide squads to be set up in New Delhi' (2002) *Outlook Magazine*, 13 December, p 42

Thomas, D and Jones, S (ed), *A Modern Form of Slavery: Trafficking of Burmese Women and Girls into Brothels in Thailand*, 1993, Washington: Women's Rights Project, Asia Watch, Division of Human Rights Watch

Times of India, 'There's our bronze girl in the being' (2000) *Times of India*, 9 September

Trivedi, H, *Colonial Transactions: English Literature and India*, 1993, Calcutta: Papyrus

Tyler, H, 'Australia unmoved by detainees', *Middle East Times*, www.metimes.com/2K2/issue2002-4/reg/australia_unmoved_by.htm (visited 23 August 2002)

Valdes, F, 'Acts of power, crimes of knowledge: some observations on desire, law and ideology in the politics of expression at the end of the twentieth century' (1997) 1 Journal of Gender, Race and Justice 213

Vance, C, 'Pleasure and danger: toward a politics of sexuality', in Vance, C (ed), *Pleasure and Danger: Exploring Female Sexuality*, reprint, 1989, Boston: Routledge, pp 1–27

Vanita, R (ed), *Queering India: Same-Sex Love and Eroticism in Indian Culture and Society*, 2002, New York: Routledge

Vanita, R and Kidwai, S (eds), *Same-Sex Love in India*, 2000, New York: St Martin's Press

'Vienna declaration and programme of action', World Conference on Human Rights, Vienna, June 14–15 1993, UN CocA/CONF157/24

Vijayan, PK, 'Outline for an exploration of Hindutva Masculinities', in Bose, B (ed), *Translating Desire: The Politics of Gender and Culture in India*, 2002, Delhi: Katha, pp 82–105

Viswanathan, G, *Masks of Conquest: Literary Studies and British Rule in India*, 1989, London: Faber and Faber

Volpp, L, '(Mis)identifying culture: Asian women and the "cultural defenses"' (1994) 17 Harvard Women's Law Journal 57

Volpp, L, 'Talking culture: gender, race, nation, and the politics of multiculturalism' (1996) 96 Columbia Law Review 1573

Walker, A, 'Shock of the East' (1994) *Evening Standard*, 12 May

Walker, F, 'Sailor hero betrayed as truth takes a dive' (2002) *Sydney Morning Herald*, 24 February

Weiner, M, *The Global Migration Crisis: Challenges to States and to Human Rights*, 1995, Reading, Mass: Addison Wesley

White, L, 'Feminist microenterprise: vindicating the rights of women in the new global order?' (1998) 50 Memphis Law Review 327

Wijers, M, 'Keep your women home', in Rossilli, M (ed), *Gender Policies in the European Union*, 2000, New York: Peter Lang Publishing, pp 209–29

Wijers, M and Lap-Chew, L, *Trafficking in Women, Forced Labour and Slavery-Like Practices in Marriage, Domestic Labour and Prostitution*, 1997, Utrecht: STV

Williams, R, *The American Indian in Western Legal Thought: The Discourses of Conquest*, 1990, New York: OUP

Young, R, *White Mythologies: Writing History and the West*, 1990, London and New York: Routledge

Younge, G, 'Britain is again white' (2002) *The Guardian*, 18 February

Zastoupil, L, *John Stuart Mill and India*, 1994, Stanford: Stanford UP

Zlotnik, H, 'The global dimensions of female migration', Migration Information Source, 1 March 2003, www.migrationinformation.org/Feature/display.cfm?ID=109

agnipariksha	The trial of purity by fire that Sita, wife of Lord Ram, in the brahmanical epic *The Ramayan* (*Story of Ram*), is forced to undergo in order to prove her honour and fidelity.
Arthashastra	A text written in the 4th-century BC discussing the theories and principles of governing a state.
Ayodhya	A town in the northern state of Uttar Pradesh where the Hindu Right is seeking to construct a temple to Lord Ram on the spot where they destroyed the 16th-century Babri mosque in December 1992. The movement is being spearheaded by the Vishwa Hindu Parishad and the Bajarang Dal.
Bajarang Dal	The Squad of Hanuman, the Hindu monkey god in the epic *The Ramayan*. Set up by the Vishwa Hindu Parishad in 1984 in the northern state of Uttar Pradesh, to awaken the Hindu youth and to agitate for cultural nationalism and the construction of the Ram temple in Ayodhya.
Bharatiya Janata Party (BJP)	The Indian People's Party and the political wing of the Hindu Right. It espouses Hindu nationalism and draws its ideological creed from the Rashtriya Swayamsevak Sangh. It is dedicated to the cause of Hindutva which it currently defines as cultural nationalism, but historically is about the establishment of a Hindu state. The party emerged from the Bharatiya Jana Sangh, which was established in 1951 and stood in opposition to what it perceived as the evils of western cultural imperialism. These principles were retained, though modified, when the party was renamed the Bharatiya Janata Party in 1980.
Durbar Mahila Samanwaya Committee	The Unstoppable Movement for Women's Equality. A sex-workers-based organisation in Calcutta, representing over 60,000 sex-workers in the Indian state of West Bengal.
karva chauth	A fast kept by Hindu wives in the northern and western parts of India to ensure the longevity of their husbands.

Mahabharata	A brahmanical epic composed between 300 BC and 300 AD, which contains the fabulous account of a dynastic struggle and great civil war in the kingdom of Kurukshetra. The philosophy incorporated into the text is enormously complex, though it emphasises social duty and ascetic principles.
Mahila Morcha	Women's Front and the women's wing of the BJP.
Radha	A central character in the *Mahabharata*, Radha, a married woman, falls in love with the main protagonist in the text, Lord Krishna, and carries on a long-term erotic and spiritual relationship with him.
Rashtriya Swayamsevak Sangh (RSS)	National Self-Service Organisation and ideological wing of the Hindu Right. It is a Hindu nationalist movement which bases itself on the ideology of Hindutva, the establishment of India as a Hindu state, and stopping what it describes as the government's appeasement of the Muslims. It was started in 1925 by Dr HB Hedgewar. It has been instrumental in the rise of the Bharatiya Janata Party.
sati	The practice through which some widows are voluntarily or forcibly burned alive on their husband's funeral pyre. A rare practice in a few communities in India. It was banned in 1829.
Shiv Sena	The army of Shiva, a Hindu god. A political party founded in 1966 which has been led by Bal Thackeray ever since its establishment. Its vision is nationalistic and it is committed to the idea that the Indian nation is at its core a Hindu culture.
Sita	The wife of Lord Ram and a central character in Valmiki's version of *The Ramayan* (150 AD). The epic evolved through an oral tradition and many versions of the story exist. Sita is traditionally held out as the ideal Hindu woman, who is selfless, devoted and gentle. However, when Sita is accused of adultery by Ram, she is forced to undergo a test of purity by fire – the *agnipariksha* – to prove her virtue. She passes the test. In this version, Ram remains unconvinced of her fidelity and Sita goes into the forest and inters herself in the earth. However, there are many competing versions of this story, including a folk version where Sita refuses to undergo the *agnipariksha* and spurns Ram.
Vishwa Hindu Parishad (VHP)	World Hindu Council and religious wing of the Hindu Right, established in 1964.

Index